Lightbulb Moments in Human History

From Peasants to Periwigs

Lightbulb Moments in Human History

From Peasants to Periwigs

Scott Edwin Williams

Winchester, UK
Washington, USA

JOHN HUNT PUBLISHING

First published by Chronos Books, 2024
Chronos Books is an imprint of John Hunt Publishing Ltd., No. 3 East St., Alresford,
Hampshire SO24 9EE, UK
office@jhpbooks.com
www.johnhuntpublishing.com
www.chronosbooks.com

For distributor details and how to order please visit the 'Ordering' section on our website.

Design: Lapiz Digital Services

UK: Printed and bound by CPI Group (UK) Ltd, Croydon, CR0 4YY
Printed in North America by CPI GPS partners

We operate a distinctive and ethical publishing philosophy in
all areas of our business, from our global network of authors to
production and worldwide distribution.

Contents

For my children,
Sarah, Sebastian, and Cate,
I love you guys.

Praise for *Lightbulb Moments in Human History*

This book is expertly written and packed with interesting information and educational insight into the past. Whether you're a history buff or looking to expand your historical horizons, this book is a great read.

How It Works **magazine**

Here's your chance to learn and enjoy Big History in a slightly "deranged" romp.

Dr Karl Kruszelnicki, Australian science communicator, author, and populariser

Quite brilliant in terms of the depth and fun analysis—this is NOT the history I learned at school—BUT I wish it had been.

Terry Melia, author of *Tales from the Greenhills*

—Introduction—

You Ain't Seen Nothing Yet

I was losing the argument. Badly.

"Look, I promise you, we're *not* devolving as a species!" I'd already had a couple of beers, but had enough presence of mind to know that wild gesticulations would signal vulnerability, so I stuffed my hands into my pockets.

But it was already too late.

"You're kidding, right? Trump? Brexit? Flat-earthers? Anti-vaxxers?" C.J. knew I had no answers and sensed the blood in the water. "You can't believe humans are still evolving. You just can't."

"Mate, we're living in the most prosperous time ever."

"Bullshit! We're being sucked down the plug-hole." He looked me square in the eye, then slowly, theatrically facepalmed.

"You'd rather live a hundred years ago?"

"Maybe? I dunno," he paused for a beat. "Look, I'm going to the bar. What are you drinking?"

As I watched C.J. stalk away, I knew he'd unilaterally declared victory. The conversation was over and I felt defeated. I knew in my heart I wasn't wrong, but I'd always been hopeless at constructing an argument on the fly. It was one of the many reasons I was a teacher and not a lawyer.

Fig. 1: Not sure C.J. ever bought into the idea… (BernardBobo and S.E.W.)

On C.J.'s return with beers in hand, the night continued amiably enough. There was no recurrence of the discussion and the night passed without further incident.

But deep down inside, I seethed.

A restless night's sleep did nothing to ease my mood. How *could* I have choked like that? Even worse, during all the tossing and turning, I'd somehow managed to muster an argument, replete with supporting evidence.

But I'd missed my chance. The French have a term for this: *Esprit de l'escalier*, the feeling you get when a witty comeback springs to mind after the chance to make it has passed. I belatedly had an argument, but I could hardly call C.J. now to continue the discussion.

Or could I?

No. That would only make me look like a psycho.

Then I had an epiphany: I'd been looking for a writing project for some time. Perhaps I could use *this* as inspiration. The *Lightbulb Moments in Human History* series is my tardy and long-winded response to that argument.

* * *

Welcome to the Jungle

If you've already read *Lightbulb Moments in Human History: From Cave to Colosseum* (hereafter referred to as *From Cave to Colosseum*), congratulations—you have discerning taste. Welcome back. If you *haven't* read *From Cave to Colosseum,* then I strongly encourage you to purchase it in paperback or ebook wherever good (or even mediocre) books are sold.

But while I'd certainly appreciate you purchasing *From Cave to Colosseum,* there's no required reading for this book. One of the beauties of history is that it makes sense wherever you pick it up.

However, it won't hurt to bring you up to speed...

Big Ideas and Big History

In *From Cave to Colosseum,* I outlined my contention that despite our perceptions of the negative events of the last few years, human existence is gradually improving. I explained David Christian's concept of Big History, a discipline which examines history from a far remove to assemble a big picture view of the past. In Big History, a century is the mere blink of the eye. It handles years by the millions and billions, from the beginning of time to the present day. Big historians combine sociological, scientific, geographical, and historical concepts to investigate long-term patterns, and it is structured around eight fundamental thresholds.

Because we are dealing with humans in this series, we were able to skip the first few thresholds (what's thirteen billion years between friends?) and *From Cave to Colosseum* entered at David Christian's Threshold 6: Humans, and then moved to Threshold 7: Agriculture. We start *Lightbulb Moments in Human History: From Peasants to Periwigs* back at Threshold 7, before moving to Threshold 8: The Modern Revolution. In the wide scope of these thresholds, the fate of individuals, even the most significant ones, is totally inconsequential.

Over the entire thirteen-billion-year scope of Big History, the meanest peasant is no more exalted than the grandest king. Or, for that matter, a single-celled organism. In fact, they're all equally *insignificant*. It's the great leaps forward that matter: Tool making; the taming of fire; the emergence of agriculture; and the beginnings of the Industrial Revolution, for example. But of course, we're zooming-in a bit closer. The *Lightbulb Moments in Human History* series will cover around a million years of world history, but in this particular book, we narrow it down to around 1,300 years.

At that magnification, individual lives become more significant. The best and brightest, the notable and the great, the malicious and the malevolent all loom large over our story. But *only* if their ideas helped shape human development. In the same way, we won't overly concern ourselves with wars and conquest. These are important in histories that chart the rise and fall of countries, but unless they initiated massive paradigm shifts in human development, they won't figure in this book. Conversely, we'll look at many people you may never have heard of, but who played a role in the evolution of collective learning.

Sometimes the consequences of Big History are even bigger than that…

For centuries, Western cultural biases have obscured the role of the near and far East in human development. We saw in *From Cave to Colosseum* that China and India made breakthroughs that were later attributed to Westerners (I'm looking at *you*, Johannes Gutenberg). In this book, we'll investigate the role of the Islamic Golden Age in preserving and developing the knowledge of the ancients so that it could be reintroduced to the West. While this has been accepted by historians for some time (it's one reason we don't refer to medieval times as "the Dark Ages" anymore) it hasn't always trickled down into the Western consciousness.

Big History is about big ideas and monumental movements which shift the zeitgeist, usually improving the lot of the human race. Hominids began living in caves and had limited language capabilities. Across hundreds of thousands of years of collective learning, humans developed from inconsequential apes to the most powerful creatures on the planet, all through iterative development. The bottom line is that, when viewed dispassionately from sufficient distance, humanity is on a gradual, quantifiable, and albeit slightly wonky uptick.

Surprised? You should be. Thinking about current events such as pandemics, wars, and climate change, rightly fills us full of dread. We are fed a panic-inducing diet of calamity through the 24-hour news cycle, and that's not even counting *fake news*. Then we obsessively scroll through our social media feeds. Worse still, our leaders are driven to myopic short-term decisions based on the paranoia and fear induced by these constant negative media reports.

Fig. 2: Eventually, the 24-hour news cycle will end… (Midjourney and S.E.W.)

It's no wonder that politicians are influenced by our negative reactions to the news because that's all *we* seem to care about. They need our votes to stay in power, and we are frustratingly short-term thinkers. When given the choice between our immediate wants and needs and the long term needs of our descendants, most of us choose the former. The very best politicians try to educate us, but being didactic isn't a proven vote winner.

Of course, the worst of these politicians deliberately seed the news with stories to distract us, or manipulate our opinions with lies. Demagogues like Donald Trump go further, weaponizing the fear-factor of the news, while somehow degrading our trust in the media:

> *There is great anger in our Country caused in part by inaccurate, and even fraudulent, reporting of the news. The Fake News Media, the true Enemy of the People, must stop the open & obvious hostility & report the news accurately & fairly...*
> Donald J. Trump (@realDonaldTrump) October 29, 2018

Significantly, what The Donald doesn't mention here, is that the "great anger" he refers to was stirred up by him for his own nefarious purposes. The movement *away* from democracy and liberty, towards autocracy and subjugation is paved by such bastards, even as they cloak themselves in their nation's flag (often literally) and cry "Freedom!"

It will be an earthshaking lightbulb moment when some bold human frees us from media and political manipulation in a positive way. That person will bring a big picture view based on quantifiable truth and long-term planning. They will lead, not simply follow the fickle mob.

It's not an easy task.

However, just because change is difficult doesn't mean the world will end on our watch. The narcissism inherent in the idea that, after untold generations of humans, *we* will be the humans to see the end of the world, is staggering. In reality, most of those generations have known far worse times than us. The people of the Byzantine Empire thought the world was ending when the Plague of Justinian decimated Constantinople between 541 and 549 AD. Medieval peasants felt the end times were upon them during the Black Death as well.

And yet here we are.

A simple Google search of "end times prophecy" yields 73,600,000 results, most claiming that we are living at the end of history. There are thousands of reasons listed, and most of them are rubbish. Every looney cult from Heaven's Gate to Jim Jones' Jonestown has predicted the end of the world. I suppose eventually, one day, one looney cult will be right. Even the more reputable religions get in on the act. Christians in particular, have had an unhealthy obsession with Armageddon and the Second Coming since Jesus shuffled off this mortal coil.

Fig. 3: Apocalypse Now? (Milkovasa, Konradbak, and S.E.W.)

In America, prepping for the apocalypse is big business. Places like Costco will sell you anything you need to survive the end of the world; you can even purchase special pre-packaged survival kits. For a price. I wonder what Costco and the other businesses who profit from selling supplies to the perpetually paranoid preppers know that we don't?

What good is profit if the world is ending? It's safe to conclude that big business doesn't believe the end of the world is nigh.

But that doesn't mean that massive change isn't coming. Things won't necessarily go back to what we have come to regard as "normal." For all we know, democracy will fail and climate change will fundamentally alter the world as we know it. England, America, Canada, and every other country (even China and Russia) may wither and die, with other, yet to be envisaged entities taking their place.

All of this means that you, dear reader, can take little immediate comfort from the idea that humanity is on an upwards trajectory. Let's face it, there's no way that in 1346 when the Black Death raged through Europe, that buboe-covered peasants said to themselves: "Oh well, our squalid lives are over, but the Renaissance is around the corner. Chin up lads, everything will be alright for our descendants!"

However, what I *am* saying is that I believe humanity will survive, and eventually prosper. In fact, it is often these moments of crisis that provide the greatest impetus for innovation and change. I'm no futurist, so I won't speculate on what such innovation and change might look like, but I'm sure the solutions will be a creative elaboration of old ideas, with some new ideas... and many brilliant "Aha!" moments.

The only people capable of this kind of thought are the ones with big ideas.

WHEN AN 'AHA!' MOMENT HITS

Fig. 4: Today's society is the result of humanity's big ideas. (Midjourney and S.E.W.)

The Domains of Lightbulb Moments

As in *From Cave to Colosseum*, I will categorize lightbulb moments into four domains: STEM (Science, Technology, Engineering, and Mathematics), Religion, Educational, and Cultural. I don't get too carried away with using these terms, but they can be helpful in understanding how big human ideas can combine and evolve into new big ideas. All of history's lightbulb moments fall into at least one of these domains (see Table 1), but many can be categorized under more than one domain, such as building megaprojects like St. Peter's Basilica (Religious, Cultural, and STEM), and, importantly, collective learning (STEM, Religious, Educational, and Cultural).

STEM	Religious	Educational	Cultural
Tool use	Life after	Speech	War
Mathematics	death	Writing	Political
Agriculture	Hinduism	Teaching	theories
Weaving	Buddhism	Reading	Sports
Pottery	Judaism	Collective	Art
	Christianity	learning	Narratives

Table 1: The Four Domains of Lightbulb Moments. (S.E.W.)

Collective Learning

In the beginning, collective learning lurched slowly and uncertainly into being. For thousands of years, humanity's intellectual capital appeared limited to survival tactics and flaking rudimentary stone tools. Nevertheless, early humans invented language, teamwork, teaching, and many other things we take for granted. Gradually, the pace of humanity's plodding progress increased. Stoked by constantly growing stockpiles of intellectual fuel, collective learning eventually became a locomotive, barreling down the tracks at mounting speed.

And once collective learning *really* kicked into gear, human knowledge grew exponentially.

In 1982, the American author, architect, philosopher, futurist, and inventor of the geodesic dome, Buckminster Fuller, theorized that up to the year 1900, the body of human knowledge had been increasing twofold every hundred years, or so. By 1945, it was doubling every 25 years, then by 1982, every twelve to thirteen months. Based on Fuller's estimation, the corpus of human knowledge is now believed to double every *twelve hours*. The pace that we are accumulating human intellectual property is frightening.

Fig. 5: These guys would never keep up nowadays. (Erica Guilane-Nachez and S.E.W.)

This phenomenon is obvious when looking at the shrinking scope of my books. My first book, *From Cave to Colosseum*, which covered the period from the earliest hominids to the fall of Rome, spanned a couple of million years. This book, *From Peasants to Periwigs*, documents big human ideas from the Middle Ages to the Scientific Revolution, a period of roughly one thousand, three hundred years. My next book (which was initially supposed to be the final of the series) will cover about one hundred and fifty years. A final book will cover from the twentieth century up to the present, and speculate a little about the future.

However, it's entirely possible that at the rate humans are amassing intellectual capital, I will *never* finish this Sisyphean task.

My Lightbulb Moment...

My lightbulb moment was to trace the upward arc of history via its big ideas, from ancient civilization to ancient civilization, through the lens of Big History. It's hardly a new idea, and any *bona fide* historians reading this now will be chuckling at my outdated, Whiggish historiography. In my defense, I don't believe I present history as a journey from a dark and inglorious past to a modern Nirvana. I simply believe Big History allows us to see the overarching positive growth.

And it's my job to prove the validity of this claim.

So far, I believe I've achieved a limited version of this aim. Unfortunately, in *From Cave to Colosseum*, it didn't help my argument that I wound up the book with humanity staring the so-called "Dark Ages" squarely in the face.

Ending on an undoubted low point was less than ideal, but it wasn't where I'd originally intended the book to finish. Unfortunately, while *Lightbulb Moments in Human History* was envisaged as a single book, fate (and spiralling word count) dictated that it realistically had to be split into more. This meant that logically, the first book ended where ancient history meets the Middle Ages.

And so we begin this book in the slump following the fall of Rome. However, as we will soon see, this was only a low point in the Western world.

A Brief Interlude I

(Everything I Do) I Do It for You

One of my favorite television programs as a small boy was *The Adventures of Robin Hood*, a British produced show from the 1950s. While it was already a bit long-in-the-tooth by the early 1970s when I was watching, it remained an afternoon staple on Channel Nine. I'd come home from school, plonk myself in front of the television with a doorstop hunk of Mum's chocolate cake, and watch the escapades of Robin Hood, Maid Marian, Friar Tuck, and Little John. Richard Greene starred in this child-oriented romp, which fed into my already growing obsession with the past.

The Adventures of Robin Hood began with a brief fanfare of trumpets, the twang of Robin Hood's bow and the thwack of his arrow hitting home. It then kicked into one of the most insidious television theme earworms of all time:

Robin Hood, Robin Hood,
Riding through the glen,
Robin Hood, Robin Hood,
With his band of men,
Feared by the bad, loved by the good,
Robin Hood! Robin Hood! Robin Hood!

If you've ever heard it, you're singing it in your head right now. If you've never heard it, look it up on YouTube. Once heard, never forgotten.

Like many children of the era, I had a bow and arrow set, complete with rubber suckers, with which I would re-enact Robin's adventures. However, this was a personal pursuit. When it came to general popularity as a playground game, it didn't hold a candle to Cops and Robbers or Cowboys and Indians. It was very niche.

This portrayal of the legend of Robin Hood gallops headlong into all of the medieval cliches: All knights (particularly crusading ones) are good guys. Lords were split fairly down the middle between evil exploiters of their serfs (who supported King John), and kind and fair father-figures (loyal to King Richard). Then there was the Lionheart himself, depicted as the epitome of English royalty, but who in reality barely set foot in England and spoke only French. On the other hand, his dastardly brother, King John the Usurper, is rendered as a dishonorable coward. The Church itself was often corrupt, but most individual churchmen, like Friar Tuck, had hearts of gold.

And, of course, the landless multitude needed an incorruptible superhero to look after them. Someone who'd rob from the rich and give to the poor. A hooded vision in Lincoln green. Enter one Robin of Locksley, whose story is so well known, it doesn't need repeating in these pages.

Fig. 1: The title card and Richard Greene (Public domain and S.E.W.)

During research for this interlude, I rewatched five episodes of *The Adventures of Robin Hood* on YouTube. A recurring trope is a main character pretending to be someone else. In one episode, Maid Marion masquerades as a man. In another, she swaps roles with her homely handmaid to expose the avarice of a potential suitor. In order to help a knight cruelly indebted to the Church, the roly-poly Friar Tuck pretends to be the knight's squire. And, of course, Robin frequently rescues people from under the Sheriff of Nottingham's nose wearing laughably flimsy disguises.

Fig. 2: *Not all the Merry Men were so merry… (Public domain and S.E.W.)*

After the rousing title song, each episode begins with a faux-medieval ballad, sung to the tune of the seventeenth-century English folk song *Early One Morning*. The lyrics of these ditties always outline the story ahead, like in this example:

When Robin Hood and Little John
Contrive by means of a charade,
To save a young man's honour
And unite him with his maid.

Hello? Spoiler alert! This four-line ditty literally gives away the entire plot of the episode. Of course, most kids wouldn't have noticed, so I guess it's okay.

Being a creation of the 1950s, *The Adventures of Robin Hood* didn't bother to steer clear of television tropes, likely because it was creating quite a few of them. The rotund Friar Tuck was at once, goofy, amiable, and perpetually ravenous. He was also fat-shamed on a regular basis. The fair Maid Marian somehow managed to radiate virginity, even though she was the only woman hanging out in the woods with a bunch of sex-starved outlaws. Little John was a working-class hero who cheerfully took orders from his "betters." Meanwhile, the Sheriff of Nottingham chewed every bit of scenery in sight, as a moustache-twirling villain of the highest order.

Robin Hood himself, was something of a smug, upper-class, boy scout. In the very first episode, he returns from the Crusades to find King John has taken his lands and he is forced to hide in Sherwood Forest. Once there, Robin of Locksley encounters a ragtag group of lower-class outlaws, who almost immediately anoint him as their leader. Despite their blind allegiance, he often mocks the ignorant, superstitious nature of his less educated Merry Men.

Robin always managed to outsmart the hapless Sheriff, whose cause wasn't helped by the fact that Maid Marian was something of an undercover agent. She maintained friendly terms with the Sheriff, while surreptitiously passing his nefarious plans on to Robin. While a marksman of Robin's caliber could have assassinated the Sheriff any time he liked, he chose instead to outsmart and humiliate his adversary at every turn.

After all, Robin Hood was an English nobleman, not a common murderer.

Even though *The Adventures of Robin Hood* was made in England, it was heavily affected by the 1950s Hollywood blacklist. Resulting from the communist witch-hunt which was the House Un-American Activities Committee, the blacklist denied employment to entertainment industry professionals who were considered communists or communist sympathizers. As these film makers couldn't make a living in the United States, it's not surprising some of them made their way to England. Left-wing activist Hannah Weinstein (thankfully, no relation to the disgraced Harvey Weinstein) was one of these radical refugees, and she became the producer of the series. She used her clout to commission scripts from blacklisted Hollywood scriptwriters, who were credited under pseudonyms.

This communist connection gives a whole new significance to Robin's "robbing from the rich to give to the poor" ethos. Of course, nine-year-old me knew nothing of this, only that I liked the *The Adventures of Robin Hood* very much.

The tale of Robin Hood has been mined by Hollywood since the early days. From the original 1922 *Robin Hood*, starring Douglas Fairbanks, to Errol Flynn's *The Adventures of Robin Hood* in 1938 (which many consider the definitive version), through 1991's *Robin Hood: Prince of Thieves* with Kevin Costner in the titular role, all the way up to Russell Crowe's forgettable *Robin Hood* in 2010. Mixed amongst these more traditional depictions of Robin and his Merry Men, were: Comedies, such as Mel Brook's *Robin Hood: Men in Tights;* and Dramas, like *Robin and Marian*, with Audrey Hepburn playing an older Marian alongside Sean Connery's pensionable Robin. There was even a Disney cartoon adaptation starring a fox as the scourge of the Sheriff of Nottingham.

All of these movies (even the Disney cartoon) had vastly superior production values to TV's *The Adventures of Robin Hood*, but for me, the quintessential depiction of Robin of Locksley was that of Richard Greene. It may not be the best, grittiest, or sexiest, but it holds a place in my heart, and was for many years, the way I visualized the Middle Ages.

−1−

A Hard Day's Knight

The European Middle Ages

From a certain perspective, the Middle Ages get a bum rap.

The Middle Ages were once referred to as the "Dark Ages" because many Western historians bemoaned the fall of Rome and perceived lack of subsequent progress. The darkness continued, these pundits believed, until it was lifted by the rebirth of culture in what we call the Renaissance. Such observers regarded the thousand-year gap between the cultural high watermarks of Europe as a harsh time, bereft of intellectual achievement.

By most definitions, the Middle Ages, or medieval period, occupies the time between the end of the Classical era, often signified by the fall of Rome, and the beginning of the Renaissance. So, roughly between 500 AD to 1500 AD. The etymology of the word "medieval" shows it to be composed of its root words: medi-, meaning "middle," and ev-, meaning "age," and so "medieval" literally means "of the Middle Ages."

It doesn't seem like much creative thought went into *that* naming process.

Representations of the Middle Ages in popular culture tend to dwell on dungeons and torture chambers. So much so that "medieval" became a synonym for barbaric cruelty and human suffering. So, in Quentin Tarantino's *Pulp Fiction*, when Marsellus Wallace tells his hillbilly rapist that he's going to "get medieval" on his ass, you know his retribution will be slow, bloody, and painful. Pop culture also has a lot to do with how we continue to perceive this time: Be it the pseudo-Middle Ages of *Game of Thrones*; all Robin Hood movies; or every sword-and-sorcery movie ever made—most of us have an image in mind of what life was like in the Middle Ages. Our concept of this time is all castles, chivalrous knights, inhuman punishments, literal witch hunts, hooded monks, the Black Death, and people living in the squalid conditions depicted in *Monty Python and the Holy Grail*:

Large Man: *Who's that then?*
Dead Collector: *I dunno. Must be a king.*
Large Man: *Why?*
Dead Collector: *He hasn't got shit all over him.*

And much of this isn't far off the mark. Filth was just a part of the rich and varied tapestry that was the Middle Ages in Europe. Nevertheless, medieval Europe wasn't all doom and gloom. Although it's also fair to say the reputation of the medieval era as a vile cesspool of filth, violence, ignorance, and disease suffers because of terrible PR. This is most often because of the aforementioned "Dark Ages" tag that has dogged it through the centuries.

The term "Dark Ages" was coined by the Italian poet Petrarch (1304–1374) to bemoan the dearth of quality Latin literature since Classical times. However, it entered the zeitgeist as a term used to stigmatize a period of a thousand years of civilization.

And if the Middle Ages were sub-par developmentally, where does this leave my thesis of human development?

What Happened to Continual Human Improvement?

The Middle Ages is the obvious place to counter the argument that human society is a continuum of gradual improvement. Rome, the cultural touchstone of the ancient world, had just fallen. Barbarians were supposedly dismantling the finely tuned mechanisms of government throughout the ex-Roman Empire, with colonial outposts like Britannia shrugging off Roman ways reverting to their natural, pagan states. Surely this massive plothole makes a joke of the unbroken line of human achievement.

My answer is this: I never claimed an *unbroken* chain of constant growth. The analogy I used in my first book is that human cultural improvement was like the stock market. There are falls and adjustments, but its long-term trajectory is north.

Also, let's be realistic. For all the "glory" of Greece and Rome, violence and poverty were still rife, and these civilizations left a lot to be desired by modern standards. Despite the sophistication and wealth of the upper classes, the vast majority of the population were poor, illiterate, and ignorant of everything except their trade. Although there is great architectural beauty of the Parthenon and the Colosseum, most small towns in antiquity were just as ramshackle as our mental images of filthy medieval villages. It's also unlikely that these mental images are fully accurate. Having said that, it *is* doubtful that the personal hygiene of medieval peasants was comparable to suburban Romans, who had easy access to public bathhouses.

In fact, the world of Greece and Rome was not some white-washed nirvana where spectacular architecture, art, and literature abound, and no one ever got dirty or did anything wrong. The Classical world was at the cutting edge of devising inhuman punishments such as crucifixion and decimation.

Fig. 1: The men of Middle Ages weren't all hunky Lancelot lookalikes, either. (By Artem Mazunov, Guerrieroale and S.E.W.)

So, contrary to popular belief, the entire Western world didn't descend into butchery and barbarism the minute Rome fell. That's because, by most standards we'd recognize today, it was *already there*. Anyone who read *From Cave to Colosseum* will know the Greeks were a warlike bunch who practiced institutionalized pedophilia, and the Romans were an even more warlike bunch, who weren't averse to feeding a few innocent people to the lions. Or nailing them to crosses if they didn't like the cut of their jib. They also weren't squeamish about knocking off their emperors—twenty percent of their eighty-two emperors were assassinated while on the throne, hardly the hallmark of a peaceful, enlightened age.

Nevertheless, there are good reasons some people consider that the world went swirling down the plughole in medieval times.

Okay, Some Things Definitely Got Worse...

Medieval Art: Artwork is the most outward manifestation of the cultural black hole that separated the medieval era from its predecessors. A brief glance at medieval sculpture shows how it suffers by comparison to its Greek and Roman counterparts. Gone is the realism, movement, and flowing lines of Classical sculpture, their places taken by stilted, static and unrealistic depictions of humans. There was definite beauty in medieval art, which featured gorgeous, illuminated manuscripts, stained glass, and metalwork. However, for the best part of seven hundred years, realistic portrayals of the human body were not to be seen.

Then, in the late thirteenth century, Nicola Pisano began sculpting marble works displaying Classical realism, and Giotto's early fourteenth-century Romanesque paintings also showed an evolution in both realism and perspective. Both Nicola Pisano and Giotto had taken their respective crafts to the next level, setting the stage for the Renaissance era, one hundred years in the future.

Philosophy was also a casualty of the medieval period. Until the early twelfth century, medieval thinkers only had access to ancient Greek philosophy through the filter of writers such as Augustine (of whom, more in a moment), who were guided by Christian theological thinking and weren't particularly keen on reading Greek. The reason for this emphasis on religion was clear, because after the fall of Rome, the Roman Catholic Church was the only force capable of providing anything approaching social unity. And so, the medieval period often presents a picture of a society attempting to find political structure based on spirituality. Because of this, the most prominent philosophers of the time were theologians, and their religious bent stifled secular thought. Such ideas would not be explored until the humanists of the Renaissance.

However, as we have seen with art, Renaissance thinking didn't just pop into existence in the fifteenth century without preamble. It happened over time as learning was rediscovered and/or imported from the East, where it had been preserved and expanded upon by Muslim scholars (see Chapter 2). Oxford University emerged around 1200 AD and began assimilating this Greco-Arabic philosophy, medicine, and science. These scholars tried to reconcile their ideas with Christian dogma. The arts faculty, in particular, valued the reason and logic of Aristotle, incurring the wrath of ecclesiastical types in the rare places where Aristotelian teachings clashed with accepted theology.

Family Feudalism

Medieval Europe had been perfecting the seemed-like-a-big-idea-at-the-time concept of feudalism since the eighth century. It was introduced to England by William the Conqueror after his victory in the Battle of Hastings in 1066. The Norman Conquest is immortalized in the incredibly biased Bayeux Tapestry, which, at 70 meters long, is the world's longest piece of cartoon propaganda. William took control of England's lands and then split them up among his loyal supporters in return for services rendered.

An early example of "jobs for the boys."

Fig 2: *The moment William saw English treasury: A (fake) detail from the Bayeux Tapestry. (Midjourney and S.E.W.)*

In 1085 AD, William I sent battalions of assessors across the country to get a good accounting of what he *owned* and what he was *owed*. The information was used to create the *Domesday Book*, or in modern English, the *Doomsday Book* (which doesn't sound menacing at all). All those worried by the intrusion of big government into our lives today can blame William the Conqueror for the invention of the surveillance state.

His Domesday database knew all.

Prior to William, Anglo-Saxon England had been divided into three classes (not including the king). The Anglo-Saxon thanes were the upper class and had money and land but were slightly more egalitarian than subsequent feudal nobles. Below them were the churls, who made up the bulk of the population and were free people who worked in trades or rented land from a thane. They ranged from relatively prosperous men with a chance of upward mobility, all the way down to dirt poor shitkickers.

Below the churls were the thralls. Some thralls were slaves to a thane for life, others were only enslaved (or *enthralled*) until they discharged a debt. The distinction between the Saxon system and the Norman system imposed by William might seem trivial from our perspective, but it was earth-shaking for medieval Englishmen.

The big losers were the thanes, who were mostly killed in battle or fled the country, leaving their lands for William to redistribute to his backers. Churls morphed into the peasant class, but with less chance of social advancement. And thralls became serfs, who were no better or worse off than they had been before.

The easiest way to think of the feudal system is as falling somewhere between a multi-level marketing scheme and a protection racket. Like a good MLM scheme, it had a pyramidal structure, with the king at the top, the nobles below him, and then the peasants and serfs at the bottom. Like a protection racket, the powerless paid the powerful a price for their safety. Think Amway meets the Mafia.

It was "good to be the king," because he occupied the top spot on the hierarchy and owned all the land. However, in exchange for loyalty and military aid, the king divided his land up into smaller *fiefdoms*, which he awarded to the nobles who supported him. These nobles were known as vassals.

However, not all vassals were created equal. Nobles such as lords, barons, earls, and counts were at the top. These high-level nobles could then create their own vassals by handing out portions of the land the king had given them. This second tier were the knights, who did the fighting for the lords and so were simultaneously vassals and lords.

Peasants made up between 75 percent and 90 percent of the population. They came in two varieties: free tenants and serfs. Free tenants rented their land from a lord and were at liberty to conduct their own affairs or leave the land without the lord's consent. Their lives were difficult, but their labor was their own, and they'd have been grateful they weren't serfs, the lowest of the low.

Serfs were effectively slaves who belonged to the land, a reality borne out by the term serf being derived from the Latin *servus* or "slave" (*servus* is also the root word of "servant"). They couldn't marry or, God forbid, leave the land without their lord's say-so. Serfs were allowed a small allotment by the lord but had to pay a tax in return. This tax was calculated on the size of the land the serf worked on and was based on a third of the land's value. Serfs labored five or six days a week for their lord to pay this debt. The good news was that on these days, the lord fed his serfs well. The bad news was that serfs had to complete their lord's work before they could work for themselves.

The even *worse* news was that while a lord theoretically couldn't kill or maim a serf, they could legally inflict corporal punishment. Such punishments varied depending on the jurisdiction. In some places, you could punish your serf "moderately," but could not "torment" them. In parts of France, you could kill your serf if they argued with you, but could not shed their blood. Unhappily for French serfs, there are many ways to murder a person without bloodletting.

Fig. 3: Some lords tormented their serfs anyway. (Acrogame and S.E.W.)

The Peasants Are Revolting

If this all seems unjust to you, you're not alone. Peasants and serfs weren't overly fond of it, either. In 1381, they rose up, protesting a new poll tax that had been levied on all adults, peasants, and nobles alike. As the Crown imposed a poll tax on *all* adults, regardless of their wealth, it was seen as inequitable as peasants paid the same as their lord. But while this unfair tax was the trigger for the revolt, the peasants had greater aims. They wanted liberty and social change.

They wanted an end to feudalism.

Revolution by the lower classes was a radical idea, and there were uprisings across England. Unfortunately for the peasants of 1381, it was an idea whose time had not yet come. On June 13, rebel peasants from across the country fell upon London. They crossed London Bridge and rampaged through the city, killing suspected government officials, destroying records, freeing prisoners, and looting houses.

Two days later, having cooled down a little, the peasant forces from Kent, under the leadership of Wat Tyler, met the king's forces outside London. Tyler and other Kentish leaders parlayed with the fourteen-year-old Richard II and his advisors. While the meeting initially went well, Tyler's rough manners towards the king offended some of Richard's posse of nobles. A violent scuffle ensued, and Tyler was stabbed repeatedly, once by the Lord Mayor of London. Somehow, Tyler escaped, but not for long.

Meanwhile, the young king rode out and addressed the peasants: "You shall have no captain but me," he cried, and led the peasant army away. The injured Wat Tyler was tracked down, beheaded, and (to add insult to injury) had his head displayed on a pike on London Bridge. Richard II's men hunted down any lingering agitators and had them executed too.

Despite Wat Tyler's demise, the revolt succeeded in stopping the poll tax. However, liberty and equality would have to wait till a later era.

Funky Monks: Poverty, Chastity, and Obedience

If you were wondering how the clergy fitted into the King/Nobles/ Peasants model, the short answer is, they didn't. The Church had its own, parallel MLM happening. The Pope in Rome occupied the king's position, followed by archbishops and bishops (who were the nobility of the church), and finally the nuns and monks occupied the lowest rung of the ladder. All this Holy infrastructure was paid for by a 10 percent tithe on the people.

How could serfs pay a tithe when they earned little or no money? They paid in kind, usually in harvested grain or animals. The Church ran a spiritual protection racket too, because failure to pay tithes meant an eternity in the fiery pits of Hell. Whether or not the Church was a religious organized crime syndicate, brown-robed monks became as synonymous with the Middle Ages as knights, grubby peasants, and unrealistic art.

Christian monasteries first appeared in fourth-century Egypt but were such a hit, it only took a century for them to spread to the western parts of Europe. Early monasteries were isolated, single-sex, religious communities. They were populated with men who cut themselves off from their friends and families, devoting their lives to prayer and the study of scripture. These monks shunned worldly goods and lived holy lives of abstinence. This chiefly meant they took vows of poverty, chastity, and obedience, although some of the nuttier monks chose to go all out and live as hermits, ostensibly to prove their devotion to God.

From our viewpoint in today's secular world, it's very difficult to see the attraction of such a lifestyle. However, when viewed in context, religion was the most important thing in the lives of medieval people. This was because every day medieval life was pretty shitty, and the idea of eschewing the material trappings of the world wasn't much of a sacrifice. A monk had a roof over his head and a reliable source of food. At least until the establishment of mendicant orders in the twelfth century, whose members begged for food and clothing.

Although initially focused on personal devotion to God, as time passed, monks began providing services to their local community. They also became teachers, manuscript copyists, artists, and even missionaries. As a result, monasteries provided most of the educated and influential thinkers of the Middle Ages.

Fig. 4: Mistakes in the monastery lasted centuries. (Midjourney and S.E.W.)

St. Augustine: Number Two with a Bullet

When it comes to the Top 40 of all-time most influential Christian theologians, **Augustine of Hippo** (354–430 AD) is a strong second place after the standout number one, St. Paul. Better known as St. Augustine, this philosopher and theologian wrote many influential works, such as *The City of God, On Christian Doctrine*, and *Confessions*. His influence on the early Christian church was such that over five million words of his writing have been passed down to posterity.

Religions are nothing without stringent rules and the Christian monasteries were no different. Around 400 AD, Augustine devised the first known code of monastic rules in the Roman Church. It sets out the core rules of monastic life, such as obedience, chastity, poverty, and detachment from the material world, among others. This code became the early basis for monastic life.

Augustine was born in North Africa, in what is modern-day Algeria. A bit of "a lad" in his youth (he fathered an illegitimate son before the age of 21), it was Augustine who famously prayed "Lord, make me chaste—but not yet." However, after converting to Christianity in 386, he never looked back: It only took him eight years to rise from new convert to Bishop of Hippo. Augustine's thinking about theology profoundly influenced the Church, and therefore, the medieval world, particularly the concept of the Holy Trinity.

One of Augustine's biggest influences on modern thought is the idea of free will. He began by pondering why God allows evil in the world. His answer was that evil only exists because God allowed humans to have free will, and because humans are bastards, evil naturally ensues from these choices. Augustine even manages to give God a leave pass for "natural evils" such as disease, which he indirectly attributes to humans because disease is only bad when it interacts with people.

If you ask me, that's really drawing a long bow.

Nevertheless, along with Jerome, Ambrose, and Gregory the Great, Augustine is considered one of the Fab Four of church fathers. However, his pre-eminence is such that he is Lennon and McCartney combined, and the other three are all Ringos (no offense, Ringo. You're still my fave).

Other Funky Monks

Because this book is a history of big ideas, not a history of monks and monasteries, I'm only going to lightly touch on some of the other monks who advanced medieval thinking. Clearly, this is not an exhaustive list, just the ones I find significant.

St. Benedict of Nursia (480 AD–547 AD) was the founder of the Benedictine Order of monks in Italy and is considered the father of Western monasticism. After his education, he went on a gap year as a hermit in a cave outside Rome. Ironically, Benedict's desire to be alone somehow attracted followers, and soon he emerged from his cave and founded a monastery. Because these followers had disturbed his peace, he set some of the ground rules, based in part, on Augustine's code. By the ninth century, most Western monasteries were guided by Benedict's rules. Side note: Despite what you may have heard, the liqueur D.O.M. Bénédictine is not meaningfully associated with the Benedictine Order. That was just a nineteenth-century marketing ploy.

St. Bede (672–735) was a member of the Benedictine Order who would go on to become the first English saint and be universally known as "the Venerable Bede." Bede was a significant scholar, whose writings covered history, music, grammar, science, and theology. Though far from the first to express the idea, he observed that "the Earth is, in fact, a sphere," putting this seventh-century man well ahead of today's flat-earthers. His historical works are of particular note and led to him being labeled the "Father of English History." Death took Bede in 735, while sitting on the floor deliriously singing that old chestnut: *Glory be to the Father.*

St. Francis of Assisi (1182–1226) was the founder of the Franciscan Order of Monks, but his early years were a bit of a mixed bag. He led a privileged life until nineteen, when he went to war and was captured. He was imprisoned in a dungeon for a year before his dad coughed up the ransom. This experience appears to have changed Francis (PTSD?), and he began having visions from God. These visions were a bit confusing: Was Francis being called to fight in the Crusades, help the sick, or repair the church? He couldn't be sure.

What St. Francis *did* know was that he loved the natural world, and there are many tales of his affinity with animals. One of these stories has him single-handedly dealing with a rogue wolf which had been terrorizing a town. All it took were a few kind words and the sign of the Cross, and Francis had wolfie eating out of the palm of his hand, like a saintly Steve Irwin.

Fig. 5: St. Francis confounded expectations. (Public domain and S.E.W.)

St. Thomas Aquinas (1225–1274) was an Italian friar of the Dominican Order, a philosopher, theologian, and a Doctor of the Church (basically an important religious dude). He was born to a noble family with connections to European kings and two Holy Roman Emperors. Somewhat understandably, Thomas' decision to join a begging order of monks was frowned upon and discouraged by his snooty relatives.

St. Thomas Aquinas was a hulking man who spoke slowly, leading him to be derided as "the dumb ox" by his (so-called) friends in the seminary. Despite what this nickname suggests, he was an exceptionally deep thinker open to all the intellectual traditions known in the thirteenth century. Alongside the Christian scriptures, his theological works reference Greek philosophical tradition, often through interpretation of Roman, Jewish, and Muslim texts, as well as the work of St. Augustine and other early church fathers. It is difficult for a layperson like me to understand (or more importantly, make interesting) the significance of St. Thomas Aquinas' contribution to medieval thought. Suffice to say, his theological influence was considerable.

William of Ockham (1287–1347) was an English theologian, Franciscan friar, philosopher, and one of the major intellectual figures of the Middle Ages. Today he is most famous for Occam's razor, a methodological principle that encourages thinkers to make the least assumptions possible when considering a proposition.

Fig. 6: The best a man can get. (Public domain, Jeksonjs, and S.E.W.)

Meanwhile, in Ireland...

On the Emerald Isle, St. Patrick had done more than allegedly rid the country of snakes. His introduction of monastic life in the fifth century saw the beginnings and growth of monastic schools. Irish scholars such as Columbanus, Aileran the Wise and John Scotus Erigena, were celebrated as some of the most learned men in Europe.

It makes you wonder how the cliche of the Irish being ignorant, violent drunks got started.

Fig. 7: St. Patrick won the hearts and minds of the Irish people.
(Sergey Kohl and S.E.W.)

Holy Orders, Batman!

In some "good" news for women, it wasn't medieval men who got to have all the fun. Medieval nuns enjoyed a higher status than peasant women, and girls who took Holy Orders were taught to read and write. A big tick.

In fact, although male monasteries were ubiquitous in the medieval world, it's thought that nunneries were even more so. These nunneries were not only inhabited by those of a religious bent, but also girls forced into it by their families, and "illegitimate, deformed or half-witted" girls. In addition, widowed women were accepted to help improve their lot. The nuns were bound by similar rules to those of the monks, taking vows of chastity, poverty, and devotion to prayer. They were also dedicated to helping the needy.

However, by some contemporary accounts, not all nunneries (or monasteries) were considered the Godly places one might expect. In *Medieval English Nunneries*, Eileen Power recounts instances of unsavory behavior in nunneries, including a prioress who was "caught in the act" with a priest, and the case of the nun Margaret, who was not allowed back into a nunnery because she was pregnant... again.

The fourteenth-century satirical poem, "Why I Can't Be a Nun" tells the story of a young wannabe nun, thwarted by her father who believed that nunneries were places of carnal sin and vice rather than holy devotion. Naughty nuns and mischievous monks were, it seems, a medieval trope. A marginal illustration in a fourteenth-century illuminated text, the *Roman de la Rose*, depicts a nun picking dicks off a penis tree. Another shows a nun and a man *in flagrante delicto*. As it was, the monks illuminating these texts must have seen this as a running ecclesiastical joke.

Fig. 8: Who can blame Daddy? (RedUmbrella&Donkey and S.E.W.)

But Most Nuns Weren't Naughty

However, as you can probably imagine, "naughty" nuns were the exception rather than the rule. There were many exceptionally learned and upright nuns in the medieval times.

St. Scholastica (480–543) was reputedly St. Benedict's twin sister. Tradition has it that she founded the Benedictine order of nuns. No small feat. **St. Hilda of Whitby** (614–680) was the knowledgeable abbess of the monastery at Whitby and was consulted for her wisdom by various kings. **St. Hildegard of Bingen** (1098–1179) was an intellectual giant. This Benedictine abbess bestrode the late Middle Ages as a mystic, writer, music composer, natural philosopher, and medical practitioner. Hildegard is generally considered to be at the pointy end of German science. **St. Clare of Assisi** (1194–1253) was one of St. Francis of Assisi's first followers. Inspired by Francis, she founded the Order of Poor Ladies, who are known colloquially as the Poor Clares. The rules Clare drafted for this order are the first known monastic rules written by a woman.

Like the monks, nuns helped keep collective learning alive in Europe.

Collective Learning in the Middle Ages

As I explained in *From Cave to Colosseum*, collective learning has been the driving force behind human growth. Very early in their development as a species, humans had learned to transmit learning from generation to generation. To appreciate the growth of education from the early-to-late medieval times, we must track the state of teaching and learning during this period.

After the fall of Rome, Theodoric, king of the Ostrogoths, ruled the remnants of the Western Roman empire from Ravenna. While there was still a Senate in Rome, that once august body now meekly endorsed whatever their imperial overlord decreed (all-in-all, not dissimilar to how it worked for the previous five hundred years). For a time, more and more Goths spoke Latin and they sent their upper-class lads to Rome for lessons in rhetoric and grammar. However, as time went by, this kind of education was eventually considered a weakness, and the Byzantine historian Procopius of Caesarea observed that the Goths believed that *real* men "ought to be freed from the timidity which teachers inspire and to take his training in arms." From this point, the road to advancement was no longer seen as being through education as it had been in Classical times; real power lay in being as big of a bullying asshole as possible.

A definite step backwards.

Holy Roman Emperor, Batman!

Charlemagne (743–814 AD) became the first Holy Roman Emperor in 768 AD and was renowned for reviving and promoting education. While some consider this reputation overblown, he did much to help scholarly traditions survive in an era not celebrated for its sophistication. When Charlemagne came to the Frankish throne, he despaired at the poor standard of Latin being taught in the kingdom. Obviously, a fluent knowledge of Latin was required for interpretation of the Bible, so he mandated that priests be persuaded or compelled to be educated to a higher standard. Charlemagne's emphasis on educational reform resulted in a higher standard of education and morals than any prior generation of clerics.

At this time there was a recurrence of interest in Classical learning during the Carolingian Renaissance. Alcuin of York (735–804 AD), *another* English monk and an influential scholar and teacher at the Carolingian court, worked to revive Classical knowledge through focusing on the seven liberal arts: Grammar, Rhetoric, Dialectic, Astronomy, Arithmetic, Geometry, and Music. He advocated the restoration of old schools and the founding of new ones. Later, in the twelfth and thirteenth centuries, many of those schools would develop into universities.

Holy Ass-whipping, Batman!

He that spareth his rod hateth his son: but he that loveth him chasteneth him betimes.
Proverbs 13:24

This Bible verse launched a thousand whips and is the basis of the adage "Spare the rod and spoil the child." The "rod" in this case was a birch rod, which was a bound bundle of leafless birch twigs. While this may sound relatively harmless, the birch rod was not only used in schools. In some prisons, birching was more feared than the cat-o'-nine-tails. For children, the rod was applied to the bare bottom as seen in the illustration below:

Fig. 9: The Ass at School—Pieter Breughel with assistance.
(Public domain, S.E.W.)

If we are to believe this illustration (and others which have come down to us), all this whipping didn't necessarily have a beneficial effect in the classroom. Pieter Breughel's *The Ass at School* depicts the medieval schoolhouse as a place of chaos, violence, and madness. In true medieval style, he represents the children as grotesque mini adults, which only increases the surreal appearance of this artwork. There is little in the depiction of classroom pandemonium that today's teacher might recognize unless they are a substitute teacher at a school for the criminally insane.

Brutalizing students was not just a medieval tradition, but quite possibly goes back to prehistory. Such beatings were used not only to reprimand students for poor behavior, but for students demonstrating stupidity and making mistakes. So, the teacher was literally trying to beat sense into his students. However, a schoolmaster's concerns went way beyond the behavioral or academic. In the seventh century, the Archbishop of Canterbury, Theodore of Tarsus, recommended that students who "fornicate among themselves" should be flogged, and that a boy who "pollutes himself" should be similarly punished. Quite how the archbishop discovered these transgressions is unclear. Maybe he went undercover.

Clearly, getting an education, something so integral to human development, was no picnic in the Middle Ages. Dutch philosopher and theologian Erasmus of Rotterdam wrote of school as a "torture-chamber" and took a dim view of teachers who dominated their students with a "menacing face and terrorizing voice" in a classroom where all one could hear was "the whistling of birches, the wailing and sobbing, the savage threats." Medieval schooling sounds like *a Tom Brown's School Days*/*Fifty Shades of Grey* mashup.

It was in the late sixth century that the grand traditions of the English public school began to emerge. The King's School was founded as a cathedral school and is said to have been founded in 597 AD, making it reputedly the world's oldest continuously operating school. As one might expect from a school of such antiquity, it has some arcane traditions. Unfortunately, the custom that enabled the school captain to keep a goat in the quad is no more. However, the rules that allow this same august personage to cultivate a beard and bring his wife to class remain on the books.

Power has its privileges.

Of course, during this period, there were a lot more important things on people's minds than goats, wives, and beards.

Death, Disease and Societal Change

In the late medieval period, average life expectancy wasn't high: around thirty years of age for upper-class men. However, if one survived until twenty-one, life expectancy jumped up to sixty-four. This is not substantially different from life expectancy in ancient Greece or Rome. This makes sense, because the child mortality rate in the Middle Ages has been estimated to be between thirty and fifty percent, which is equivalent to the estimated child mortality rate in the Classical era. Although this high death rate is to be expected in a world without antibiotics, modern medicine, and basic hygiene, it's still staggering. The simplest cut or abrasion could lead to a life-threatening infection, so it's no wonder medieval people prayed a lot.

Tuberculosis and leprosy were among the most fearsome diseases of the day, as was a non-sexually transmitted version of syphilis (that took all the fun out of it). But, of course, no discussion of disease in the Middle Ages would be complete without mention of the Plague. Not only was it a fearsome disease, but the societal destruction it wrought forced the medieval world to reinvent itself.

Out of death and misery came positive change and some big ideas.

Avoid Cliches Like the Plague

We all know the plague cliches: Rats and fleas; beaky plague doctor masks; ragged, dirty peasants; buboes; wholesale death. Yet, until COVID-19, it was difficult for twenty-first-century people to fully imagine the experience of living through such a pandemic. Not that the coronavirus is even vaguely as lethal as the *Yersinia pestis* bacterium, which had a fatality rate of up to sixty percent. Nevertheless, we have a better appreciation of what life was like for those medieval people trying to avoid the plague. It must have been terrifying.

Despite the enduring notoriety of the Black Death, this outbreak was just one of many during the Middle Ages.

The Early Medieval Pandemic

The Early Medieval Pandemic began in 541 AD as the Plague of Justinian in Byzantium. Proving it was no respecter of rank, the Byzantine Emperor Justinian (the lucky guy for whom it was named) was stricken with plague, but miraculously recovered. Over the next two hundred years, plague spread in up to eighteen major waves across the Mediterranean Basin and up into Northern Europe.

In 686, plague had made its way to Jarrow in the northeast of England. It hit the Jarrow monastery particularly hard, with only two monks living to tell the tale. One was an adult monk named Ceolfrith, and the other was a boy of around fourteen years. Together, these two continued to perform mass until new monks could be trained. The boy grew to be our old mate, The Venerable Bede.

Fig. 10: The Venerable Bore (Midjourney and S.E.W.)

The belief at the time was that this plague was sent by God as a punishment for human misdeeds. If this was the case, it suggests that the God of the Old Testament had come out of retirement, although He finally gave the world some respite around 767 AD.

However, this vengeful deity hadn't finished with the Middle Ages yet; oh no, not by a long shot.

The Black Death: The Plague Strikes Back

Plague returned with a vengeance in the fourteenth century. This time, it was the Black Death, the most lethal pandemic in recorded history, which peaked in Europe between 1347 and 1351. As much as one third of the population succumbed to its depredations.

Some towns in which most of the residents had died were simply abandoned. Contemporary reports often state that there were "hardly enough living to care for the sick and bury the dead." Even though many believed the plague was God's judgment on humanity, religious rites such as funerals were ignored due to a lack of living clergy. Survivors resorted to mass graves to dispose of the victims' bodies.

Fig. 11: Cedric the Plague Doctor wasn't quick on the uptake.
(Midjourney and S.E.W.)

Understandably, there was a significant decrease of faith in a God that could allow such carnage. Those who survived learned that life was fleeting and there was little point delaying gratification. Laughing in the face of death, people ate, drank, and were merry. And had a lot of sex: Many cast their moral codes aside, because what the hell, why not live a little before a grisly, agonizing death?

This new world order didn't just affect sobriety, chastity, and scruples. The population decrease had a dramatic effect on the workforce, with significant, long-lasting social and economic ramifications. Despite official attempts to keep the cost of labor at pre-plague levels, the lack of workers (as well as the difficulty and danger of producing goods) eventually drove up rates of pay. Serfs who had been bound to one lord were suddenly mobile and could negotiate more favorable conditions from another master. This was the harbinger of the end for the feudal system.

The plague also wiped out entire noble families, but it wasn't all good news for society's most lowly. Instead, the dead noble's land left vacant by the ravages of the Black Death was simply incorporated into the estates of distant relations. This concentrated wealth even more than pre-plague days. Of course, I'm a "glass half full" kind of person, so I'm going to point out one upside of this phenomenon. It contributed to the emergence of mega-rich merchant princes, like Lorenzo de' Medici. Now, I'm no fan of concentrating all wealth and power in the top one percent of society, but in the case of Lorenzo and men like him, I'll make an exception, because of the role they played as patrons of the arts during the Renaissance.

But I'm getting ahead of myself.

Holy War: The Last Crusade?

Although we are looking for lightbulb moments, the Crusades were definitely not one of them. They were, however, very influential and have implications right up to the present.

It all seems to have begun with a beleaguered pope.

Pope Urban II had a lot on his plate. He had an arch-nemesis, the awesomely named Antipope Clement III; he had to manage disputes between a number of Christian nations; and he had to stare down the spread of Islam into eastern Europe. Perhaps in an attempt to draw attention away from the church's internal troubles, in 1095 he began to advocate for a Holy War to rid the Holy Land of the "pagans." He made the whole affair very attractive to God-fearing nobles:

All who die by the way, whether by land or by sea, or in battle against the pagans, shall have immediate remission of sins. This I grant them through the power of God with which I am invested.

This generous offer set off a succession of religious wars known as the Crusades, that would continue for hundreds of years. The best known of these Holy Wars took place between 1095 and 1291 as Christian armies from Europe attempted to "liberate" Jerusalem and the Holy Land from Islamic rule.

They believed they were on a mission to civilize.

Contrary to what we might expect, most Crusaders were not gleaming, gracious knights. A significant number of filthy, ignorant peasants came along on the road trip as well. The historian Albert of Aachen wrote that this "stupid and insanely irresponsible" rabble believed that a particular goose and goat were "inspired by the Holy Ghost," and followed wherever they led.

If this was not what the leaders of the crusade expected, some nobles were no less embarrassing. The Frankish contingent didn't cover themselves with glory when paying their "respects" to the Byzantine Emperor Alexius I. One of the Frankish counts took it upon himself to sit on Alexius' throne and threw shade at the emperor when asked to get off: "This must be a rude fellow who would alone remain seated when so many brave warriors are standing up." Alexius wisely said nothing to the discourteous, heavily armed man.

Despite these hiccups, from a Christian perspective, Pope Urban II's First Crusade was significant and successful. Jerusalem was conquered, as well as the cities of Antioch and Edessa. A second, unsuccessful crusade was launched in 1147, when the Turks took back Edessa.

The news got worse for the Christians. Pope Urban II keeled over dead when he heard that Saladin had reconquered Jerusalem. No matter. The new pope, Gregory VIII, called for a Third Crusade in 1189. This was a veritable who's who of crusaders, featuring the boy-band supergroup of Holy Roman Emperor Frederick I, King Philip II of France, and Richard the Lionheart of England. Unfortunately, poor old Frederick died *en route*, which wasn't particularly auspicious. And things didn't get better for the Crusaders. This ill-fated venture saw Saladin victorious and keeping his hold on Jerusalem.

The Fourth Crusade (1202–1204) was perhaps the most moronic crusade of all, which is a big call after all the goose-following in the First Crusade. The crusaders had intended to go to Egypt and fight Muslims but got a teensy bit distracted on the way. Instead of attacking Egypt, they sacked Constantinople, the largest Christian city in the world.

Oopsy.

This was largely due to Byzantine court intrigue and unpaid debts, but there was a healthy dose of racism and stupidity involved as well.

Fig. 12: A misguided massacre about to take place.
(Erica Guilane-Nachez and S.E.W.)

In an era of bad ideas, this one was spectacular in its foolishness. The ill-advised attack caused the schism between the Catholic and Orthodox churches that has continued until today. Not only that, but by weakening the Byzantine Empire, it left them sitting ducks for Ottoman conquest, hastening the collapse of Christendom in the Middle East.

Nice work, boys.

There were at least nine crusades, none of them particularly successful. You'd think the Christians would've learned their lesson sooner.

The Significance of "Magna Farta"

One of the most significant lightbulb moments of the Middle Ages occurred in 1215 AD, with the signing of the Magna Carta (or "Great Charter") by the deeply unpopular King John. It is, hands down, one of the most influential documents in history. Revered particularly in English-speaking democracies, Magna Carta guaranteed the rights of individuals, including the right to a fair trial. It also established the principle that all people, even the king, are subject to the law.

King John did not willingly give up these rights. Rather, he was dragged kicking and screaming to the negotiating table after a group of rebel barons rose up against him and captured London. Letting go of some of his royal privileges was the only way he could secure peace and remain sovereign.

Hence Magna Carta.

However, true to his reputation as England's worst ever king, Bad King John then stabbed the barons in the back. He wrote to Pope Innocent III, asking him to annul the agreement. The Pope, who had excommunicated the king in 1209 (then re-communicated him after John paid a "tribute") duly obliged. The argy-bargy induced by this papal interference led to a civil war which John continued to wage until, at last, he shat himself to death in 1216. The compromise peace after John's messy demise allowed his son to be crowned Henry III, the rebel barons to be restored to their rank, and Magna Carta to remain the law of the land.

Fig. 13: Despite this illustration, King John did not physically sign Magna Carta. (Midjourney and S.E.W.)

Although Magna Carta enjoys a stellar reputation in the modern age, it wasn't always so popular. In the seventeenth century, the Lord Protector Oliver Cromwell was less impressed with the document, which he derisively referred to as "Magna Farta" (apparently Cromwell had a scatological turn of phrase: he also referred to the Petition of Right as the "Petition of Shite").

Robin Hood: Fictional Freedom-Fighter/Terrorist?

Before King John crapped himself into the afterlife, English folklore insists he had an antagonist in the form of Robin of

Locksley, otherwise known as the outlaw Robin Hood. We've already examined my childhood memories of *The Adventures of Robin Hood*, but there have been many attempts to establish Robin Hood as a *bona fide* historical figure. However, the "Robin Hood" Wikipedia page lists him as "legendary" and that's good enough for me. However, as he is at least 99 percent fictional, one might well ask, "For which lightbulb moment could he *possibly* be responsible?"

It's the pervasiveness of Robin Hood's egalitarian legend which is the big idea here. Robin and his Merry Men have always been portrayed as heroic outlaws. Their "misdeeds" were really justified resistance to the corruption of a tyrannical king and his minions. They remained loyal to the crusading King Richard the Lionheart. Robin and his men redistributed wealth from the rich to the poor, thwarting the dastardly designs of the evil Sheriff of Nottingham. Further, even though Robin Hood was himself a noble, he slummed it in Sherwood Forest with Friar Tuck, Little John, Will Scarlet, and the rest of the Merry Men. These things made Robin something of a working-class hero in a time before the concept of "working class" even existed.

The legend makes historical sense when we consider the real-life backdrop of the rebel barons fighting King John: dispossessed nobles fighting an unjust king. However, the idea that the powers-that-be aren't always right and could (and indeed *should*) be opposed was subversive. Robin would serve as a role model for many future freedom-fighters/terrorists.

Rightly or wrongly, this was a very big idea.

Fig. 14: Rich travellers held up by a merry, gay, subversive outlaw.
(Public domain and S.E.W.)

Medieval Literature: A Cultural Black Hole?

As readers of *Lightbulb Moments: From Cave to Colosseum* will be aware, the ancient world was a source of amazing literature, from the *Epic of Gilgamesh*, through *The Iliad* and *The Odyssey*, up to the poetry of Virgil and Ovid. Given the reputation of the Middle Ages as a cultural black hole dominated by the early Christian church, one might be forgiven for thinking medieval literature would be non-existent or just plain dreadful.

Nothing could be further from the truth. In addition to the plethora of religious writing (and to be fair, there was an awful lot of that) there were many significant literary texts produced.

Beowulf

Beowulf is thought to have been set down in writing around 1000 AD and is regularly cited as the first major work of literature in English. While *technically* true, this is drawing something of a long bow, as it was written in Old English and is unintelligible to modern readers. That's probably why it's one of the most frequently translated works of Old English literature. *Beowulf's* writer is unknown, so is usually referred to as the "*Beowulf* poet." However, it's likely the story had been transmitted orally for many years before being committed to parchment.

Beowulf is the story of Beowulf, the hero of a tribe of Swedish seafarers known as the Geats. When the monster Grendel attacks the mead hall of King Hrothgar of the Danes, Beowulf comes to the rescue and defeats the beast. This seriously pisses off Grendel's mum, who mounts her own attack. Unperturbed, Beowulf kicks Mum's ass as well, then goes home to his tribe where he becomes king. And lived the rest of his life in peace.

Or so he thought.

Fifty years pass, and Beowulf is called out of retirement to fight a dragon. Although victorious, he's mortally wounded in the battle and dies with a heroic speech on his lips:

After they burn my body, tell my warriors to build a great burial mound on the cliffs that stick out into the sea. The sailors steering their ships on the gloomy waters will see it and call it Beowulf's barrow, and my people will remember me.

Stirring stuff indeed.

Marco Polo: Bullshitter Extraordinaire

One of history's first and greatest travelogs was that of Venetian merchant and explorer Marco Polo (1254–1324). His book, *Travels*, outlines his journeys into India, Persia, Japan, and traveling the Silk Road into China, where he spent over seventeen years. In total, Marco's travels lasted twenty-four years.

At the end of that time, Marco returned to Venice having made his fortune as a trader, and during a war between Venice and Genoa, he paid for (and captained) his own personal warship. He was captured and held for ransom by the Genoese, and during his captivity Marco dictated *Travels* to Rustichello of Pisa, a fellow prisoner. As *Boy's Own* adventure as all this sounds, *Travels* is not a page-turner, its plodding pace making it something of a yawn-fest. As Rustichello was a professional writer of romances, the lack of panache is surprising.

Over the years, the veracity of some of Marco's more "out there" claims have come under scrutiny. He maintained that he was buddies with the Mongol Emperor. He even claimed to have governed a Mongol city, but there is no corroborating evidence for these assertions. One of Marco's most dubious assertions was that he gave the Mongols tips on warfare (as if they needed them).

While it seems pretty clear that Marco Polo was a total bullshit artist, *Travels* is, when viewed with proper skepticism, a valuable historical document and provides an insight into the medieval world.

Sir Gawain and the Green Knight

Who doesn't love a good Arthurian legend?

With their genesis around 500 AD, these tales of gallant knights, magic swords, sorcery, courtly love, and (of course) the quest for the Holy Grail, have become woven into Britain's mythological tapestry. Arthurian legend was basically a cross between *Game of Thrones* and the Marvel Cinematic Universe. Arthur is portrayed as a just and wise king, and his court at Camelot is a magic place, full of brave knights and courtly love. Sir Lancelot and Queen Guinevere are the prototypical tragic star-crossed lovers.

Sir Gawain and the Green Knight is a story from this tradition, written in the late fourteenth century as a narrative poem by an unnamed writer. Arthur's nephew (and Knight of the Round Table) Sir Gawain is the main protagonist of the tale, which begins when a mystical Green Knight presents himself at the court of Camelot.

The Green Knight challenges Arthur to hit him with an axe. There's one condition: Arthur must vow to allow the Green Knight to reciprocate the axe blow in a year's time. Arthur thinks this challenge is silly, but the Knight then impugns the honor of Camelot. Incensed, Sir Gawain steps forward and administers the blow, neatly lopping off the Knight's head. This leaves the Green Knight less impaired than Gawain might have hoped. The knight picks up his head and reminds Gawain of his promise: they must meet again in twelve months at the Green Chapel.

One of the greatest, most enduring medieval tales ensued.

Fig. 15: And so it begins… (Erica Guilane-Nachez and S.E.W.)

The Canterbury Tales

One of my most enduring memories of high school was when, without preamble, my English teacher, Mrs. Finney, walked into the classroom and began speaking a weird language in an equally weird accent. We all hoped she was okay, but she *hadn't* had a stroke. Instead, she was reciting the beginning of Geoffrey

Chaucer's (1345–1400) *The Canterbury Tales* in the original Middle English. This was her party-piece and she looked forward to this lesson every year. It had the desired effect: Mrs. Finney had our attention and held it for the rest of the lesson.

We learned that Chaucer's long-form poem tracks the pilgrimage of thirty-one people, including the writer himself, from an inn in London to Canterbury Cathedral to visit the shrine of St. Thomas à Becket. At the innkeeper's suggestion, the pilgrims agree to pass the time on their journey telling each other their personal tales. Given that the contingent includes a knight, a prioress, a carpenter, a cook (the so-called Wife of Bath), and a miller, a wide range of stories are told.

The knight tells a high-minded narrative of courtly love, but this is countered by the miller's bawdy tale, which is punctuated with fart jokes. The ten-times-married Wife of Bath regales the party with an Arthurian legend, which is related to another poem about Gawain, *The Wedding of Sir Gawain and Dame Ragnelle.*

Fig. 16: Fart jokes can only take you so far... (Archivist and S.E.W.)

While Chaucer's great work remains a timeless insight into English life towards the close of the fourteenth century, it tragically was less than a quarter complete when he died. The writing of *The Canterbury Tales* was roughly contemporaneous with the writing of *Sir Gawain and the Green Knight*, but at least we know the name of the author. There are still ninety copies from the 1400s in existence, meaning that, by medieval standards, *The Canterbury Tales* was a massive bestseller.

Notre-Dame and the Brilliance of Medieval Architecture

Watching the BBC documentary *Rebuilding Notre-Dame, Inside the Great Cathedral Rescue*, I was inspired to reflect on the brilliance of medieval architecture. In the program, Lucy Worsley interviewed the team rebuilding Notre-Dame de Paris after the 850-year-old structure was tragically gutted by fire in 2019.

Built between 1163 and 1250 AD, Notre-Dame is the epitome of Gothic architecture, and the rebuilding effort showcased the technical knowledge and ingenuity of the original designers. This building is heroic in scope. The interior of the cathedral is 130 meters long by 48 meters wide, with the roof 35 meters above. Two hulking gothic towers flank the western facade.

To achieve this truly epic construction, the architects and engineers pioneered use of flying buttresses (graceful arched structural supports) and rib vaulting (arched ribs that enable a ceiling to cover a large open area), which allowed Notre-Dame to effortlessly soar (with the addition of the spire) to a height of ninety-six meters. Its enormous stained glass rose windows are, on their own, amazing artistic statements. Clearly, given the splendor of this cathedral, the restoration team has undertaken a daunting task, but this isn't the first major renovation rescue performed on the old girl.

During the French Revolution, Notre-Dame was desecrated and left in disrepair. It took public interest in the building spurred by the publication of Victor Hugo's *The Hunchback of*

Notre-Dame to rally Parisians behind their fallen icon, and the old girl was restored between 1844 and 1864.

Yep, this is my hot take: Quasimodo saved Notre-Dame.

Fig. 17: *From the 1923 MGM movie* The Hunchback of Notre Dame. *(Public domain and S.E.W.)*

While I appear to be singling Notre-Dame out for praise, the truth is the medieval era gave the world many truly awe-inspiring religious buildings. Cathedral building was a mania in the Middle Ages, and these huge, long-term building projects were the moonshots of their day. They took decades to construct and cost massive sums of money, overtly signaling the wealth and power of the Catholic Church.

Hundreds of skilled tradesmen and laborers toiled with the most basic of tools, to erect these masterpieces of medieval architecture. It wasn't a safe or easy job, either: Industrial health and safety rules were 900 years in the future, and life was cheap. A few lives lost to the Glory of God was a small price to pay.

A Man's Home Is His Castle

The iconic castles of the Middle Ages did double-duty as monumental defensive structures and prestigious (albeit by medieval standards) residences for noblemen. However, the earliest incarnations of these structures were not quite so swanky. The basic concept behind them dates back to Roman siege fortifications, with the simplest version of a castle consisting of a wooden palisade and earthworks. However, this architectural simplicity didn't last long.

The classic features of medieval castles are familiar to any child who's built a sandcastle at the beach, even if their names are not. Firstly, there are the curtain walls and towers that make up the perimeter defensive wall. Then, there's the gatehouse at the entrance of the castle. Inside the walls, the keep, the largest tower behind the walls, was the most secure part of the structure. This was where damsels in distress were confined. The bailey is the courtyard area inside the walls.

And what castle, sand or otherwise, is complete without a moat? These artificial ditches surrounding the walls were filled with water. A less well-known design feature of the castle, long-drop toilets built into the curtain wall overhanging the moat, ensured the water quality was less than pristine. Other than purpose-built siege engines, drawbridges were the only safe way to cross these open sewers.

While towers were an important aspect of any fortress, their size increase over the years was not for any good reason. Having the biggest tower didn't provide any tactical advantage to the castle's defenders—it was merely part of a lordly dick-measuring contest.

Fig. 18: They're both correct (Ruskpp and S.E.W.)

Leaning Tower of Pisa

This attractive bell tower in Pisa was not intended to be a curiosity, but it was destined to become one. It was constructed in three stages over a period of two hundred years, beginning in 1173, when the foundations were laid. But that was where the problems began.

The foundations were poorly designed and the subsoil unstable, so the building had already begun to sink by 1178. This construction problem, plus Pisa's almost constant state of war with surrounding city-states, meant that building was halted for nearly one hundred years. Luckily, this hiatus gave time for the soil beneath the tower to settle, saving the tower for posterity.

Construction recommenced in 1272, and the builders designed the upper floors to have one side higher than the other in an attempt to disguise the listing of the tower. But rather than hide the problem, it just added a less obvious imperfection: the Leaning Tower of Pisa is also slightly banana-shaped.

Another war brought construction to a standstill in 1284. The world had to wait till 1319 for the completion of the seventh floor. By then, the tower was leaning 4 degrees from the perpendicular.

Four major earthquakes have rocked the Pisa region since the late thirteenth century, each of a magnitude that could've brought down the tower. Ironically, the dodgy soil, which caused the lean, may have minimized the effect of the quakes through "dynamic soil-structure interaction." So the Leaning Tower may owe its continued existence to its imperfection.

Much later during the Renaissance, Pisa resident and scientific rockstar Galileo Galilei, used the tower to perform a famous experiment. He dropped cannonballs of different masses from the tower, demonstrating that their speed was independent of their mass.

Fig. 19: And the rest is history... (Beatrice Preve, Public domain, and S.E.W.)

Medieval builders expertly used an arcane suite of skills, that today we would refer to as physics, engineering, and mathematics, in the construction of their jaw-dropping buildings. This positioned them at the cutting edge of the beginnings of modern science, right up alongside wizards, alchemists, and necromancers.

Magic and the Occult: The Beginnings of Modern Science and Medicine?

The Middle Ages saw the beginnings of modern medicine and science. While this is truer of the medieval Muslim world, there were still inklings of it in the West. Of course, these important, respected fields weren't as we know them today. In the Middle Ages, they took the form of occultism and magic. Yep, medieval alchemists, necromancers, wizards, wise-women, and witches were the precursors of today's rocket scientists and brain surgeons.

Despite the images we see of medieval witches in popular culture, the practice of magic (dark or otherwise) during the Middle Ages was, in general, the province of humans with penises. Court records from the late Middle Ages show that most people accused of necromancy or dark magic were men. This doesn't mean that medieval men were more evil than women (although they probably were). Rather, it can be accounted for by the inequality of educational opportunities at that time, as the ability to read the Latin incantations from books of magic spells was a prerequisite for the performance of necromancy.

For those uninitiated in the ways of the dark arts, the practice of necromancy involves conjuring the dead for divination or prophecy. I'm not sure about the success rate of this practice, but it's clear that those necromancers who were caught, tried, and executed were not conjuring the right dead people.

*Fig. 20: Conjure the **right** dead person. Every time.*
(Samiramay, Zsolnai Gergely and S.E.W.)

When it came to the "occult," it seems most medieval women had to content themselves with either dancing naked and nymph-like in the forest or healing the sick. Most sick people in the Middle Ages saw nothing like what we would consider as a doctor. Instead, the sick were often attended to by a local "wise-woman" who was skilled in using herbal or traditional remedies. They might also offer the afflicted a magical charm to help their patient, which at the very least might have acted as a placebo. Like most vocational skills in the medieval times, these healing arts were passed down from mother to daughter. Although in the early Middle Ages, this type of magic was often accepted as a necessary part of life, in later years the church considered such wise women to be servants of Satan. This often resulted in them being tried as witches and burned at the stake.

Fig. 21: "Burn the witch! Burn her!" (Erica Guilane-Nachez and S.E.W.)

Another semi-occult pursuit popular in the Middle Ages was alchemy, which was a heady mixture of natural philosophy, mysticism, and naivety. It was not a new concept and in a European context dates back to around 300 BC. While over time, alchemical research would lead towards "real" science, alchemy was based on a flawed Aristotelian idea that all matter was composed of four elements: earth, air, fire, and water. Alchemists took that belief to its "logical" conclusion that the right combination of these elements could create any substance. It was from this belief that the idea of turning lead into gold arose. Some alchemists also thought that they could create potions that could extend life or even cheat death. Another common assumption was that to have success in the alchemical field, its practitioners must display purity of mind, body, and spirit, a suite of traits that may have kept alchemists from falling foul of zealous clerics. However, because of its heathen origins, alchemy was ultimately condemned by church authorities.

It didn't help matters that medieval alchemists guarded their secrets by using an obscure system of symbols and arcane names for the materials they studied. The popularity of alchemical research survived well beyond the Middle Ages and, as we shall see in Chapter 4, involved some *very* famous names

You Have Chosen ... Wisely

What would a discussion about the Middle Ages be without mention of the Holy Grail? Chances are you may have heard of it: you know, the cup that Jesus Christ drank from during the Last Supper? It was also supposedly used to collect JC's blood after he was stabbed with the centurion's spear during his crucifixion. The Grail was then given to some dude called Joseph of Arimathea, who inexplicably whisked it off to Britain.

Ninety percent of this is a medieval invention. Sure, Jesus must have drunk from a cup at the Last Supper, and it would be a sweet piece of Jesus memorabilia if you could get your hands on it. Unfortunately, all the other stuff is enthusiastic Jesus fanfic. There's no mention in the Bible of Jesus' sippy cup being brought to the crucifixion to catch his blood, or of Joseph of Arimathea swiping it to take to an obscure foreign land.

While not at all true, the legend of the Holy Grail spawned a thousand stories. As some readers may have guessed, *Monty Python and the Holy Grail* and *Indiana Jones and the Last Crusade* are two of my favorites, and I can quote both verbatim. There's a good reason the Pythons and Spielberg chose the Holy Grail as the subject of these films. It's because of the Grail's place as the pre-eminent trope in medieval literature, most particularly Arthurian legend.

Fig. 22: Particularly when you don't choose the cup of the carpenter...
(Luis Louro and S.E.W.)

Medieval Music

No lesser light than Charles Darwin believed that music had been around since the first hominids howled tunefully (or otherwise) while attempting to attract mates. While the musical notation of some ancient music has come down to us, it's not until the Middle Ages that people think they know how the music of the era sounded. Mostly, this is because of movies and television shows, but surprise, surprise, these—ahem—"recreations" are not accurate.

We *do* know the melody and the lyrics to some popular folk songs, but we really don't know what the instrumental accompaniment sounded like. Perhaps they sounded more death metal than *Greensleeves*, but with the instruments they had (lyres, harps, lutes, bagpipes, trumpets, flutes, organs, drums, cymbals, tambourines, and bells), this seems unlikely. In any event, most medieval music wasn't written down, and it wasn't until the late Middle Ages that composers started transcribing their music. The best documented music of this era is church music, with the Gregorian chant being an early chart-topper.

Fig. 23: Top of the Medieval Pops (Midjourney and S.E.W.)

For most of the medieval period, music was composed with a single melody, a style known as monophony. A musical big idea of the later Middle Ages was the beginnings of polyphony, which consists of two or more simultaneous lines of melody. The oldest, and possibly most famous example still known is the thirteenth-century English six-part round, *Sumer is icumen in*. However, most polyphonic compositions at the time were religious, and this music was known as *ars antiqua*, which translates as "ancient art" (not "ancient arse").

The End of the Darkness

So, while the Early Middle Ages *were* the Dark Ages of Europe, it would be foolish to say that nothing good happened during those thousand years. The years between 500 and 1500 AD were not a homogenous lump of ignorance, violence, and disease:

there was slow, but undeniable, social, philosophical, and artistic growth. This process of gradual change and progress picked up speed over the years until reaching terminal velocity in the fifteenth and sixteenth centuries. This kind of incremental development does not take place in a vacuum: collective learning *had* been taking place.

The main takeaway from the medieval period is that after the undoubted setback of the fall of Rome, human society clawed its way back, although it wasn't quick or easy and it certainly wasn't fun. Collective learning based on a dangerous combination of violence, fundamentalist religion and sexual discrimination played a major part in that revival.

However, this "dark" and sometimes less enlightened era in Europe was in stark contrast to what was occurring in the Islamic world, which was going through something of an awakening.

* * *

—2—

Rock the Casbah

The Islamic Golden Age

Western perceptions of Islam are often of an intolerant and almost medieval faith. It is seen by outsiders as a fundamentalist religion that is anti-women, anti-science and anti-progress. There are reasons Westerners might feel this way. Some are valid. Others... not so much. Without doubt, there are faults on both sides, ranging from Christian Crusades to ISIS, and all the colonization and terrorism in between.

But it's not my job to wade into *that* bun-fight.

And when the East wasn't being vilified, it was often viewed in the West with a kind of fetishized otherness, which Edward Said, founder of postcolonial theory, would later term "Orientalism." The Western fascination with the East had been around for hundreds of years but took off in the eighteenth century with Galland's translation of *One Thousand and One Nights*. This compendium of tales featured a mysterious, sexy, and edgy world of scimitars, turbans, fezzes, and pointy, curled-up slippers. The tropes of the Orient figured in the work of great poets Byron, Shelley, and, of course, well-known opium addict Samuel Taylor Coleridge's *Kublai Khan*. They also featured in the fiction of luminaries such as Wilkie Collins, Charles Dickens, and Rudyard Kipling. Edward FitzGerald's translation of *the Rubaiyat of Omar Khayyam* also exacerbated this misguided Islamophilia.

In 1978, Edward Said published *Orientalism*, one of the seminal works of postcolonial theory and among the most significant books of the twentieth century. Said contended that the West's view of the "Orient" traded on Islamic stereotypes that supported the West's paternalistic, imperialist policies.

The man had a point.

To this day, popular culture depictions of the Islamic world rely on lazy tropes such as "all Muslims are Arabs who ride camels," or look like sheiks, terrorists, or belly dancers. Even before 9/11, Muslims were often depicted as sleazy, untrustworthy villains, unless they were subservient sidekicks to the blond-haired, blue-eyed hero. Popular films such as *The Mummy*, the *Indiana Jones* series, and Disney's *Aladdin* cartoon and its live-action remake demonstrate all these cliches. In all honesty, when I was searching photo libraries for illustrations for this chapter, it was difficult to avoid such stereotypes. Sometimes, like in other chapters, I steered into the cliche.

Yet, in *this* chapter, it is my job to ignore the stereotypes and show the important, rich, and often unappreciated history of the Islamic world. They had plenty of big ideas. And one particular idea which, as we will see, ensured that we live in a developed world today.

Fig.1: Like I said, sometimes I steered into the cliches. (1001nights and S.E.W.)

A Very Short History of Islam

Even Islam's Public Enemy Number One, Sir Salman Rushdie, describes Muhammad (570–632 AD) as "one of the great geniuses of world history." And it is easy to see why: Muhammad's lightbulb moment grew to become the world's second largest religion. He was also a social, political, and military leader with few equals.

The Prophet Muhammad was born in the Arabian town of Mecca. His father died before he was born, and his mother passed away when he was only six years old. This left young Muhammad to be brought up by his grandfather, and then later, his uncle. It was a difficult beginning, but things got better when he was around twenty-five, when the soon-to-be prophet met and married a rich older woman by the name of Khadijah.

Khadijah was a successful businesswoman in her own right and is herself an incredibly significant person in Islamic lore, as she is considered Muhammad's first follower, and is referred to as the "Mother of the Believers." This marriage allowed Muhammad some upward mobility, wealth, and prestige, but it wasn't all about money and power. The couple had six children, and in an era where many men had multiple wives, Muhammad and Khadijah's marriage was monogamous until her death in 620 AD.

Ten years before that, Muhammad had a vision of the archangel Gabriel who told him: "You are the messenger of God." This was the first, but not the last message that he received from higher beings. Inspired, Muhammad began preaching in Mecca. He told his audience they should worship only one God, Allah. He also proclaimed that his followers should be generous as a way of expressing their appreciation to Allah. This new religion became known as Islam.

The Arabic word *islām* directly translates as "surrender," underlining the fundamental nature of the faith—that the believer surrenders to the will of Allah. Allah revealed his will to his final messenger, Muhammad, who then disseminated this knowledge through setting down the sacred scriptures, the *Qur'ān*.

Islam is one of a group of three religions that worship the God of Abraham. These three Abrahamic religions, Judaism, Christianity, and Islam, trace their lineage to Abraham's sons. The Jews and Christians look to his second son, Isaac. Muslims claim descent from his eldest son, Ishmael. Islam accepts that the main protagonists of the Christian Bible (including, but not limited to, Adam, Noah, Abraham, Moses, and Jesus) were prophets sent by Allah. They believe that, in addition, Muhammad is Allah's last and most significant prophet, whose message is the culmination of His revelations.

In these early days, Islam drew no distinction between the religious life and public life (and sometimes still doesn't, #sharialaw). Muslims believed it was their mission to take their values to the world through *jihād*, which literally translates as "exertion" but can also be translated as "holy struggle" or "holy war." Effective military conquest and an uncompromising commitment to core religious practices explains the astonishing success of the early spread of Islam. Less than a century after Muhammad's death in 632 AD, Islam had spread through the Middle East, then on to Africa, Europe, the Indian subcontinent, and South-East Asia.

By the end of the Umayyad Dynasty in 750 AD, the Islamic Caliphate included Spain, Portugal, North Africa, Egypt, Arabia, the Levant, and Persia. Not long after, during the Abbasid Dynasty, Baghdad became a significant center of learning. It was a place where the collective knowledge of the Roman, Greek, Indian, Chinese, Persian, North African, and Egyptian civilizations was collated, translated, and used to drive new discoveries. Despite what Latin scholars might try to tell you, from the mid-eighth century right up to the beginning of the twelfth century (and arguably, beyond), Arabic was the scientific language of humankind.

Holy War had played a key role in the initial expansion of the religion. However, in the twelfth century, Sufi missionaries spread it even further. Islam even gained a reputation as being tolerant of other religions. Yes, you read that right. Tolerant. In fact, Jews and Christians were given a special status as the "people of the Book" and were allowed to continue practicing their religions under a policy of leniency.

This period is considered "the Golden Age of Islamic Civilization" and is roughly concurrent with the period which we refer to as Europe's Dark Ages.

Fig. 2: A Muslim scholar gets news about witch-burning from the West. (Midjourney and S.E.W.)

The Golden Age of Islamic Civilization

Harun al-Rashid (766–809 AD), the fifth caliph of the Abbasid Dynasty, came to power emphasizing the importance of knowledge. He established the library known as the *Bayt al-Ḥikmah* or House of Wisdom, which was initially focused on Islamic learning. Despite his intellectual bent, Harun wasn't averse to lowbrow entertainment. He would slum it incognito through the back streets of Baghdad-after-dark with his rat-pack that included his court executioner, and the poet Abu Nuwas (because when *hasn't* bringing an executioner and a poet been handy on a debauch?).

Harun's son and successor, al-Ma'mun, was even more progressive. He expanded the House of Wisdom into an academy, opening it up to new schools of thought and to knowledge from the outside world. This included sponsoring the translation of Greek philosophical and scientific works, and the importation of other important books that did not exist in the Islamic world. As a result, the House of Wisdom flourished as a hub of knowledge and culture: the ideal place for scholarly men to excel in mathematics, astronomy, geography, medicine, physics, and chemistry. Due to its location in the Abbasid capital, it benefited from the influx of Islamic scholars from across the caliphate.

Muhammad ibn Musa al-Khwarizmi

Persian polymath Muhammad ibn Musa al-Khwarizmi (780–850 AD), whose name is sometimes Latinized as Algorithmi (yes, we have him to blame for algorithms), was influential in the worlds of astronomy, mathematics, and geography. Around 820 AD, he was appointed chief astronomer and head of Baghdad's House of Wisdom.

Al-Khwarizmi's *The Compendious Book on Calculation by Completion and Balancing* (c. 813–833 AD), quite apart from being the most awesomely named math textbook of all time, set forth the first system for solving linear and quadratic equations. European universities used *The Compendious Book on Calculation by Completion and Balancing* until the sixteenth century as their go-to math textbook.

As late as the twelfth century—nearly *four hundred years* after al-Khwarizmi's death—Latin translations of his arithmetic textbook, *On the Calculation with Hindu Numerals*, introduced the decimal positional number system to Europe and ensured that Hindu-Arabic numerals replaced Roman numerals.

In case you're unsure, Hindu-Arabic numerals are the ten digits we currently have in our decimal number system. However, in 2019, the American market research company Civic Science polled the question: "Should schools in America teach Arabic numerals as part of their curriculum?" The results were eye-opening. Seventy-two percent of Republican respondents believed Arabic numerals had no place in American classrooms. Forty percent of the Democrats polled agreed. What these people thought should replace 0, 1, 2, 3, 4, 5, 6, 7, 8 and 9 is not recorded.

Fig. 3: ...but it's probably a little something like this. (Sly and S.E.W.)

Mathematicians from the Middle East, such as Abu'l-Hasan al-Uqlidisi, expanded the decimal system to include fractions. Decimal point notation was pioneered by Sanad ibn Ali, a colleague of al-Khwarizmi, who also wrote the earliest work on Arabic numerals.

Abu Nasr Al-Farabi

Abu Nasr Al-Farabi (872–950) was a renowned early Islamic philosopher, known in Europe as Alpharabius. He had a wide field of expertise, being active in the study of mathematics, metaphysics, political philosophy, ethics, logic, science, cosmology and music theory. Like many polymaths up until the Scientific Revolution, he dabbled in alchemy, and wrote the book *The Necessity of the Art of the Elixir*, which I'm sure flew off the bookshelves in tenth-century Baghdad.

His followers referred to him as "the Second Teacher," a name acknowledging that only Aristotle (aka the First Teacher) was his superior. His commentaries ensured the preservation of ancient Greek philosophical and scientific texts, which allowed them to influence other important philosophers. Although Al-Farabi was an adherent of Aristotle, the school of philosophy he founded, Alfarabism, diverges from the works of Plato and Aristotle, and foreshadows modern philosophy by moving from metaphysics towards methodology.

Al-Jahiz: The Boggle-Eyed

Abu Othman Amr bin Bahr (776–868) is, sadly, more famous by his nickname: Al-Jahiz ("boggle-eyed"). He was born in Basra and rose above his humble beginnings to be a talented writer, who had a gift for expressing himself through humor. After spending his early life in Basra, Al-Jahiz moved to Baghdad in 816 AD, ostensibly to work in the library of the Bayt al-Ḥikmah. He authored over two hundred books, the most famous being the seven volume *Book of Animals*, a scholarly work that deals with aspects of animal classification and food chains. He even touches on the idea of evolution and natural selection, more than a thousand years before Darwin.

After spending half a century in Baghdad, Al-Jahiz retired back home to Basra. Still a lifelong learner at ninety-two, he met his end in a most appropriate fashion. He'd been working in his private library, when he was unfortunately crushed to death by an avalanche of books. Something tells me Al-Jahiz would've seen the humor in this.

Fig. 4: It only seemed appropriate… (Midjourney and S.E.W.)

Hasan Ibn al-Haytham

Hasan Ibn al-Haytham (965–1040), was an Arab Muslim mathematician, astronomer, philosopher, theologian, medical researcher, and physicist. Al-Haytham made important contributions to human understanding of sight and is considered "the father of modern optics."

Between 1011–1021 AD, Ibn al-Haytham (or Alhazen, as he was known in the West) wrote his most influential work: *The Book of Optics*, which explained how sight occurs when light is reflected from an object and into one's eyes. It was a book so well known that it's mentioned by Geoffrey Chaucer in *The Canterbury Tales*. Ibn al-Haytham demonstrated that while the eyes gather input, vision actually occurs within the brain. He was also one of the first to use a hypothesis in his experiments, making him a trailblazer in the scientific method, a full five hundred years before the Renaissance scientists who usually get the credit.

Interestingly, before Ibn al-Haytham's work on optics, one common theory used to explain sight was the "emission theory." This theory had been around since classical antiquity, and had been championed by Euclid and Ptolemy, among others. It held that sight occurred because the eye *emitted* rays of light, like Superman's X-Ray vision.

Well, we have Ibn al-Haytham (and common sense) to thank for debunking that one.

Ibn Sina

Ibn Sina (c. 980–1037), known in the Western world as Avicenna, was a Persian scholar regarded as one of the paramount thinkers of the Islamic Golden Age. He was a philosopher, astronomer, and a physician of such stature he is considered the father of early modern medicine.

Born in the city of Bukhara, Ibn Sina was a precocious child, who by 10 years of age had committed the entire *Qur'ān* to memory. He was, however, briefly stumped by Aristotle's *Metaphysics*, which he is said to have re-read forty times until he had memorized that as well. Even so, its meaning eluded him until he chanced upon a brief commentary by Al-Farabi, which finally gave him understanding.

Ibn Sina, like Al-Farabi, was influenced by Aristotelian philosophy. He is believed to have written over four hundred works, but only two hundred and forty have survived until today. This was a man who really didn't know the meaning of staying in his lane. Ibn Sina wrote books on mathematics, alchemy, astronomy, philosophy, medicine, psychology, geography, geology, theology, logic, and physics. He even had time for poetry, writing a medical textbook in verse just for the hell of it.

Most notable of Ibn Sina's works were *The Book of Healing* and *The Canon of Medicine*, a medical encyclopedia. The latter was a standard medical text for hundreds of years and was used until the seventeenth century. These medical texts outline advanced ideas including a procedure for cataract surgery and the advocacy of human drug trials, revealing just how far Ibn Sina was ahead of his time.

The Rubber Yacht of Omar Khayyam

If you've heard of Omar Khayyam (1048–1131 AD), it is most likely in relation to the *Rubaiyat of Omar Khayyam*, a nineteenth-century collection of his poetry, translated by Edward FitzGerald. It is written in quatrains such as

WAKE! For the Sun, who scattered into flight
The Stars before him from the Field of Night,
Drives Night along with them from Heav'n, and strikes
The Sultan's Turret with a Shaft of Light.

There is controversy over whether these poems were exclusively the work of Omar Khayyam. They probably all weren't. However, it's clear that Islamic scholars were obsessed with writing poetry.

During his lifetime, Omar Khayyam wasn't famous for his balladry. He was known as a groundbreaking mathematician, philosopher, and astronomer, who merely flirted with poetry. Khayyam's mathematical works include: *A commentary on the difficulties concerning the postulates of Euclid's Elements*, the stunning *On the division of a quadrant of a circle*, and the immortal page-turner *On proofs for problems concerning Algebra*. There is evidence he wrote a book, now lost, on binomial theorem, which I'm sure was gripping reading for those who understood its meaning.

Razia Sultana

Razia Sultana (1205–1240 AD) is famous as the first female Muslim ruler, and she briefly ruled the Delhi Sultanate in the north of the Indian subcontinent. I say briefly, because the big idea of feminine rule was way ahead of its time, and, unfortunately, it doesn't end well.

It all began while Razia's father, Sultan Shamsuddin Iltutmish, was away on a military campaign. She ruled Delhi in his stead from 1231 to 1232 AD, and legend has it that when Daddy got home, he was so happy with her stewardship he made her his heir. Despite this, when the Sultan died, it was Razia's half-brother Ruknuddin Firuz who took the throne. At Razia's urging, the people revolted against Ruknuddin's rule. He was deposed, and Razia took the throne 1236.

Many of the nobles who supported Razia's sultanate were shocked and disappointed when she began asserting her power. This was not the rubber-stamp figurehead they had expected. But less than four years into Razia's rule, the nobles revolted against *her*, and she was deposed. Not done yet, Razia married one of the rebels and tried unsuccessfully to regain the throne. Her successor was her half-brother, Muizuddin Bahram, who had her killed not long after.

Fig. 5: What did I say earlier about lazy stereotypes? (1001nights and S.E.W.)

Mansa Musa: The Richest Person in History?

The Golden Age of Islam was not confined to the Middle East. If being super-rich is a big idea, then arguably the richest man in human history was a West African emperor who took his enormous entourage (to my knowledge, not a euphemism) on a road trip to Mecca in the fourteenth century.

Mansa Musa (1280–1337), was the ninth *Mansa* (emperor) of the Mali Empire, and a devout Muslim who wanted medieval Mali to partake in sophisticated Islamic culture. Money was no object. Mali was immensely rich from mining salt, copper, and gold, as well as trading in elephant ivory. Of course, as emperor, Mansa Musa was the beneficiary of much of this wealth. While the common assertion that he was the richest person ever is impossible to quantify, as we'll see, the manner of his pilgrimage to Mecca (or *hajj*) makes the claim feasible.

To be sure, Musa wasn't the first West African king to travel to Mecca. However, the opulence of his *hajj* ensured his notoriety across Northern Africa and the Middle East. The emperor undertook this expedition between 1324 and 1325, a journey spanning nearly 4400 kilometers.

And he didn't travel light.

Musa's procession included doctors, lawyers, teachers, craftsmen, ten thousand soldiers, sixty thousand porters, twelve thousand slaves (each carrying 1.8 kilograms of gold), and heralds dressed in silk and carrying staffs of gold. There were also eighty camels each carrying 136 kilograms of gold dust. All-in-all, Mansa Musa was transporting over two tons of gold. It's easy to imagine that all this wealth made Musa's caravan a tempting target for raiders, but his troops were well armed and numerous. Only a fool would've attacked them.

Besides, why would anyone need to rob Mansa Musa's caravan? He generously handed out gold to the many poor people he encountered along the way. In fact, his largess was such that Musa's crossing of North Africa resulted in the price of gold crashing by twenty-five percent. It would take more than twelve years to recover its value.

Mansa Musa's devotion to his faith, if not already obvious from the magnitude of the *hajj* and his extraordinary charity, was underlined in other ways. He had his people build a mosque every Friday, so that he and his followers could worship. On his return to Mali, he built several large mosques, and constructed many schools for both boys and girls, where they learned Arabic and studied the *Qur'ān*.

If it was Mansa Musa's goal to promote Mali on the world stage, he succeeded beyond his wildest dreams. In fact, he literally put Mali on the map: In 1375, Spanish cartographers created the *Catalan Atlas*, which depicted Mansa Musa dominating West Africa (see below). His conspicuous affluence also ensured his name was right up there with those of Croesus, Midas, Crassus, Rockefeller, and Musk when obscene wealth is discussed.

Fig. 6: Mansa Musa—Richer than Trump? Sorry Donny, it's not even close. (Public domain and S.E.W.)

Ibn Battuta and the Brotherhood of the Traveling Pants

Ibn Battuta (1304–1368) was a renowned Moroccan traveler and writer. His full name was Shams al-Din Abu 'Abdallah Muhammad ibn 'Abdallah ibn Muhammad ibn Ibrahim ibn Muhammad ibn Yusuf Lawati al-Tanji ibn Battuta, so it made sense to shorten his name. However, Ibn Battuta translates to "Son of Duckling" which surely requires some explanation.

Alas, I have none.

Ibn Battuta received a traditional Islamic education in Tangier, and his obsession with travel began with his 1325 pilgrimage to Mecca. Once the wanderlust hit, he decided to visit as much of the world as possible, resolving "never to travel any road a second time." He was uncommonly successful in this aim and became known as "the traveler of Islam." In fact, he covered more territory than any explorer before the Age of Discovery, with his 117,000 kilometers easily beating Chinese Admiral Zheng He, who sailed around 50,000 kilometers, and well-known fibber Marco Polo who supposedly traveled 24,000 kilometers. In contemporary terms, Ibn Battuta traveled to forty-four countries in a twenty-seven-year period, including such USA-friendly places such as Iraq, Iran, Somalia, and Arabia.

During his travels, Ibn Battuta often acted as a judge, zealously attempting to make local customs conform to Muslim law. This meant that he routinely sentenced men who didn't attend Friday prayer to be whipped in public, and thieves to have their right hands chopped off. In the Maldives, Judge Battuta banned women from appearing bare breasted in public, which had been the norm. Understandably, this upset fans of toplessness and Ibn Battuta's tenure in the Maldives was short lived.

When he returned home, he clearly had a lot of travel stories to relate. He set down these recollections in a travelog with a name nearly as long as his own: *A Gift to Those Who Contemplate the Wonders of Cities and the Marvels of Traveling*. Mercifully, this is more concisely known as *The Rihla*.

In *The Rihla*, Ibn Battuta tells the story of his wanderings. He relates that he was married numerous times, leaving one wife because he had an argument with her dad. Because of his years of study, he often acted as a *qadi*, or judge, in the places he visited. This brought him into contact with the high and the mighty, including a few sultans who were a couple of slices short of a loaf.

Of course, traveling 117,000 kilometers in the fourteenth century inevitably put Ibn Battuta in harm's way. His journey through India and Sri Lanka was particularly problematic. At one point, Ibn Battuta was chased by ten mounted Hindus. He escaped them, only to be captured by forty more Hindus, who relieved him of his valuables, kindly allowing him to keep his clothes. Having given up nearly everything, he was allowed to leave, only to be captured by more robbers who wanted his clothes as well, although for the sake of decency, they left him his trousers. After eight days wandering, clad only in his pants, Ibn Battuta was rescued. Unfortunately, fate had more humiliation in store for poor old Ducky.

At the conclusion of an otherwise successful trip to Ceylon, where he met with the king, Ibn Battuta had more bad luck. On his departure, his ship was beset by pirates. The crew were soon overwhelmed and the ship plundered. "They seized the jewels and rubies which the king of Ceylon had given me," Ibn Battuta wrote, "and robbed me of my clothes and provisions [...] They left nothing on my body except my trousers."

I suspect that Ibn Battuta selectively edited these stories to cover up the fact he was twice left naked by robbers. And that's far more generous than some historians, who suspect he didn't travel to all the destinations he mentions in *The Rihla*.

Fig. 7: Ibn Battuta: World traveler extraordinaire...
(Léon Benett, Public domain and S.E.W.)

Islamic Architecture

Islamic architecture in the seventh and eighth centuries developed under the influence of Roman, Byzantine, Persian, Mesopotamian, Chinese and Mughal architecture. Over time, Islamic builders developed their own architectural style, which included elements such as minarets, muqarnas, pointed arches, onion domes, pointed domes, and arabesques. These unique features are responsible for the many masterpieces of Islamic architecture, such as the Dome of the Rock; the Great Mosque of Samarra; the Citadel of Aleppo; the Great Mosque of Cordoba; Taj Mahal; Blue Mosque of Istanbul; and the Alhambra.

The Alhambra is a palace and fortress in Granada, Spain, constructed in the Moorish style for the Nasrid Dynasty. It is a UNESCO World Heritage Site, described as "a rich repository of Moorish vernacular architecture, into which the traditional Andalusian architecture blends harmoniously." The name Alhambra, which translates as "the red" in Arabic, is due to the reddish color of the rammed earth of which the outer walls are constructed. It was initially a small fort constructed on the remains of Roman fortifications, on a plateau overlooking the city of Granada. It is a complex of palaces and courtyards surrounded by a fortress. The basis of the Alhambra we see today was built between 1238 and 1358 during the Nasrid Dynasty. In 1333, Yusuf I, Sultan of Granada, converted it into his royal palace. After the Moors were expelled from Spain in 1492, the Alhambra was vandalized and fell into disrepair. Later, parts were remodeled in the Renaissance style.

The Alhambra became the site of the Royal Court of Ferdinand and Isabella, and was the place where Christopher Columbus got the royal go-ahead for his little expedition. Later still, Napoleon decided it would be a hoot to use a bomb to blow up the Alhambra, because when you're a military dictator, why not? Legend has it his plans were thwarted by a proto-John McClane, a Spaniard who, in true *Die Hard* fashion, was hidden in the building and single-handedly diffused the bomb, thus saving the Alhambra for posterity.

Fig. 8: For obvious reasons, Die Hard: Alhambra is not a Christmas movie.
(Jose Ignacio Soto, Tiler84, and S.E.W.)

The Dome of the Rock

The oldest example of Islamic architecture is the famous Dome of the Rock in Jerusalem. It was built between 691–692, the Arabs having conquered Jerusalem just over fifty years previously. While borrowing heavily from Byzantine architecture, the Dome of the Rock was also beginning to display a distinctly Islamic architectural style. The most striking feature of this building is the gilded dome crowning the octagonal base. The site itself is special, sacred to Jews and Muslims alike. Readers of *From Cave to Colosseum* will be interested to know that it's supposedly built on the spot where Old Testament God had gaslit Abraham into nearly sacrificing his son Isaac. In the Islamic world, the site is famous as the place where Muhammad ascended to heaven.

When it comes to religious real estate, it's location, location, location.

Fig. 9: Great moments in architecture (Anna Kucherova, Peter Sobolev,
Mistervlad, Shchipkova Elena, and S.E.W.)

One Great Mosque Deserves Another...

The Great Mosque of Samarra was built in Iraq around 850
AD. If size matters, no mosque could match it, as it covered a
whopping forty-two acres, and was constructed of baked brick.
Unfortunately, most of the mosque was destroyed during the
Mongol invasion of 1258. Luckily for posterity, an intriguing
52-meter high cone-shaped minaret survived the destruction.
The most interesting feature of this minaret is the ramp that
spirals its way to the top.

The Great Mosque of Córdoba, Spain, was initially built on the
site of a Christian church between 784–786. During the ninth
and tenth centuries, it was extensively remodeled and extended.
One of this mosque's most unique features is the hypostyle hall

(a large interior space whose roof rests on pillars or columns) consisting of approximately eight hundred and fifty columns made of jasper, porphyry, and marble. In one of history's great moments in recycling, most of the columns and capitals were repurposed from earlier buildings.

Honorable Mention One: Hagia Sophia. While Turkey's Hagia Sophia mosque is undoubtedly a medieval building, some readers might question its place in this chapter for a couple of reasons. For one, it was originally built as a Christian church in late antiquity (531 AD) by Emperor Justinian, *before* the advent of Islam. The other reason is that, not only did it begin life as a church, it remained one for nearly a thousand years. For the vast majority of this time, it was an Eastern Orthodox church, except for the fifty-five years it was a Catholic cathedral after the idiotic Fourth Crusade had sacked Constantinople and looted Hagia Sophia in the thirteenth century. It was restored to Eastern Orthodoxy in 1204, when it was returned to Byzantine control.

However, in 1453, Constantinople fell again, this time to the Ottoman Empire. For the next five hundred years, Hagia Sophia served as a mosque. Then, in 1935, the Turkish government converted it to a museum, until 2020, when it was controversially *reconverted* into a mosque. This latter event left Pope Francis feeling "very pained" and caused the Patriarch of Moscow to claim it "a threat to the entire Christian civilization."

So far, "Christian civilization" hasn't fallen... but give it a little time.

Hagia Sophia's most striking architectural feature is its thirty-two-meter main dome, which is supported on pendentives (four triangular corner devices that help suspend the dome over a square base) and two semi-domes (half domes often used at either end of a barrel-vaulted ceiling). After it became a mosque, the now characteristic minarets were constructed around the ancient structure.

Honorable Mention Two: The Taj Mahal. Why does the most beautiful and famous example of Isalmic architecture only warrant an "honorable mention"? It's because it post-dates the topic of this chapter, the Islamic Golden Age. Nevertheless, it's certainly one of the most iconic buildings ever created by humans, so it deserves recognition.

The story behind the Taj Mahal is a tragic one. When the favorite wife of the Mughal emperor, Mumtaz Mahal, died giving birth to their *fourteenth* child, the emperor was shattered (although clearly not as shattered as his wife must have been). He commissioned a grand mausoleum to be created in her memory. And *what* a mausoleum: The dome is fully seventy-three meters tall, and the white marble tomb is breathtaking. It is legend that Shah Jahan intended to build himself a black granite version of the Taj Mahal, mirroring the grand building across the river. There is no existing evidence for the truth, or otherwise, of that claim.

Fig. 10: A uterus can only take so much. (Oksana Byelikova and S.E.W.)

The One Thousand and One Nights

The Islamic Golden Age also gave us great literature. *One Thousand and One Nights* (also known as *Arabian Nights*) is a collection of folk tales that has survived to influence popular culture right up to the present. It gave us immortal characters such as Aladdin, Ali Baba, and Sinbad the Sailor, among others.

One Thousand and One Nights was assembled over centuries and comprises stories with origins in North African, Arabian, Egyptian, Persian, and Indian folk tales. Not all editions of the collection include the same narratives. In fact, the best-known stories to Western eyes: *Aladdin's Wonderful Lamp*, *Ali Baba and the Forty Thieves* and *The Seven Voyages of Sinbad the Sailor*, were not featured in the original Arabic collection but were added later.

The narrative common to all versions of *One Thousand and One Nights* is the story of *Scheherazade and Shahryar*, which frames the collection. Shahryar is a king who finds his wife screwing around and does what any all-powerful monarch would do… he has her executed. Clearly a gifted, psychopathic misogynist, the king takes this to the next level when he decides that *all* women must be executed… but only after he's taken their maidenhead. So, he makes a habit of marrying attractive young virgins, bedding them, and then beheading them the morning after. After an unspecified number of chaste young women are violated and violently dispatched, Shahryar marries another beautiful virgin (he *definitely* has a type) named Scheherazade, fully expecting another pre-breakfast execution.

But Scheherazade is aware of Shahryar's MO and devises a cunning plan. On their wedding night she regales Shahryar with a fascinating story, which she cannily neglects to finish as the sun begins to rise. Desperate to hear the resolution, the king postpones his bride's decapitation so he can hear the end of the tale.

Scheherazade, clearly seeing that she was onto a winning formula, finishes the story the next night, then begins another, which, again, she does not finish. She avoids post-coital decapitation a second time. This pattern continues for one thousand and one nights, after which time, Scheherazade's ability to delay her husband's gratification has changed him from serial killer to loving husband.

And they all lived happily ever after.

Yikes.

One Thousand and One Nights is full of big ideas: "real strength comes from within" (Aladdin); "never let greed overtake you" (Ali Baba); and "always keep your wits about you" (Sinbad). But the overarching lesson is when Scheherazade teaches us: "if your husband is a homicidal maniac, a good cliffhanger will keep him at bay."

Fig. 11: Scheherazade: the inventor of "the Cliffhanger" (D-Keine & S.E.W.)

Djinn and Tonic

A recurring creature in the *One Thousand and One Nights* tales is the *Djinn* or *Jinni* (which is usually Anglicized as "Genie"). *Djinns* were mercurial: catch one on a good day, and he would be Robin Williams' jovial Genie from Disney's *Aladdin*, offering you three wishes. However, on a *bad* day, you'd better watch out—these powerful magical creatures really knew how to be vindictive. In one of the *One Thousand and One Nights* stories, a man finds himself face-to-face with an enraged *djinn* after his son accidentally killed the *djinn's* son with a discarded date pit. This susceptibility to date pits may be why dates are still considered by some Muslims to provide a shield against demons. As Muhammad said: "Whoever consumes seven *Kurma 'Ajwah* (dates) in the morning, then on that day he will not be exposed to poison or magic."

I imagine they'd be pretty damned regular too.

Fig. 12: Happy Genie: Pants optional (ZoneCreative and S.E.W.)

In pre-Islamic days, *djinns* were believed to be fiery mythical spirits which haunted the Arabian desert. Of particular concern were the *shaitan*, a malevolent class of djinn which could be male or female, looked absolutely hideous, and to round things off, loved to chow-down on excrement (presumably not excrement stimulated by breakfast dates). Later on, in the *Qur'ān*, the *shaitan* became associated with the Judeo-Christian-type devil known as

Iblīs (or in Arabic *ash-Shayṭān*). Iblīs and his hordes of shaitan are known to whisper wicked suggestions into men's ears in a bid to tempt them into sin. However, given the shaitan's shit-eating diet, I imagine their close presence was easy to detect.

But on to more palatable substances...

Coffee: The Wine of Araby

Coffee is one of the world's most popular beverages and has been the fuel for innumerable big ideas. But there was a time, not so very long ago, when it was unknown outside the Ethiopian plateau. It seemingly took an eternity for coffee to emerge out of Africa and onto the Arabian Peninsula. By the fifteenth century, it was being grown in Yemen, and then in Egypt, Syria, Persia, and Turkey.

Before long, special public coffee houses became popular, delivering the caffeine jolt that kept the Islamic world buzzing. But these proto-Starbucks were not only for drinking coffee. The patrons engaged in learned conversation, watched performances, listened to music, and kept up with current events. Coffee was just the stimulant required in a world in which alcohol was forbidden.

Fig. 13: Life in the Coffee House (Nastasic and S.E.W.)

There's a persistent meme circulating the internet claiming that in fifteenth-century Turkey, a wife could divorce her husband if he failed to provide her with an adequate supply of coffee. As widespread as this "factoid" is, there isn't a primary source confirming it, only meme after meme copying the same BS story. In some versions, the law is attributed to Saudi Arabia, but it's equally baseless.

Which is unfortunate, because it's a great story.

Surprisingly, some people didn't love coffee as much as these apocryphal Turkish wives. Robert Evans in *the (Brief) History of Vice*, tells of Kha'ir Bey, a Mamluk pasha who took it upon himself to ban coffee in Mecca. Not only was this move unpopular with the people, it was also wildly unpopular with the sultan. Like millions to come, the sultan loved his morning cup of joe and really hated the withdrawal headache that banning coffee inevitably caused. The prohibition was soon overturned.

Of course, this didn't stop the killjoys in Mecca, who seemed desperate to spoil everyone's fun. A few years later, a wild-eyed cleric stirred up a mob which set fire to coffee houses. Incensed at this "sacrilege," a pro-coffee mob assembled, and intense *Gangs of New York*-style clashes ensued. Only after coffee's legal status was confirmed did the mob violence cease. Even then, there were further attempts to prohibit coffee drinking.

In the end, though, coffee was saved for all Muslims.

"Suicide Squad, assemble!"

Some guys who didn't need to be caffeinated were the Nizari Ismailis, a heretic group of Persian/Syrian Shiite Muslims from between the eleventh and thirteenth centuries. While these guys didn't enjoy overwhelming military strength, they used more covert means to secure victory. Their preferred game plan was to mobilize undercover knife-wielding teams to murder key enemy figures. These teams were often disguised as beggars or monks. Such political murders were intentionally done in crowded, public locations to maximize the impact, by undercover operatives who understood their low probability of survival.

They were the original Suicide Squad.

The Nizari Ismailis didn't need the effects of coffee because they allegedly used more potent drugs. There was a general belief that before embarking on a murder mission, they would eat hashish, which supposedly acted as a performance enhancing drug, and accounted for their remarkable success. This reputation for drug use led to them being referred to as *hashashun*, or hashish eaters. It doesn't take much imagination to see that *hashashun* was corrupted into "Assassin," the name by which Nizari Ismailis are better known. Not surprisingly, the word assassin came to be synonymous with political murder.

It's a great origin story. But did the Assassins' hash-eating really enhance their performance? I ask this because THC, the psychoactive constituent in hashish, is not renowned for inducing a murderous rage. Rather, it's famous for causing a lack of motivation and feelings of euphoria. It also can impair motor control, increase appetite, and cause lapses of memory. Call me crazy, but I doubt it would energize berserk suicide assassins.

However, while these Assassins didn't *invent* assassination (it had been around as long as humanity), they were pioneers in the art of covert murder. This idea would be duplicated in the future, by groups whose need for victory was greater than their scruples.

Like I've said before, not all lightbulb moments are intrinsically positive.

Fig. 14: Too many edibles? (Erica Guilane-Nachez and S.E.W.)

Islamic Art

Let's be clear, there is no single style of "Islamic art." The art of the Islamic peoples has a long history, spanning the period between the seventh century and today. It encompasses diverse Islamic cultures across the world and is represented in a wide range of artistic fields, from painting, textiles, and ceramics, right through to architecture. Its early influences were Byzantine, Sasanian, and early Christian art, but with a major difference that would define many Islamic art forms: the way it treats the depiction of humans.

Although not strictly prohibited in the *Qur'ān*, some interpretations of Islam teach that it is idolatry to depict the human or animal form. That makes drawing people (or fluffy animals) a sin against Allah, because only He can create living forms. It certainly didn't help matters that Muhammad is reported as saying: "Those who will be most severely punished by Allah on the Day of Resurrection will be the image-makers." As a result, Islamic religious art tends to eschew the use of human or animal figures. Of course, there are exceptions: Identikit images of wanted criminals are allowed under Sharia law, as are scientific drawings of the human body for medical textbooks.

However, while it is rare, sometimes this prohibition on human images can get taken too far. Witness the fate of the 1500-year-old *Buddhas of Bamiyan* in 2001. These two monumental statues (55 meters and 38 meters tall respectively) were situated near Kabul, Afghanistan, and had been designated a UNESCO World Heritage Site. Unfortunately, that didn't stop the Taliban government declaring the images *haram* (forbidden by Islamic law) and blowing them to smithereens. This was despite a massive international campaign to save the Buddhas.

The "prohibition" on depicting living creatures is not always apparent in secular Muslim art, because some Islamic cultures follow different interpretations of the law. Even in these cases, living beings are often portrayed in a stylized rather than realistic fashion—it seems the less detail, the less controversy. While these restrictions may appear to make it difficult for Muslim artists, they responded in an ingenious fashion. By using intricate tessellating geometric, calligraphic, and floral patterns in their work, these artists have, for one thousand five hundred years, produced some of the most beautiful artwork ever created by human hands.

How Did the Islamic World View the Crusades?

Even a cursory reading of the last two chapters demonstrates that comparing medieval Islamic Civilization to medieval Western civilization is like comparing a thoroughbred racehorse to a scabrous mule. So, it's no surprise that, at the time, Muslims in the near East viewed the unwashed peasant hordes who invaded the Holy Land and indiscriminately killed many thousands of innocent people, as inferior barbarians.

Nowadays many Muslims look back on the Crusaders as the predecessors of waves of Western colonialism, up to and including the two Gulf Wars. From this perspective, Crusaders were marauders who were only driven away by a well-organized jihad. This viewpoint was fueled by a combination of innumerable real atrocities and perceived slights, and eventually inspired the rather unfortunate big idea of Islamic Fundamentalist Terrorism.

While there is some truth to this view of the Crusades, the Al-Jazeera documentary *The Crusades: An Arab Perspective* offers another perspective: In addition to the bloody battles, there was frequently a climate of cooperation. Muslims and Christians often lived together in harmony, sharing sacred spaces, forging political alliances, engaging in commerce, and even exchanging scientific concepts.

It all just went to hell at some point.

Probably the greatest Muslim hero of the Crusader era was Al-Nasir Salah al-Din Yusuf ibn Ayyub (1137–1193), better known simply as Saladin. He was the first sultan of Egypt who led the Islamic military campaign against the Crusaders in the Holy Land. Saladin's forces reconquered most of the Crusaders' gains in the Levant, including the biggest prize of all, Jerusalem. Before that, he had, through a combination of military force and diplomacy, united a large part of the Muslim world under his rule.

Despite Saladin's fierce military reputation, he displayed great chivalry towards his opponents. He earned King Richard's respect by making his personal physician available to help nurse Richard through an illness. Also, when King Richard's horse was killed in battle, Saladin offered him a replacement mount in the interests of fairness. Considering these barbarians were invading his homeland, he showed admirable kindness and restraint.

Fig. 15: And the West never meddled in the Middle East again...
(Public domain and S.E.W.)

Why Didn't the Islamic World Continue Their Intellectual Dominance?

Given the Islamic world's advances in all realms of academic endeavor, it is clear they had a significant head start on the West *and* they were fired up on caffeine (and possibly other substances). They certainly weren't anti-science or anti-progress, although they *were* anti-women, although the West can hardly claim the moral high ground at that time.

So why didn't Arab astronauts land on the Moon in 1869?

There is no single answer as to "what happened?" although the 1258 AD sacking of Baghdad and destruction of the House of Wisdom by Hulagu Khan's Mongols can't have helped. Survivors of the attack claimed so many books were thrown into the Tigris that it ran black with ink. While this is, no doubt, an exaggeration, when it comes to information-related tragedies, the desecration of the House of Wisdom is right up there with the burning of the Great Library in Alexandria.

This destruction is considered by some academics to be the endpoint of the Islamic Golden Age. Although others argue that a decline in creative thinking and a rise in religious fundamentalism and madrasas (religious schools) in the eleventh and twelfth centuries also played a role. Still others, usually those with a vested interest, reject the idea that religion played a part and put the decline down to a raft of varied economic and political factors.

It was certainly problematic that mechanical printing in Arabic script was resisted by some Muslim legal scholars. It was essentially prohibited in the Ottoman empire between 1483 and 1729 due to objections to the mechanical reproduction of Arabic script. Given the supercharging effect that the proliferation of printed books had on collective learning during the Renaissance in the West, this must have been a significant reason for the stalling of Islamic dominance.

Likely, it was the cumulative effect of all these factors.

*

Whatever the reasons for the relative decline of the Islamic world, its Golden Age was highly significant in the world of big ideas. The contributions of Golden Age scholars to collective knowledge on the planet are incalculable. The achievements of the scientists of the Islamic Golden Age covered a wide range of disciplines, especially mathematics, astronomy, and medicine. These were all big ideas on their own, but the true brainchild of the early Islamic scholars was the preservation and expansion of the teaching of the ancients. Without their work, it's probable that the Renaissance and subsequent human advances would have been delayed, or perhaps have never even occurred.

But before we examine the European Renaissance, let's have a peek at what was happening in Central and South America around this time...

* * *

A Brief Interlude II

White Lines

Just when I thought I was out, they pull me back in!
Michael Corleone, *The Godfather, Part III*

Readers of *From Cave to Colosseum* will remember my loathing of Erich von Däniken, elder "statesman" of the ancient aliens theory. For those who need a refresher, his theory claims that all significant human endeavor in the past was not the work of humans, but was, in fact, performed or inspired by visiting aliens. As a boy, I'd been obsessed with *Chariots of the Gods?*, von Däniken's first book about the subject.

When my old school friend Brian read *From Cave to Colosseum*, he reminded me of something that I had somehow totally forgotten about when reflecting on my youthful obsession with von Däniken's body of work. Brian and I attended Cronulla Public School in the early 1970s, and he pointed out that our classes had been taken on a *school excursion* to see the movie version of *Chariots of the Gods?* No *wonder* I took it to heart so much. I had been preoccupied with the moon landings for some time, and already had an unhealthy relationship with the book *Chariots of the Gods?* Then my teachers reinforced it all by somehow shoe-horning it into the school curriculum.

It all makes sense now.

Eventually I realized my foolishness, and in *From Cave to Colosseum* I devoted quite a lot of space to poking fun at the man and his ideas. I despise the way he stripped away the respect and dignity due to ancient peoples for their lightbulb moments. As far as he was concerned, ancient humans didn't have the intellectual and physical wherewithal to erect Stonehenge, invent writing, or build the Great Pyramid of Cheops, among a myriad of other achievements.

Imagine my joy then, when I recently stumbled across the podcast *Science Vs*, an episode of which, *Science Vs Ancient Aliens*, assailed the ancient aliens theory head-on. The program interviewed paleoanthropologist Dr. Shelby Putt, Egyptologist Dr. Mark Lehner, and archaeologist Prof. David S. Anderson, who all used facts and logic to debunk the idea that aliens intervened in human affairs. In my favorite segment, the host, Wendy Zukerman, interviewed the man himself: Erich von Däniken. While she was far more polite than I would've been, she pulled no punches:

Wendy Zukerman: Are you the reason that people think the aliens helped build the pyramids?
Erich von Däniken: I think so, yes.
Wendy Zukerman: All the experts that we spoke to said we just don't need aliens to explain how we have the Great Pyramid; we have all the evidence in front of us. Why do you think differently?
Erich von Däniken: No, we don't have all the evidence, and all the scientists who say we have all the evidence (and) we do not need extraterrestrials [...] never understood the story of Erich von Däniken they probably never read (my books). In the meantime, it's forty-one books.

Yeah, that's right, people. Erich von Däniken's rebuttal to scientific evidence was that the experts just didn't understand him, because they hadn't read any of his *forty-one* books. It was as if he thought the sheer volume of his bullshit was enough to counter facts. Sadly, it's an attitude we've come to see more often in recent years, particularly in the world of the internet.

I'm bringing von Däniken up this one last time (I promise) because we're about to examine the big ideas of the Aztec and the Inca, two civilizations he routinely mined for his books.

As usual, he misinterpreted and misrepresented evidence to suit his interpretations.

As usual, he made it all about aliens.

As usual, he was dead wrong.

*

Von Däniken tends to conflate the Mayans and the Aztecs, and *From Cave to Colosseum* already addressed his misinterpretation of Ancient Mesoamerica, so there is no need to revisit it here. However, his interpretation of civilizations of Pre-Columbian Peru is another thing entirely.

Fig. 1: *The Nazca Desert was fertile ground for crazy Uncle Erich...* (*Jarnogs and S.E.W.*)

Erich found himself particularly aroused by the Plains of Nazca, on which are carved the famous Nazca Lines, most of which depict stylized animals. These white lines were made in the soil of the Nazca Desert between 500 BC and 500 AD, inscribed by the local Nazca people. The remarkable thing about these geoglyphs is that their subject matter is only fully visible from the air. Since their discovery, there has been one overriding question: what was their purpose?

One theory speculates the lines are aligned with various remote Nazca temples, tying into a common idea that they're related to religious observance. Another, notes they follow the paths of aquifers, perhaps helping the Nazca manage scarce water resources. Yet another, now disproved, theory links the glyphs to astronomical observations. A popular idea contends they are messages from the Nazca people to their gods.

These latter two ideas overexcited von Däniken's fertile imagination, almost bringing him to the verge of climax:

> *If you fly over this territory—the plain of Nazca—you can make out gigantic lines, laid out geometrically, some of which run parallel to each other, while others intersect or are surrounded by large trapezoidal areas.*
>
> *The archaeologists say that they are Inca roads. A preposterous idea! [...] Seen from the air, the clear-cut impression that the 37-mile-long plain of Nazca made on me was that of an airfield!*
>
> *What is so far-fetched about the idea?*

What is so far-fetched? Oh Erich, where do I begin? Before we get onto the idea of gods, they were not "Inca roads." They were created by the Nazca people over a thousand years before the Inca Empire emerged, not as roads, but for a yet unknown reason. As for his assumption that humans couldn't have worked out a way of creating these lines that didn't require the intervention of "gods," as we've seen, all research so far calls this bullshit. And really, why would aliens, flying interstellar spaceships, require drawings of arrows, monkeys and hummingbirds to guide them to a safe landing in a godforsaken desert?

Fig. 2: "What is so far-fetched about the idea?" Everything, Erich. Everything.
(Forcdan and S.E.W.)

Von Däniken was also excited by the impressive mortarless masonry practiced by the Inca. Rather than shaping regular stone blocks like other ancient peoples, the Incan artisans used irregularly shaped rocks and fitted them together in an organic and seamless manner. As always, Erich expressed incredulity at how mere humans could have managed this "impossible" feat. Surely, he posited, such precise work could only be accounted for by the arrival of extraterrestrials with laser cutters.

As per usual, Herr von Däniken's disbelief in mundane explanations is expressed in words to the effect of "scientists have been unable to explain how [add ancient wonder here] was built." The problem for ancient aliens conspiracy theorists is that ninety-five percent of the time, scientists *have* been able to explain the construction methods. It's just that conspiracy nuts pooh-pooh these logical explanations, because they really spoil their fun.

The truth behind Inca stonework techniques is surprisingly simple. Here they are set out by the University of California's Jean-Pierre Protzen in his paper, "Inca Quarrying and Stonecutting":

Inca construction techniques have long been the subject of wild speculation. Investigations of ancient quarry sites and of numerous cut-stone walls reveal that the amazing Inca constructions were built with very simple means. Stones were selected out of rock falls or just broken out of a rock face with pry-bars. [...]

The fitting of one stone to another was done by cutting the already laid stones to receive the next ones in a trial-and-error fashion. Experiments show that with this process stones can be mined, cut, dressed, and fit with little effort and in a short time.

Such low-tech explanations upset von Däniken and his acolytes, because they are long on practicality and human ingenuity, and distressingly short on aliens and heat-rays. The fact is that all this spectacular stonemasonry required from the Inca was good, old-fashioned know-how and untold years of back-breaking labor. Of course, ancient aliens theorists would rather ignore such inconvenient truths, and instead, rely on their convoluted ideas.

It's infuriating.

The good news is that we're now moving past the period of history that interested Erich von Däniken. Thank God. I've had my say, and I hope I haven't upset too many people in the process.

I'm out, and I'm not getting pulled back in again. Let's hope I'm more successful than Michael Corleone in *The Godfather Part III*.

Let's get on with some *real* history.

* * *

—3—

Stop Draggin' My Heart Around

The Aztecs and the Incas

Mesoamerica: What Came Before

In *From Cave to Colosseum*, I looked at the lightbulb moments of ancient Mesoamerica. We saw that, building on the achievements of the Olmec civilization, the Mayan civilization developed a system of writing, a base twenty mathematical system that included the concept of zero, advanced astronomical observations, and a sophisticated calendar. The Mayans created significant megastructures in the form of pyramidal temples. They were also the first civilization to use chocolate and tobacco, two substances that went on to have a profound influence on the future development of humanity for both good and ill.

Of course, not all the big ideas of Mesoamerica were so benign (if one can count a significant carcinogen like tobacco as benign). The Olmec and Mayans practiced extreme body modification, including molding infants' heads to unnatural shapes, and elaborate forms of human sacrifice that would have caused the most hardened medieval torturer to throw up into his mouth a little bit.

The Mayan civilization lasted for a thousand years, but fell into decline in the eighth to ninth century AD. No one is exactly sure how this occurred, but theories include potential overpopulation, depleted soil, and climate change. There may even have been devastating wars between competing Mayan city-states. Whatever happened, the rich civilization of the Mayans collapsed, leaving something of a power vacuum.

But not for long.

All Hail the Toltecs ... Maybe

Who were the Toltecs? The Aztec people revered a civilization they referred to as the Toltecs, who ruled the city of Tula in the central highlands of Mexico. It is speculated that they existed somewhere between 900–1521 AD. The name Toltec derives from the Aztec word for "artisan," *Tōltēcah* (or the other way around... all things regarding the Toltec appear shrouded in mystery). We don't get an unbiased view of the Toltecs because most of our knowledge comes from Aztec sources.

As far as can be known, the rise of the Toltec civilization roughly approximates to the end of Mayan domination of Mesoamerica. Their city of Tula bears some striking similarities to the architecture and art of the grand Mayan city of Chichén Itzá, so there are more than a few questions about their relationship. Did the Toltecs conquer the Mayans and do some impromptu redecorating of Chichén Itzá? Did the Mayans influence the Toltecs? Or, did the Toltecs and Maya have a trading relationship and cross-pollinate each other with ideas? Short of new discoveries, it is likely we'll never know for sure.

Of course, there's another, somewhat crazier theory. In recent years, scholars such as Susan D. Gillespie and Michel Graulich have questioned if the Toltec Civilization actually existed at all, and suggested instead that they were merely a part of Aztec mythology. But, hold on... What about the city of Tula? A non-existent civilization can't construct a city, can it? Gillespie and Graulich's answer to that question is that Mesoamerica had a number of civilizations who may have built Tula, not least the Mayans. That would go a long way to explain the similarities between Tula and Chichén Itzá.

Fig. 1: *An interesting question (Nailotl Mendez, Softlightaa, and S.E.W.)*

Whether the Toltecs were a figment of the imagination or not, they loomed large in the Aztec mind. Of course, the Olmecs, Mayans, and Zapotecs shared many basic cultural traits with the Aztecs, so these civilizations likely had an influence on the Aztecs as well. Not least of which was their homicidal religious urges.

The Aztecs took these bloodthirsty influences to a heightened level.

All the Earth Is a Grave, and Nought Escapes It

This cheery title is an excerpt from Daniel G. Brinton's translation of an Aztec poem which, when quoted out of context, seems to sum up the death fixation of the Aztecs. After all, these guys *really* loved death. The full text is a little more poetic:

All the earth is a grave, and nought escapes it; nothing is so perfect that it does not fall and disappear. The rivers, brooks, fountains and waters flow on, and never return to their joyous beginnings;

*they hasten on to the vast realms of Tlaloc, and the wider they
spread between their marges the more rapidly do they mold their
own sepulchral urns.*

Granted, it is still dark, but it has a beauty not usually associated
with practitioners of human sacrifice. Nevertheless, the morbid
sentiment underlines the debt this Mesoamerican culture
post-classical period owes to its forebears, the Mayans. Death
remained very much a part of life for the Aztecs. It's believed
they sacrificed around twenty thousand people a year, but when
they dedicated new temples to the gods, the death toll could be
much higher. This staggering yearly death toll was required to
appease the gods and ensure a better future.

It certainly wasn't a better future for their untold thousands
of victims. But the Aztecs thought the gods were right on board.

You see, the Aztecs saw offering the heart of a screaming,
squirming victim as fair repayment to the gods for the sacrifices
they made in creating the world. What kind of sacrifices did
these gods make? Well for one, when the gods Quetzalcóatl
and Tezcatlicopa created the world from the body of the
giant crocodile Cipactli, Tezcatlicopa had his foot bitten off in
the struggle. Then, during a meeting of deities regarding the
creation of the solar system, the god Nanahuatzin took one for
the team, throwing himself into celestial flames so he could be
reborn as the sun.

In Aztec religion, one good sacrifice deserves another.

Yet, as abhorrent as human sacrifice is to modern day
sensibilities, the Aztecs believed that the gods were nourished
by the flesh and blood offered up to them. It's a belief that's not
as unusual as you might think. Many world religions have at one
time or another engaged in human sacrifice. The very symbol
of Christianity commemorates the method in which Jesus was
sacrificed, ostensibly by his Father, so Christians can't get too
judgy. But then, neither can most "modern" religions.

Fig. 2: The Aztecs learned a thing or two from the Mayans.
(Midjourney and S.E.W.)

Skin in the Game

Like many other cultures before them, the Aztecs worshiped a pantheon of gods. If you don't count the bloodbath required to appease them, these deities were strongly connected to the well-being of the Aztec people. For instance, a plentiful supply of food was of obvious interest to the community, so there was a god of their main food staple, maize. Other gods looked after aspects of food preparation, agriculture, and rain. The Aztecs also had a clear religious interest in astronomy, and this was reflected in the number of gods associated with their observations of the night sky.

In the same way the Romans appropriated and adapted the Greek gods, the Aztecs did much the same with Mayan gods. The most well-known example of this was the feathered serpent god, Quetzalcóatl, who was effectively a recycled version of the Mayan god Kukulkán. Quetzalcóatl was powerful (after all he *had* helped create the world). He also moonlighted as the god of agriculture, is credited with discovering maize (in an Aztec legend), invented a complex calendar (which was actually devised by the Mayans), and was identified with one of the most significant features in the heavens, the planet Venus. He was also closely associated with learning, science, crafts, and the arts. If that wasn't enough, Quetzalcóatl was the god of priests and merchants. No wonder he had a favored place in the hearts of the Aztec people.

Which is appropriate, because the preferred method of sacrifice was relieving the sacrificial victim of their still-beating heart. In 1487, at the four-day blood-bath that was the re-consecration of the Great Pyramid of Tenochtitlan, it's estimated the Aztecs sacrificed up to 80,000 prisoners. If true, this averages out at fifteen coronary extractions per minute—which, you've got to admit, is extremely efficient murdering. A much lower estimate of the body count of this ceremony is four thousand individuals, which is still an impressive one thousand victims a day.

It's possible that as many as a quarter of a million people had their hearts sliced out per year, one in five of which were children.

But it wasn't just hearts which interested the priests.

Xipe Totec (aka "Our Flayed Lord") was a god who bedecked himself in freshly flayed human skin and required that his priests do the same during the springtime festival of rebirth, "The Festival of the Flaying of Men." This jolly celebration took place in the eighteenth month of the Aztec calendar, and was depicted by the sixteenth-century Jesuit missionary Juan de Tovar in the *Tovar Codex* (see illustration below). I'm sure you agree, dear reader, that nothing says "rebirth" quite like a temple populated with clerics wearing human skins.

It certainly makes Easter eggs and bunnies look lame by comparison.

Fig. 3: Xipe Totec's priests made this Festival fun for all the family.
(Juan de Tovar, Public domain, and S.E.W.)

In fact, many Aztec gods had weird idiosyncrasies. Tezcatlipoca had a number of unpleasant ones. For a start, he would wander the land at night, appearing as a skeleton with a beating heart suspended in its ribcage. This proved a great temptation to Aztecs, who never saw a heart they didn't want to rip out, and this one was just sitting there in plain view. Tezcatlipoca promised to richly reward any Aztec who could manage to "steal his heart." For reasons best known to himself, he also liked to make certain villagers dance until they dropped dead.

Tezcatlipoca wasn't just quirky though; he was downright evil. In a move which is again reminiscent of Greek gods like Zeus, Tezcatlipoca dragged Xochiquetzal, the goddess of fertility and flowers, down into the underworld and brutally raped her. As Tezcatlipoca rested after his horrific crime, Xochiquetzal managed to escape and return to Earth to resume her place in the Aztec pantheon.

But while Xochiquetzal was the goddess of the somewhat hippie domains of flowers and fertility, peace and love really wasn't her thing. Her festival during the month of Toxcatl had consequences every bit as horrific as any other Aztec ceremony. Before the festival took place, a young maiden was chosen to play the part of Xochiquetzal in the celebration. This fake Xochiquetzal was then married to a warrior playing the part of her rapist, Tezcatlipoca.

So, a happy ending, Aztec style.

Just kidding. Remember, we're discussing the affairs of the Aztec gods.

The ritual marriage of the fake Xochiquetzal and the fake Tezcatlipoca lasted a year until the *next* Toxcatl festival, at which time the priests of the goddess took the fake Xochiquetzal and had her sacrificed and flayed. Then one of the priests wore her skin and pretended to weave cloth. As you do. Added to the gruesome tableau were Xochiquetzal's other priests, who danced around confessing their sins. I'm guessing they had quite a lot to get off their chests.

I could go on, but you get the idea: The Aztec gods were at least as bloodthirsty as the Aztecs themselves. However, despite bonding over their over-the-top religious practices, the Aztecs weren't necessarily a homogenous lot.

A Total Eclipse of the Heart

The Aztec people comprised several of the ethnic groups of central Mexico. Like the Ancient Greeks, the Aztecs' big idea was to organize themselves into smaller city-states which they referred to as *altepetl*. These states then joined together in shifting political alliances.

Aztec cities were organized in neighborhoods known as *calpulli*. These were communities of people in small rural villages or in cities who communally owned and administered shared spaces such as farming plots. The people living in the *calpulli* were on the lowest rung of Aztec society.

Like many cultures, both now and in the past, there was a distinct class system within the Aztec Empire. The nobility, or *pipiltin*, a class comprising military and government leaders and the high priests, lorded it over the commoners, the *macehualtin*, who were basically serfs. If a *macehualtin* fell into debt, they had the attractive option of selling themselves into slavery. The other class of people that could become slaves were captured enemy combatants who didn't end up as a human sacrifice.

Apart from being drawn solely from the *pipiltin* class, the priesthood had a further hierarchy all their own. However, unlike the other nobles, they refrained from drinking alcohol and had to remain celibate. Because the punishment for breaking these rules was death, I'm guessing these guys kept their vows better than modern Catholic priests.

All Aztec men were conscripted into the military, but women could not serve as warriors. Women were also excluded from serving in religious orders, with the exception that they could act as priestesses for select female gods. It's possible some females were allowed to work in lower administrative roles or in markets. A select few could also work as healers or midwives.

As you can imagine, most of these jobs required education. The Aztec Civilization recognized this and provided ample opportunities for learning.

I Don't Like Mondays

Unlike their medieval counterparts in Europe, Aztec children were required to attend school. If this seems forward thinking, it was... to a point. In a somewhat less enlightened way, the type of education children received varied greatly according to gender and social class. However, for the lower classes, there was none of that fancy reading, writing, and 'rithmatic for which the Aztecs were known.

For a start, boys and girls spent the first fourteen years of their life being home-schooled by Mom or Dad. After they turned fifteen, the male children of the commoners (*macehualtin*) attended schools called *telpochcalli*, whose main role was to train male youths in religion, agricultural skills, trades (such as pottery or metal work), and farming. They were also taught to be warriors. The girls were sent to a different school, where they were taught the Aztec version of Home Economics, learned how to perform religious rituals, brushed up on their singing and dancing, and learned arts and crafts. Girls who showed real promise were trained in the healing arts and midwifery.

Of course, if you were an Aztec of noble birth, you underwent a different education. These fortunate sons went to *calmecac* schools from the age of six. *Calmecac* schools specialized in academics and religious studies, which was perfect training for a life as a government official or priest. There was, however, a smattering of military training provided and discipline was tough, so the noble kids didn't get a free ride.

Calmecac schools also taught their students to play the ballgame, which was often a matter of life or death.

The Ballgame

Readers of *From Cave to Colosseum*, might recall the Mesoamerican Ballgame, which was among the World's first codified popular sports. The ballgame was already ancient by the time the Aztecs began playing it, with the earliest evidence of the game going back to 1400 BC. The ballgame held a religious significance for the Aztec, who regarded it as a battle between the sun god, Huitzilopochtli, and the forces of night. Researchers Taladoire and Colsenet suggest that in some cases, the ballgame served as a substitute for full scale warfare between city-states, with disputes settled (and even kingdoms decided) by the outcome.

Either way, win or lose, the stakes were serious.

Fig. 4: The style and skills of the ballgame
(Christoph Weiditz, Public domain, and S.E.W.)

In Tenochtitlan, the Aztec capital, the most prestigious ball court was known as the *teotlachco* or holy ballcourt. Not only was it the Wembley or Yankee Stadium of the ballgame, it also provided a convenient venue for religious festivals and ceremonies. This goes some way to explaining the dual sporting/religious significance of the ballgame in Aztec life.

While nowadays no one is precisely sure how the game was played, it's speculated that two teams faced each other across the court, with the ultimate goal being to somehow get a heavy rubber ball through a stone hoop to score. Sounds easy, right? Basketball players do it with monotonous regularity in the NBA.

Unfortunately for the ballgame players, they could not control the ball with their hands or feet, and could only use their knees, elbows, hips, and head. These limitations didn't make shooting goals easy. In fact, it was *so* difficult that if a goal was scored, the game was won—a bit like the Seeker catching the Golden Snitch in Quidditch.

Fig. 5: Given the Aztecs' thirst for blood, it's no surprise they took to the ballgame. (Ivan and S.E.W.)

The ballcourt was known as a *tlachtli* and was often shaped like the capital letter I, although there were regional differences. The court was between 30 and 60 meters long, and surrounded by walls around 2.5 to 3.5 meters high, with a stone hoop attached high up on one of these walls. Around the court, viewing areas were provided for judges, spectators, and Aztec bigwigs (such as priests and administrators).

In 2020, archaeologists from the National Institute of Anthropology and History were investigating a Mayan temple when they uncovered details about the balls used in the ballgame. The temple, located in the city of Toniná, appears to have been the manufacturing center for the balls, as containers were found filled with raw materials. These were mostly filled with rubber, but among other organic matter, they also contained… human ashes. Yep. The Mayans mixed the remains of dead people into their sports equipment. In theory, this was to help vulcanize the rubber, but it's not difficult to imagine more sinister reasons for this additive. Sure, this was not on an Aztec site, but it's a fair bet that given their love of the ballgame and their more lethal nature, the Aztecs made their balls in exactly the same fashion.

If playing a lethal game with human remains wasn't enough, another gruesome aspect of any ballcourt complex was the obligatory skull rack.

Keeping Score with Skulls?

The skull rack, or *tzompantli*, is exactly what it says on the label: a rack of skulls. These were made up of two wooden uprights that held horizontal rows of wooden poles displaying an array of skewered human skulls, like a macabre rotisserie. While skull racks have been documented in several Mesoamerican cultures of all eras, they were taken to a new and exalted level by the Aztecs.

Skull racks are often associated with the display of the skulls of enemy combatants or victims of sacrifice. This is because one of the goals of Aztec warfare was to capture as many enemy warriors as possible to use as sacrificial fodder. The *tzompantli* was a very obvious way of keeping track of the enemy death toll. In Tenochtitlan, the *Hueyi Tzompantli*, or Great Skull-rack, may have been made up of 60,000 skulls, which is probably a world record for the number of skulls displayed like a human abacus.

Tzompantli and ball courts usually went hand-in-hand. As the ballgame was often a substitute for all-out war, it's easy to imagine these racks displaying the decapitated heads of the losing team as a kind of makeshift scoreboard. Although admittedly, that's not a historian's serious theory, just my ghoulish imagination.

Fig. 6: An easy way of keeping track of the score?
(Juan de Tovar, Public domain, and S.E.W.)

The Rise and Fall of the Aztec Empire

In 1427, three city-states—Tenochtitlan, Texcoco, and Tlacopan—combined to become what we now refer to as the Aztec Empire. They joined forces to defeat the state of Azcapotzalco, which was, up to then, the big dog in the Basin of Mexico. Once this was done, it didn't take long for Tenochtitlan to shaft Texcoco and Tlacopan as well.

Through a combination of trade and military conquest, the Aztecs continued to extend their empire. However, it was not a unified empire in the sense Western conquerors might recognize. Rather than occupying the land of their defeated rivals with military force, the Aztecs controlled these conquered states through the appointment of quisling puppet rulers, and the cementing of alliances with royal marriages between city-states. Because of this status, these conquered states paid taxes to the empire, rather than tribute. A subtle difference, I grant you, but one that let the friendly rulers keep face (and their hearts).

By 1519, things were looking rosy for the Aztec Empire. Their political clout reached into the southern reaches of Mesoamerica, extending from the Pacific Ocean in the west to the Atlantic Ocean in the east. The empire was rich through the taxes farmed from client states, had enough tobacco to give their population lung cancer a thousand times over, could watch all the gory ballgames they liked, and they had a massive surplus of human skulls.

What could possibly go wrong? The 1591 arrival of a bastard named Hernán Cortés and the Spanish conquistadors, that's what. But before we go there, we're going to have a look at what was happening in Peru.

* * *

Meanwhile, in Peru...

What Came Before

In *From Cave to Colosseum*, I was greatly remiss not to mention the ancient South American civilizations that paved the way for our next destination: the world of the Incas. One of these pre-ceramic Peruvian civilizations, the Caral-Supe, is South America's oldest and is roughly contemporaneous with the Sumerian, Egyptian, and early Chinese cultures. That said, we are clearly looking at another cradle of civilization. While there is evidence of Caral-Supe villages existing around 4000 BC, their first city was built approximately five hundred years later, and it was no ordinary city.

Caral was a metropolis which boasted temples, an amphitheater, circular plazas, residential zones, and six large stepped pyramids. These latter structures are remarkable in their antiquity, predating all Mesoamerican pyramids, and are even older than many Egyptian pyramids. Caral is likely the oldest urban area in the Americas, leading to some commentators regarding it as the "mother city of South America."

Archaeological evidence indicates that the Caral-Supe people were spiritual, and had a societal structure based on commerce, as they appear to have invented the quipu method of recording data with knotted string. It's speculated they were a pleasure-seeking people, as there's evidence of drug taking as well as an apparent love of music, with animal bone flutes being a common artifact. They also appear not to have been a martial culture, as there have been few weapons of war found by archaeologists.

Given their new-agey spirituality, macrame, drug-taking, flute-playing, and pacifism, one might speculate that the Caral-Supe people were a bunch of dirty hippies. However, flower children or not, there's no doubt the Caral-Supe were the first in a series of civilizations that directly led to the Inca.

Another early Peruvian civilization was the Paracas culture, an Andean society that existed between 800 BC and 100 AD. The Paracas people were geniuses with water management and irrigation, and they were no slouches with the weaving of textiles, using braiding and knotting techniques to create stunning items of clothing. We know a lot about Paracan textiles due to one of their other obsessions...

You see, the people of the Paracas culture just loved to dig shaft tombs in which they would deposit dead relatives. But these honored dead weren't just dumped into a hole and forgotten. They were lovingly wrapped in elaborate funerary bundles, composed of layers of expertly woven textiles. These mummies, and the textiles in which they were swaddled, were preserved due to the subtropical desert environment of the Paracas Peninsula, to be later discovered by archaeologists.

These mummies weren't alone, either. The shaft tombs of the Paracas were designed for multiple burials, so Grandma, Grandpa, and other relatives were literally piled up inside them. But the last time anyone saw the dear departed wasn't when they shoved them into the tomb. Sometimes the ancestors would have their heads—just their heads—taken out of the tomb for, as far as archaeologists can determine, use in religious ceremonies. When the ritual was concluded, Grandma's head was lovingly reunited with her body.

Until next time.

Fig. 7: "What nice teeth you have, Grandma!" (Carlosphotos and S.E.W.)

Following the end of the Paracas culture, and greatly benefiting from their intellectual property, was the Nazca Civilization, which built cities in southern Peru between 200 BC and 600 AD. If the name sounds familiar, it's because you just read about them in the previous *Interlude* due to their association with the UFO-loving charlatan I promised not to mention. These people settled in and around the Nazca valley, and are known for their colorful pottery and textiles, and, most famously, the aforementioned Nazca lines that inspired a thousand ancient aliens enthusiasts.

The Chimu Empire

The Chimu Empire dominated the western seaboard of South America for nearly a thousand years before being conquered by the Inca Empire around 1470 AD. The major archaeological site of the Chimu is the city of Chan Chan, which accommodated an estimated population of 30,000 people in an area of twenty square kilometers. Located on the coastal desert plains of Peru, this was a highly unusual place to build a city, particularly because of the very low rainfall in the area. To make things worse, when it rained, it *really* rained. Droughts in the area were usually broken by destructive storms that brought catastrophic deluges. Despite the unpromising landscape, nearby valleys were fertile and, with the application of ingenuity, the residents were able to irrigate fields and produce beans, sweet potato, papaya, and cotton.

The Chimu also liked to sacrifice children. And llamas. A mass burial site has been discovered less than a kilometer from Chan Chan, containing one hundred and forty children and a couple of hundred llamas, as a result of what can only be a mass sacrifice. I guess when you live in a god-forsaken wasteland periodically blasted by catastrophic storms, you'd try anything to make it stop.

Perhaps due to the difficulties inherent in their physical location (or a child and llama shortage) the Chimu were attempting to expand their territory and influence at the very time the Inca Empire arrived to take center stage. The Incas subdued the Chimu and established an indirect rule over their lands, but their rule was not destined to be a long one.

The Inca Empire

The name "Inca" is derived from the word *Inca*, which was actually the title they used to refer to their emperor. While we still occasionally use the word *Inca* in this way, nowadays it's most commonly used to denote the civilization itself. The Inca Civilization was vast, well-organized, rich, and—with the exception of conquered enemies and beautiful children (of which, more later)—known for the humane treatment of its people.

After emerging from the highlands of Peru in the early thirteenth century, the Inca quickly became the most powerful force in pre-Columbian America. While the native Inca population never exceeded 100,000 people, they managed to impose their culture on an empire of about ten million conquered people. Their empire stretched over 4,000 kilometers, from southern Colombia in the north, down into central Chile, traversing mountainous and inhospitable terrain.

The structure of Incan society was layered, with the emperor and his immediate family at the top, nobles and high-ranked clerics in the middle, and the smelly old commoners at the bottom. Nevertheless, the emperor could not have maintained control without the aid of his aristocratic administrators, who kept the *hoi polloi* in line with harsh controls. While Incan architecture and technology were of a high standard, they were not particularly original, borrowing heavily from their Peruvian predecessors. Their economy was agrarian, based on the staple crops of maize, potatoes, tomatoes, peanuts, chili peppers, squash, coca, and cotton. In a move that would horrify thousands of Western children, the Inca raised guinea pigs as a food source. They also made clothes out of llama wool and cotton.

However, the Inca failed to develop significant innovations common to most large-scale civilizations, such as the wheel, iron, steel, and a written language. They also lacked a large beast of burden such as the horse or bullock, and had to rely instead on the much less robust llama. Despite these deficiencies, the Inca established a large empire connected by an excellent system of roads. They also created impressive megastructures, even though they lacked metals harder than bronze.

Fig. 8: It was one big empire... (Drutska and S.E.W.)

Inca mythology holds that the great god Viracocha was the creator of all things. There are, as in many sacred texts, differing stories, but one tale is that Viracocha emerged sopping wet from Lake Titicaca, said "Let there be light," or words to that effect, then brought the sun, moon, and stars into being. Not satisfied, he also created Inti (the Inca Sun God), and his sister, Mama Killa (the Moon Goddess, not a gangster rapper). As is requisite in the incestuous affairs of gods, when Inti and Mama Killa grew up, they were married.

Viracocha created the first people by breathing life into large rocks and molding them into humanoid shape, but unsurprisingly, considering the building materials used, he was dissatisfied with the lumbering stupidity of Humanity 1.0 and discontinued the model. Viracocha's second attempt with smaller stones was somewhat more successful, and the Inca were the result. Nevertheless, this story goes some way to explaining why many people are still as dumb as rocks.

Maybe because his creations were so thick and ponderous, one legend has it that Viracocha unleashed a flood near Lake Titicaca, wiping out all but two beings. He then entrusted these survivors, Manco Cápac and Mama Uqllu, with the task of bringing civilization to the world. Legend has it that they founded the Inca civilization.

Mission accomplished, Viracocha then roamed the earth dressed as a beggar, teaching his people and performing a miracle or two (he was also a famous sex-pest, as we'll see later). Despite having purged the bulk of the rock-people with his flood, Viracocha's creations still proved disappointing. Many refused to follow his teachings and behaved badly, as humans are wont to do. Mightily pissed off at the moronic nature of humankind, Viracocha walked on water across the Pacific Ocean and buggered off into the sunset, never to return.

Who can blame him?

Nevertheless, the Inca prospered, rapidly growing their empire. Their conquests weren't always by the sword, and often the Inca would threaten/negotiate with their targets like mob bosses. If that failed, bloody wars certainly weren't out of the question, and the empire continued to grow. These new provinces were put under the control of Inca governors and administrators, who made sure these newly conquered people toed the Incan line and farmed taxes for the emperor. Local nobility who had collaborated with the Inca were allowed to keep their rank and position. Nobles who refused to turn quisling were summarily exterminated.

When it came to subduing conquered peoples (a terrible, yet significant big idea), the Inca clearly knew what they were doing. And this know-how came straight from the top.

Incan Emperors

At the pinnacle of Incan society was the emperor known as the Sapa Inca or "Unique Inca." As the Sapa Inca was considered to be a direct descendant of Inti, the sun god, he ruled with impunity. Everything in Inca society, from the most exquisite golden statue to the contents of the shittiest diaper, was the personal property of the Sapa Inca. Such was his magnificence, his subjects were not permitted to look him directly in the eye (rather like some celebrities today). The Sapa Inca had an array of wives and innumerable children, but he had one "primary" wife known as the Coya, who was (of course) his full sister. The Coya had a major influence upon deciding which of the Sapa Inca's sons would succeed him.

So, it should come as no surprise that when the emperor died, it was usually the son of the Coya who took over the family business of being a god-on-earth. Although deceased, the Sapa Inca continued to play a major role in Incan life. His body was mummified and left unburied, lounging around the palace

Weekend at Bernie's style. A dead Sapa Inca still had attendants to look after his every need, although usually it was just to swat away the flies. The Incan belief in the afterlife was such that dead emperors retained ownership of all they had acquired during their lifetimes. Death didn't end their public life either. The mummies of Sapa Incas were often brought to "consult" at important meetings, and on special occasions, they would be paraded through the streets.

The first emperor was Inca Manco Capac, who led his people to settle in Cusco. This tribe was unremarkable by Peruvian standards of the day and had probably plagiarized the Chimu for much of their culture. However, by the time the fourth Inca, Mayta Capac, came to the throne in the fourteenth century, the Kingdom of Cusco had begun to stretch its wings and extort tributes from neighboring tribes. Mayta Capac's successor, Capac Yupanqui, decided that it would be a hoot if Cusco took its bully-boy show on the road, extending their influence still further. By the time the eighth Inca, Viracocha Inca (not the previously mentioned god of the same name), was on the throne, they had begun a wholesale program of expansionist assimilation of other cultures.

However, up to this point, one couldn't really describe the Inca as a fully-fledged empire. But the next Sapa Inca had other ideas.

Viracocha Inca's son, and the ninth Sapa Inca of the Kingdom of Cusco was named Cusi Yupanqui. He would become better known as Pachacuti, which roughly translates as "the Earth-Shaker" or "He who remakes the world." Initially, the boy who would be Pachacuti was not intended to succeed his father on the throne, let alone shake the Earth. However, his fortunes changed dramatically when the city of Cusco was attacked by the fiercely competitive Chanca tribe. Faced with a superior force, Emperor Viracocha did what any lily-livered royal would do: he took his intended successor, Pachacuti's brother Urco, and literally headed for the hills.

Undaunted by the cowardice of his father and brother, Pachacuti stayed behind and rallied the troops enough to survive the first day of the attack. Overnight, he prayed to the Sun god Inti for assistance, and was (apparently) sent a vision. Thus inspired, Pachacuti emerged the next day, ready to lead his forces. Although vastly outnumbered, the warriors of Cusco (bolstered by a group of ordinary citizens that included women and children) held off the Chanca assault. Legend has it that even the rocks and stones rose up to fight for Pachacuti.

Witnessing this battle from their hide-out in the hills, Viracocha Inca and Urco decided that all wasn't really lost after all, and came back with their own troops to join the fray. Thus reinforced, Pachacuti fought off the Chanca. Yet, despite this achievement, Viracocha Inca remained unimpressed and still favored Urca as the next Sapa Inca.

But it wasn't over yet.

When Pachacuti saw the Chanca regrouping for another crack at Cusco, he decided to take the offensive. The army of Cusco fell upon the Chanca encampment, and Pachacuti decapitated their leader on the battlefield. One might think that this valor would've made Pachacuti a shoo-in for the next Sapa Inca, but there was a problem.

Tradition dictated that the emperor wipe his feet on the bodies of the defeated enemies, and ever the dutiful son, Pachacuti insisted this honor belonged to his craven father. However, Viracocha informed "the Earth Shaker" that any foot wiping should be done by the *next* emperor, the spineless Urco. After a heated dispute that included Viracocha Inca attempting (and failing) to have Pachacuti assassinated, Pachacuti was proclaimed Sapa Inca, and Viracocha and Urco were exiled from Cusco.

It was under the rule of Pachacuti that the business of Incan empire-building really kicked up into high gear. He conquered the Chanca, the Quechua, and the Chimu, and initiated the systems of government that would, over the course of his reign, facilitate the creation of the Inca Empire. He built magnificent roads to connect his empire and rebuilt much of Cusco. It's also believed that Machu Picchu was constructed as an estate for Emperor Pachacuti.

Pachacuti's successor, Topa Inca Yupanqui, expanded the empire still further, extending south to present day central Chile. After Topa Inca Yupanqui, Emperor Huayna Capac extended the boundaries to the north, before he was carried off by a mysterious virus that he picked up from a tribe who'd had contact with the Spanish. This precipitated an Incan power struggle, of which the Spanish would eventually take advantage.

It All Began in Cusco

The heart of the Inca Empire was the city of Cusco, its geographic and administrative center. From there, the Inca effectively controlled the western half of South America. Given their love of administration and road building, they are often considered the Romans of the New World, and Cusco was the place where the magic happened. It's clear the Inca knew the importance of their capital, because one explanation of the name "Cusco" derives from the Inca word for "navel," and Cusco certainly was the navel of the empire. However, other researchers believe the name is derived from the phrase *qusqu wanka* which translates as the "rock of the owl." This refers to an Incan myth in which one of two brothers turned into an owl which flew to the site of Cusco, then promptly turned to stone to mark the chosen capital of the new empire.

Frankly, I prefer the logic of the "navel" explanation, although the "owl" story is more poetic.

It's believed that the city was laid out in the shape of a puma, which would certainly have been a first in town planning. To the Inca, the puma symbolized earthly power, and so the significance of laying out a city in this way is obvious. But is it true? The citadel of Sacsayhuaman is the head, with its serrated walls providing the teeth of the puma. The puma's body was outlined by the rivers Tulumayo and Huayanay, and its tail was the fork where these rivers meet. Its heart was the Temple of the Sun. The concept certainly can't be disproven, because the outline of Cusco does look *something* like a crouching puma (when viewed through squinted eyes).

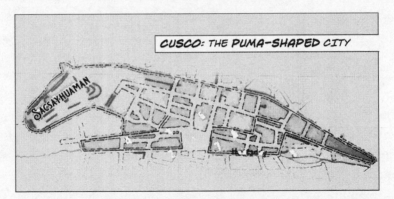

Fig. 9: More like a crouching dog? (S.E.W.)

While a puma-shaped city may seem fanciful, there's no doubt about the sacred status of the puma in Inca society, so it makes sense. One thing is for sure, Cusco was laid out meticulously. The planners' attention to detail was such that Incan engineers diverted two rivers past the site of the city. It's also likely that the design template of the city was used to plan other Inca cities. How Cusco was constructed, particularly how its large stones were quarried and transported to the site is something of a mystery.

Like many other Incan architectural achievements...

Incan Architecture
Sacsayhuaman: Putting the Costco in Cusco?

The head of Cusco's puma was Sacsayhuaman (for pronunciation, just imagine Borat saying "sexy woman"), a massive stone citadel built in the fifteenth century by Pachacuti and successors. It was constructed using huge, polygonal stones, shaped precisely to fit together without mortar. As mentioned in the previous *Interlude*, a person-who-shall-not-be-named believed this fine stonework is the result of alien intervention. While there is *some* mystery around how this stonework was completed, the idea that extraterrestrials were involved is plainly ridiculous. There is ample evidence that the stones were quarried locally, and laid using methods and tools available to the Inca at that time.

Although Sacsayhuaman could accommodate a thousand warriors, its defensive capabilities were rarely put to the test. After the Chanca invasion had been subdued by Pachacuti, the Inca had few enemies capable of besieging Cusco, and so the Inca used Sacsayhuaman for other purposes. For instance, the compound included a temple to the Sun god Inti. Sacsayhuaman was also a bulk storehouse for weapons, armor, food, tools, and precious metals, rather like an ancient, stone-walled Costco.

After the Spaniards took control of Cusco, they dismantled much of Sacsayhuaman, stone-by-stone, to provide building materials for new Spanish style buildings. It wasn't long until all that was left of the puma's head were enormous stones too large to be scavenged.

All Roads Lead to Cusco

As previously mentioned, the Inca Empire is often compared to the Roman Empire. While relevant on a number of levels, it is most apparent when looking at the network of roads they built to connect far-flung reaches of their empire. In their 1856 book, *The Architectural Instructor: Containing a History of Architecture from the Earliest Ages to the Present Time* (which in true nineteenth-century style has a subtitle which goes on for another hundred words), Lafever and Weingärtner wax lyrical about the road system of the Inca Empire:

> *Perhaps the most glorious monuments of the civilization of the Peruvians were the public or royal roads, extending from the capitol to the remotest parts of the empire [...] (T)hey broke down rocks, graded precipice, leveled hills, and filled up valleys without the assistance of powder or of instruments of iron. [...] (T)hey did, in short, what even now, with all of modern knowledge and means of action, would be worthy of the most powerful nations of the globe.*

Lafever and Weingärtner aren't just whistling *Dixie*: the Incan roads traversed all manner of landscapes, from deserts to marshlands. If required, the Inca would engineer short rock tunnels or vine-supported suspension bridges to facilitate the roadworks. However, while this *tour de force* of road building helped the Inca grow and maintain their empire, there was an unfortunate consequence. The freedom of movement the roads afforded eventually aided the Spanish conquest.

Machu Picchu

In 1911, entranced by the idea of discovering the "Lost City of the Incas," American amateur archaeologist Hiram Bingham set off on an expedition and was taken to the overgrown site of Machu Picchu by a local villager. Although not quite a "lost city," it was certainly a large, impressive site. It had been built in the mid-fifteenth century, but was abandoned during the Spanish conquest around a hundred years later. Today, it's generally accepted that Machu Picchu was constructed as a place where Emperor Pachacuti and subsequent Sapa Incas could get away from it all. It's thought to have been home to around seven hundred people, most of whom were retainers to the emperor.

Fig. 10: Pachacuti shows off Machu Picchu, his hidden getaway. (Midjourney and S.E.W.)

Built high in the Andes, at almost 2500 meters above sea level, Machu Picchu displays all the hallmarks of Incan architecture and town planning. It is mostly constructed of the classic mortarless walls of polished, tight-fitting stone, which still stands today despite being located on a fault line. Machu Picchu also boasts a sophisticated water management system, and may have been purposely sited on fault lines to allow better drainage.

In a downside to this magnificence, there's evidence that human sacrifice was practiced at Machu Picchu, which probably shouldn't come as a major surprise...

Suffer the Little Children

Like the Aztecs far to their north, the Inca practiced human sacrifice, but to a somewhat lesser extent. As we've seen, the Aztec weren't too fussy about their victims: It didn't matter whether you were a conquered enemy, unsuccessful ball-player, fanatical volunteer, criminal, or an unlucky Aztec of any age. The Aztec were equal opportunity sacrificers.

Conversely, the Inca were a little more selective about the lives they offered to the gods. They preferred to sacrifice children, a habit they may have picked up from the Chimu. The Inca had very high standards, offering up only the most beautiful children (uggos need not apply). It's thought this was because attractive kids were both aesthetically pleasing and pure of heart, therefore, more bang for your sacrifice buck. However, state-sanctioned child murders weren't a weekly occurrence. Rather, they took place in response to significant events, such as the death of the emperor or at a time of famine.

Fig. 11: It's not Mr Snuffles I'm worried about… (Midjourney and S.E.W.)

In his 1551 book, *Narrative of the Incas*, Juan de Betanzos wrote of the Inca's predilection for child sacrifice, claiming that up to a thousand children were sacrificed at a time. While he didn't witness this carnage personally, he took the word of his wife, who as Emperor Atahualpa's widow, had it on good authority.

Luckily for these children, their deaths weren't quite as horrific as the Jack the Ripper sacrifices of the Aztec priests. The Inca put a lot of care, preparation, and even a modicum of mercy, into killing children. Attractive kids from all over the empire were selected and shipped into Cusco, where they were fed like kings, dressed in expensive finery, feted like rockstars, and presented to the emperor.

So far, so good.

But then it gets weird.

Over the course of these feasts and festivals, the children were fattened up with good food and chicha beer. They'd never had it so good. Or so they thought. When the priests determined the time was right, they escorted a procession of obese, drunken children into the mountains. When they reached the place of sacrifice, they were drugged and strangled or cracked on the head. Sometimes, comatose kids would just be left in the freezing cold mountains to die of hypothermia.

Three Inca mummies discovered in 1999 provide startling evidence of this practice. The mummies, now referred to as Llullaillaco Maiden, Llullaillaco Boy, and Lightning Girl were so well preserved that a biochemical analysis of their bodies supported the evidence of de Betanzos, that ritual drug-taking played a role in their untimely deaths. For a period of up to two years prior to the sacrifice, priests used coca and alcohol to induce a catatonic state in their child victims. This was for sacred, practical, and merciful reasons. Sacred, because coca and alcohol were closely associated with Inca religious practice. Practical, because the kids were kept pliant and zombie-like for long periods. And merciful, because the kids were so zonked out that they really couldn't see what was coming.

But if this small mercy makes you think the Inca were benign by New World standards, you'd best think again.

Fig. 12: It's like she's still sleeping after five hundred years.
(Grooverpedro, Wikimedia Commons, and S.E.W.)

Skin Drums and Skull Cups

When it came to retribution, the Inca were ruthless, and took inordinate pleasure fashioning macabre trophies from the body parts of conquered foes. They made panpipes out of human bones, necklaces of human teeth, drums from human skin, and drinking cups from human skulls. These last two are particularly grisly and interesting.

The skin for the drums was obtained by flaying enemies, often while they were still alive and kicking. Rather than stretching this harvested skin across a traditional type drum, the Inca had something much creepier in mind. The skins were sewn into the approximate shape of a human body, stuffed with straw, then re-dressed in the clothes they wore in life. A drum was set in the stomach of these bizarre flesh pinatas which were strung up and left to twist in the breeze, their hands involuntarily tapping a beat. These grotesque "person drum" displays must surely have struck fear into the hearts of the Incas' enemies.

The skull cup was an "honor" reserved for conquered leaders. And *what* an honor. After decapitation, the brain was scooped out of the skull, and after some remedial work inside the braincase, a cup of beaten gold was inserted in the cavity. This was then connected to a gold tube which protruded from the skull's mouth. Thus completed, the skull cup was then filled with *chicha* beer ready for the emperor. The accepted method of drinking from this "cup" was eye-to-eye-socket through the golden straw, essentially making the skull a gruesome sippy cup. It wasn't for the squeamish, but after a long dusty battle, what better way of quenching a hard-earned thirst?

Fig. 13: When you've got a hard-earned thirst… (Midjourney/S.E.W.)

Despite the disturbing nature of the person drums and the skull cups, I'm personally most horrified by the panpipes made from human bones. Not because of the hideous nature of the instrument, but because of the detestable New Age music they must surely have emitted when played. Give me a novelty beer mug and disembodied drum solo any day.

Tied Up in Knots

As mentioned, to the best of our knowledge, none of the Andean civilizations invented a written language. Considering the supercharging effect that the development of writing had on the Sumerians, Egyptians, Mayans, and Chinese, this would seem to be a problem for the Inca.

Clearly, the inability to record numbers or words in writing was a drawback, but the civilizations of South America came up with an ingenious workaround. They recorded accounting data and phonetic language using the *quipu*. *Quipu* were assemblages of textile cords via which they were able to convey numeric information, through a combination of number and type of knots, length, type, and color of rope, and number of attached cords.

Fig. 14: Tied up on knots (Public domain and S.E.W.)

While we have an understanding of how numeric *quipu* worked, there's another type of *quipu* that no living person is able to decode. These are the so-called narrative *quipu* which are thought to have been able to convey phonetic information. By the time of the Inca, *quipus* were being used to set down historical records. Unfortunately, these could only be decoded by the bureaucrats in Cusco, and after the Spanish conquest and subsequent destruction of all things indigenous, the method of interpreting the *quipu* was lost.

When It Absolutely, Positively Has to Be in Cusco Overnight

One group of people who could certainly read the *quipu* were the Incan version of FedEx known as *chasqui*. These guys were no ordinary couriers. They were selected for duty on the basis of their intelligence, fitness, memory, and ability to interpret *quipu*. In fact, *chasqui* were often essential to the reading of the *quipu*, as a large proportion of the message was passed on orally. With relay stations set up throughout the extensive Incan road system, the *chasqui* could tag-team deliveries over distances of around two hundred and forty kilometers a day.

An essential piece of equipment for the *chasqui* was the *pututu*—a conch shell used as a trumpet to signal ahead to other *chasquis* that a runner was close. I imagine the resounding toot had the effect of a football manager ordering a substitute to warm up. The new runner would stretch his quads and do some light sprints up and down the touch line in preparation for taking his place in the big game. However it worked, the new runner was ready to continue passing on the message when the old runner arrived.

Fig. 15: Couriers were fitter in those days…. (Midjourney and S.E.W.)

The Return of the Magical Semen

Readers of *From Cave to Colosseum* will be familiar with the fascination many ancient cultures had with strange methods of insemination, which far too often occurred orally. Legends are replete with weird stories, such as when the Egyptian god Thoth was conceived after Horus serendipitously swallowed some of Set's semen during a "fight."

Well, half a world away, the Inca did not disappoint.

One Incan legend tells the story of Caui Llaca, a goddess renowned for her beauty and independent nature, who was the subject of unwanted attention from male gods who vied for her affections. Chief amongst these lecherous deities was the creator god, Viracocha, who you may remember from earlier, often took the form of a filthy tramp. He desperately wanted to claim Caui Llaca's virginity and, perhaps sensing that being an unwashed homeless man might turn off a beautiful young goddess, came up with a devious method to achieve his aim.

One day, as Caui Llaca sat beneath a shady fruit tree, the creepy Viracocha transformed himself into a bird. One thing led to another, and he "magically" relocated his semen into the fruit of the tree. Unaware of this unsavory event, Caui Llaca ate some of the fruit and became pregnant. Upon the birth of her child, she belatedly decided to determine the identity of its father. When she discovered that the child's father was a stinking bum, she did the only thing a disgraced Incan goddess would do: She grabbed her child and ran into the ocean. Realizing that his masquerade had gone too far, the lecherous old Viracocha unmasked himself and tried to catch her, but she never looked back to see the identity of the fruit-rapist. And as Caui Llaca and her son waded into the waves, they were magically transformed into two islands.

Clearly, this was not a lightbulb moment, but it *is* yet another in a long line of god/insemination-by-mouth related mishaps.

Did the Inca and Aztec Add to the Collective Knowledge of Humanity?

Given the aim of this book is to track the lightbulb moments in history that brought us to where we are today, it's fair to ask if the Aztec or Inca added to humanity's collective knowledge. They had made some breakthroughs independently of the rest of the world. For instance, the Inca invented roads and sophisticated courier networks unassisted by any other culture. The Aztec clearly made great strides in open heart surgery, although, unfortunately, none of the patients survived.

However, because they were so remote from the Asia/Europe nexus, their ongoing influence was limited. Another issue is that we simply don't know the full extent of their intellectual capital. Therefore any potential influence the Aztec or the Inca may have had was severely curtailed by the wholesale destruction of their records and learning by the Spanish. Who knows *what* they could have taught us?

But forget the Spanish, here's another thought: Given the many thousands ritually murdered by Aztec and Incan priests, how many brilliant minds were sacrificed? Could an Aztec da Vinci or an Incan Einstein have been slaughtered in the name of appeasing bloodthirsty gods? Could an Incan Napoleon who might have routed the European invaders, have been drugged and left to die in the Andes? We cannot know.

What we do know is that these Central and South American civilizations built on the knowledge of those who came before them, and (assuming they could've moved past the human sacrifice stage), would have developed further. But this was not to be.

Unfortunately for both civilizations, the end was nigh.

* * *

A Brief Interlude III

Ch-ch-changes

Nowadays, I find change easy.

I haven't always been this way, but the slings and arrows of outrageous fortune have, to a certain extent, inured me to most types of adjustments, developments, innovations, modifications, revisions, or any other synonyms for "change" that the thesaurus can throw at me. Which is just as well, because a major change in this book is upon us.

Fig. 1: A change is as good as a holiday. (Midjourney and S.E.W.)

From the beginning of *From Cave to Colosseum* until now, I've organized *Lightbulb Moments in Human History* as chronologically as possible, and for the most part, focused on one civilization at a time. There were three reasons I structured the books this way. One was so I could lay out the logical progression of human achievement to demonstrate how collective learning accumulated. Another reason was to help support my thesis that the world is inexorably improving, driven forward by the weight of cultural capital. The final reason was because this straightforward linear framework was familiar to casual readers of history, making the books easier to read.

This strategy could be seen as overly simplistic, but I believe it's served me (and my project) well. Until now.

Emerging from the late Middle Ages, the story of humanity's lightbulb moments became an even more complex web of interrelated strands. The pace of change and innovation began to speed up. Around the fifteenth century, a number of significant historical developments began to occur almost simultaneously. As a result, the Renaissance, the Reformation, the Age of Discovery, and the beginnings of the Scientific Revolution are deeply intertwined. And yet, they're also discrete historical movements.

Eventually, I realized if I continued the exclusively chronological approach, the narrative would become far too complex. A chapter on all the events that occurred between the fifteenth and seventeenth centuries (dates often associated with all the movements mentioned above) would be very complex and stretch out to three or four times the length of previous chapters. I was also concerned that it could become a little dull. One of my goals is to make *Lightbulb Moments in Human History* easily digestible and, hopefully, fun to read. Clearly, a change had to be made.

Therefore, this is where I will diverge from a strictly linear structure.

The next four chapters, on the topics of the Renaissance, the Reformation, the Age of Discovery, and the Scientific Revolution, will regularly overlap time-wise. Sometimes historical figures will appear in more than one of these chapters. Some concepts that could appear in more than one chapter will only appear in one. Others may appear in all. But I trust that this is, for me at least, the simplest and best way to structure the ongoing investigation.

Also, please be warned: this new world order is not merely for the aforementioned chapters. As I move forward with the *Lightbulb Moments in Human History* series, this is how the books will continue to be structured, as the pace of change and complexity only increases.

So, dear reader, now you are forearmed. I invite you to continue as we look at the Renaissance.

—4—

Just Like Starting Over

The Renaissance

When studying art history at high school, I remember my teacher, Mrs. Cowan, banging on and on about how the Renaissance was "the rebirth of Classical thought, architecture and art." Because the curriculum had been dumbed down so that Year 8 Neanderthals could understand, it seemed that the Renaissance flickered to life like a fluorescent tube, pretty much the second Leonardo picked up his first paintbrush.

Either that, or I wasn't paying attention properly.

Whichever it was, I bought into the "instant rebirth" story wholesale: I idolized Michelangelo, who seemed like a total badass, yet who created heart-achingly beautiful statuary, architecture, and paintings; I felt awe at the genius and wide-ranging artistic and scientific endeavors of Leonardo da Vinci, and I remember dismissing medieval art and architecture as being simplistic and boring, with no redeeming features.

However, the Renaissance was about a lot more than architecture and art. The changes that rippled through society crossed many disciplines: A social historian might note the end of the ages of feudalism and chivalry. An economist would laud the beginnings of a more modern conception of commerce. A scientist would revel in the foundation of the sciences of astronomy, medicine, anatomy, and the beginnings of the scientific method. A philosopher would ponder the rejection of medieval scholasticism and the growth of humanism. Theologians would point to the proliferation of religious art and architecture.

There was literally something for everyone.

The Renaissance was no less than a remaking of European culture. But it didn't happen overnight. Or in a vacuum. However, it must be said, it was coming from a dark place, and I'm not talking about the "Dark Ages."

The Unexpected Upside of the Black Death

By some estimates, the Black Death took place within living memory of the people of the early Renaissance. As seen in Chapter One, this deadly pandemic had cut a swathe throughout mid-fourteenth-century Europe, and the ever present threat of death engendered an ongoing fatalism. Practicing pious Christianity hadn't saved them, so there was an air of "eat, drink, and be merry, for tomorrow I die!" about these guys. They knew life was short, so they planned to make the most of it.

Religion remained a dominant theme in art in the post-pandemic world, probably because the Church in Rome was the leading patron of Renaissance artists. Yet, some artists, no doubt influenced by a combination of the rise of humanism and nouveau riche patrons such as the Medici, chose to depict scenes out of Classical myth, such as Sandro Botticelli's the Birth of Venus. But it wasn't just art that changed in this new world.

Fig. 1: If only she'd read the invitation more carefully. (Wowinside and S.E.W)

A major upshot of the Black Death was an increased pace of economic change in response to the sharp decline in population. Prior to the pandemic, Europe was still firmly in the grasp of the feudal system, with workers still bound to their lords through serfdom. Labor shortages due to the death or relocation of former peasants led to, among other things, an increase in wages and an accelerated end to Feudalism.

However you look at it, there's a strong case to be made that the Black Death helped bring about the Renaissance. It just proves you can't blame the so-called "Dark Ages" for everything.

Dark Ages?

Not all Classical philosophy, art, and learning were lost in the "Dark Ages." In fact, some hadn't been lost at all. Sure, some learning had been mislaid and, as we've seen, had been found and preserved by Islamic scholars and then reintroduced to the West. But this mostly happened hundreds of years before what we traditionally consider the beginnings of the Renaissance.

While we try to slap an approximate date of between 1400 and 1500 AD on the beginning of the Renaissance, this is merely a convenient label. There's no day that the starting-gun went off. Moreover, the DNA and development of Renaissance art are easily traceable: A range of artists rediscovered Classical methods over time, and the realism and flowing lines gradually returned, reaching their zenith in the high Renaissance.

Sculpture is arguably the art form where the loss and rediscovery of dynamic realism is most easily seen. First, let's look at one of the greatest known Classical sculptures, *Laocoön and His Sons*, (below). This marble sculpture is from the Hellenistic Period (323 BC–31 AD) and was uncovered in an Italian vineyard in 1506 AD. Characteristic of the era, *Laocoön and His Sons* tells a story from Greek mythology and depicts human anatomy and movement with stunning realism.

Fig. 2: Laocoön, his sons, and a snake (Marie-Lan Nguyen and S.E.W)

Sure, Laocoön is unnaturally large compared to his sprogs, and it's definitely odd subject matter to twenty-first-century eyes, but what a sculptural achievement.

Fig. 3: A Medieval Pieta vs Michelangelo's Pieta (Public domain)

Now compare the two statues above. Both are of the same subject, the Pieta: Mary cradling the dead Jesus. The medieval version on the left is childlike in its lack of sophistication; Jesus looks like a poorly carved marionette. In contrast, Michelangelo's Pieta with its inherent pathos, lifelike anatomy, and gently flowing robes, is arguably the most outstanding sculptural achievement in human history. Now, I'm the first to admit that this comparison is grossly unfair: I'm setting up a strawman by contrasting the medieval Pietas (there are many of them and they are usually poor examples of medieval sculpture) to the work of a great master at the peak of his powers. A fairer comparison would be to the late medieval sculpture of Nicola Pisano, whom I cited in the Middle Ages chapter as a valid forerunner of Renaissance. Nevertheless, Pisano was an outlier from a time when the Middle Ages were morphing into the Renaissance.

Anyway, my point is that a similar pattern of medieval crudity morphing into Renaissance beauty can be seen in art, literature, politics, philosophy, and almost any other human endeavor.

While the period was crammed with new and exciting ideas, there was also a fair bit of plagiarism too...

The "Invention" of the Printing Press

Readers of *From Cave to Colosseum* will remember that despite constant claims that Johannes Gutenberg invented printing, the process initially appeared in China in the first millennium AD. The first we hear about Gutenberg and the modern invention of the printing press is in 1439, after a long and secretive development process.

As someone descended from printers, and who worked in the graphic arts for twenty years of my working life, I often discounted the significance of printing. To me, it was just a boring job, not one of the most significant human inventions since the wheel. It was therefore easy to gloss over the fact that before printing, numbers of books were limited to the number a monk could copy by hand.

Fig. 4: The penny drops... (Midjourney and S.E.W.)

The invention of the printing press and moveable type led to greater ease and speed of book production. It's estimated it took a monk around one hundred days to hand copy a Bible—that's just over 3.5 Bibles per year. Gutenberg's first print run of the Bible was 200 copies in three years, about 66 Bibles per year. So the first-ever print run, with its attendant learning-curve, was already eighteen times faster than hand copying, and the speed and efficiency of printing would only improve.

By the end of the fifteenth century, there were printing presses located in approximately 270 cities throughout Europe. This precipitated an exponential growth in printing that was a major factor in the growth and accumulation of knowledge. Print media such as books and pamphlets enabled the proliferation of ideas that helped to shape changes in the Renaissance period. No longer were books an unattainable luxury item, available only in monasteries or the libraries of the mega-rich. This provided an opportunity for a growing number of people in each subsequent generation to gain knowledge and enhance it with their own contribution. The sheer number of knowable things grew at an incredible rate. This democratization of information brought about crucial changes in society, academia, religion, industry, and economy. What emerged was nothing more or less than the first information revolution.

When the printing press came into use in the fifteenth century, it is estimated that less than 10 percent of European adults were literate. As the number of printed books multiplied, adult literacy rates rose inexorably, and by 1696, it had risen to 47 percent. The implications for education were staggering. There was a reason to learn to read. The more literate individuals in a society, the more people were available to teach others to read, resulting in more literate individuals. A cycle of growth, which drove the need for more schools and in time, the need for institutionalized schooling.

This need was evidenced by the growth in the number of new schools being established. If one examines the schools chartered during the medieval period, there was a small, but increasing number of new schools each year in England. In the thirteenth century, there were only three new schools. And while there was an appreciable rise in the number of newly established schools in the fourteenth and fifteenth centuries (fifteen and twenty-four respectively), that is nothing compared to what was to come. Over one hundred-and-fifty were chartered in the sixteenth century when the effect of mass-produced books began to take hold.

However, these schools did not always embody the Renaissance's humanist ideals. Individuality, the humanist goal so prized in the modern world, did not always sit well with a harried schoolmaster teaching a classroom of unruly boys, so the birch rod was still very much in evidence. The curriculum was broadened by the greater availability of printed books, but the students still learned mostly Latin grammar, arithmetic, and rhetoric. Despite the desire to create a more literate populace, the male children of the wealthy made up most of the growth in school enrolments.

Fig. 5: The "devil's horn" hand signal isn't as "metal" as we thought.
(Acrogame and S.E.W.)

The woodcut above, purporting to show a Renaissance era classroom, is by German artist Hans Burgkmair. Woodcuts are illustrations made by using a tool to carve grooves into a wooden block, which allowed raised areas to be inked and impressed onto paper in the newfangled printing process. In this illustration, the hapless teacher, depicted in a jester's hat, is surrounded by rowdy pupils greeting him with the "devil's horns" hand-signal. Despite appearances, this is not anachronistic evidence of rock 'n' roll culture during the Renaissance. This hand gesture, favored by metal fans and subject of a failed copyright attempt by Gene Simmons of Kiss, has an ancient and appropriately satanic origin story. It is a sign known as Mano Cornuto, which is Italian for "horned hand," and it was used as a symbolic protection against the evil eye. Regardless, it would be wrong to assume that students performing an exorcism on a jester/teacher was an accurate representation of Renaissance schooling. What one can assume is that by the sixteenth century, the "classroom" trope was well established enough to be subverted for comedic purposes.

The Playing Fields of Eton

It was in England during the Renaissance that the grammar schools which eventually evolved into the famous public schools of Eton, Shrewsbury, Harrow, Winchester, Rugby, Westminster, and Charterhouse, came into being. But before we examine them, let's backtrack a little and examine the tricky definition of an English public school.

For the uninitiated, these public schools are not state schools open to the general populace, despite what the name suggests. Far from it. They are schools which charge exorbitant fees and were originally intended solely for the sons of the ruling classes. They were designed to forge the leaders of the future and were "public" only in the sense that anyone from any place, religion or background could attend if they had enough money. The most famous of these schools—Eton College (1440 AD), Rugby School (1567) and Harrow School (1572 AD)—have supplied England with an endless supply of gormless, upper-class twits for over 500 years.

It's a proud tradition.

In fact, these public schools have a large array of time-honored traditions. One such is the institution of "fagging." This practice thankfully has nothing etymologically to do with the pejorative words "fag" or "faggot" (which are an unfortunate American invention). The idea was that a "fag" (or younger student) would act as a servant for a "fag-master" or older student. If this wasn't humiliating enough, fags were bullied and sometimes physically and/or sexually abused. Of course, it was not all inhumane, but even at its best, there was an uncomfortable aspect of slavery about the practice. T.L. Jarman, in his *Landmarks* in the History of Education, compares fagging to the way that Spartan boys were encouraged to bully each other to toughness. I would add that there's also a touch of good old Greek-style pederastic mentoring (see *From Cave to Colosseum*) in the classic fag/fag-master relationship, although with less romance and more of a sex slave vibe.

Humanism: Renaissance Education in Europe

On the continent, formal education also remained the province of the well-heeled. Increasingly, however, the medieval curriculum which had favored religious texts was pushed aside. Instead, Italian schools of the fifteenth century led a revolution by reverting to the study of classical Latin texts by Julius Caesar, Cicero, Virgil, Ovid, and Terrence. Following this lead, much of Europe followed suit in the sixteenth century. Focusing on these pre-Christian writers ensured that *studia humanitatis* (or humanistic studies, which comprised poetry, grammar, history, rhetoric, and moral philosophy) led to the growth of humanism in Europe.

Humanism is a philosophy "informed by science, inspired by art, and motivated by compassion." It asserts the dignity of human life and fosters the ideal of individual liberty. Above all, it values reason. Indeed, if there was a single cause of the renewal and reawakening of knowledge in the Renaissance, it was humanism. It remained the cornerstone of the education of elites into the twentieth century.

So, what effect did the growth of schools and humanism have on collective learning?

The Education of Genius

The Renaissance is rightly famous for the sheer volume of geniuses it produced: Dante Alighieri, Giotto, Geoffrey Chaucer, Thomas Hobbes, Nicolaus Copernicus, Erasmus, Raphael, Donatello. The list goes on and on. What caused this era to produce so many great minds, with interests spanning a vast array of intellectual disciplines?

We've seen that humanism played a big part.

However, given the seeming explosion of polymaths in the Renaissance era, it might be an interesting exercise to examine what is known of their education. Why were they so prolific? What prepared them to unleash their lightbulb moments on the world? Was there a secret sauce that created a Renaissance man and if so, what was it?

Let's look at what is known of the education of four of the most prominent Renaissance figures: Leonardo da Vinci, Michelangelo, William Shakespeare, and Galileo Galilei...

The Education of Leonardo da Vinci

Leonardo had almost no schooling and could barely read Latin or do long division.
Walter Isaacson, *Leonardo da Vinci*

The term "Renaissance Man" could have been invented to describe Leonardo da Vinci (1452–1519). Not only does he routinely land near the top of the list of the greatest painters of all time, but he is revered for his remarkable contributions to science, medicine and invention. Leonardo created artistic masterpieces including the *Mona Lisa, the Last Supper* and *Vitruvian Man*; drew plans for inventions such as parachutes, an underwater diving suit, and machine guns; made detailed anatomical drawings during dissections; and performed investigations into areas as diverse as botany, cartography, astronomy, geology, and alchemy.

Fig. 6: Leonardo da Vinci and the Vitruvian Man
(Sergey Kohl, Caifas and S.E.W.)

However, despite being one of the most influential and talented individuals in history, Leonardo had received very little formal education and was mostly self-taught. While he was often touchy about being a self-described "unlettered man," he also took pride in his lack of formal schooling, as it allowed him to be a free-thinker. It might also have had another unintended but fortuitous consequence.

Being a left-hander who wrote right-to-left in mirror-reverse script, one can imagine Leonardo having that idiosyncrasy beaten out of him at school, as was done right up until living memory. Modern cognitive neuroscience has shown that converting left-handers to right-handers by force leads to a disruption in the part of the brain that integrates executive and cognitive control of skilled movements, and one can only imagine what detrimental effect that would've had on Leonardo's dexterity and creativity. This is, perhaps, the only case known where lack of education may have gifted the world a genius.

The small amount of formal learning Leonardo did receive was at a type of elementary school known as an "abacus school," which emphasized the mathematical skills useful in the world of business. If his father, Ser Piero da Vinci, had visions of him following in his footsteps and becoming a notary, those hopes were dashed as the guild of notaries would not grant membership to the bastard sons of members. In any event, Leonardo showed little or no inclination towards this path. In his classic *Lives of the Artists*, Giorgio Vasari wrote that Piero was aware of his son's disinterest in the family business and realized that Leonardo "never ceased drawing and sculpting, pursuits which suited his fancy more than any other."

And so it was that as his son neared the age of fourteen, Ser Piero prevailed upon one of his clients, Andrea del Verrocchio, to take his son on as an apprentice. However, considering Leonardo's raw talent, it was unlikely the master needed much convincing. Verrocchio, an artist, an engineer, and himself a Renaissance man who ran one of the most renowned workshops in Florence, was the perfect choice to nurture da Vinci's genius. Leonardo's studies under Verrocchio would have covered anatomy, dissection, geometry, bronze casting, drawing techniques and mathematics, which were quite enough to go on with, even for the wonder boy from Vinci.

From the age of nineteen, now a young master painter himself, Leonardo continued to live with and work for Verrocchio for a decade after the completion of his apprenticeship. It was probably far easier for him to work in Verrocchio's workshop, where he didn't have to compete for work in the cut-throat

Florence marketplace. However, by this time, the pupil had well and truly surpassed the master and Leonardo's future education was in his own hands. As we all know, a long and storied cross-disciplinary career ensued.

Even though there are plenty of other contenders, it's entirely probable that Leonardo da Vinci possessed the greatest, most wide-ranging intellect in human history. He was, after all, a sublimely talented painter, sculptor, scientist, engineer, and architect, to name but a few of his areas of interest. Whatever the verdict, there's no doubt that he was a supreme example of the triumph of nature over nurture.

The Education of Michelangelo

Michelangelo di Lodovico Buonarroti Simoni (1475–1564), or, as the world best knows him, Michelangelo, is one of the precious few individuals—like Jesus, Mohammed or Cher—who are universally recognizable by their first name. He was a Florentine sculptor, painter, and architect during the high Renaissance. While the term "Renaissance Man" provides a perfect description of Leonardo da Vinci, Michelangelo was also a prodigious polymath who had a strong claim to that title, having painted the ceiling of the Sistine Chapel; sculpted the David and the Pieta, and designed the dome of St. Peter's Basilica; as well as being responsible for many, many other masterpieces of the Renaissance. And like Leonardo, Michelangelo also made life drawings of autopsied bodies, giving him an intimate knowledge of human physiology. If Leonardo was the greatest painter of all time, then Michelangelo the greatest all round artist of all time.

You may disagree, but I'm happy to fight you for it.

Fig. 7: Michelangelo tells it like it is. (Muratart, Georgios Kollidas, and S.E.W.)

Unlike Leonardo, Michelangelo had several educational opportunities. As a young boy, Michelangelo was sent to Florence to study Greek and Latin under the tutelage of Francesco da Urbino. However, he showed little interest in school, preferring painting, drawing, and hanging out with other arty types. Michelangelo's father, Ludovico di Leonardo Buonarroti Simoni, was dismayed and considered his son's preference to be an artisan as somewhat beneath him.

At thirteen (much older than a usual apprentice), Michelangelo was apprenticed to one of Florence's most distinguished painters, Domenico Ghirlandaio. While these arrangements were supposed to be for a three-year term, Michelangelo left after around two years. It was at that time that Lorenzo "the Magnificent" de' Medici, the de facto ruler of Florentine Republic, had approached Ghirlandaio, asking for his best pupil. Ghirlandaio sent Michelangelo, and this was the beginning of a new chapter in Michelangelo's education.

For the next two years, Michelangelo studied at the Platonic Academy within the Medici household. There's evidence to suggest that Michelangelo's father Ludovico played a part in getting him this position, as he was a distant cousin of Lorenzo the Magnificent. Here Michelangelo was exposed to great literature, great minds, and to Lorenzo's incredible art collection. It's likely he was exposed to other things as well.

William E. Wallace contends that there was the rebirth of something akin to the Greek erastes/eromenos relationships: "Between the ages of 10 and 20, young men oftentimes were the object of attention of larger groups of elder males. This was not clandestine, was oftentimes open. The older males are taking an interest in the younger boys as a part of their education. Their education intellectually as well as, perhaps, sexually." Wallace believes that Michelangelo "benefitted" from this kind of homo-social relationship during time in the Medici Palace: "Michelangelo's stay in the Medici Palace fits this pattern perfectly. He became the object of attention by older men between the ages of 15 and 17, at a time when he was discovering his own sexual identity." There's no evidence of whom Michelangelo's "teacher" might have been, but I'm guessing they didn't call Lorenzo "the Magnificent" for nothing.

Apart from hobnobbing it with the glitterati of Florence, he was also exposed to new and exciting ideas and, of course, Lorenzo's amazing collection of artwork and precious objects, including many works by Donatello. It's almost certain that the two years Michelangelo spent in the Medici household, studying with leading humanist thinkers, was more valuable to his development than any potential university education. Although not fluent in Latin, Michelangelo memorized Dante during this time and took to writing poetry. He left the Medici Palace upon the death of Lorenzo, as his presence was no longer required by Lorenzo's son. But not before he had picked up the skills, knowledge and relationships he needed to move forward in his spectacular artistic career.

The Education of William Shakespeare

The immortal playwright and poet William Shakespeare (1564–1616) was born in the year of Michelangelo's death. His father, John Shakespeare, appears to have been a dodgy businessman and history doesn't record if he had any role in Will's education. William's mother, Mary Arden, seemed like a nice enough lady, but wouldn't have troubled biographers if it weren't for her talented son.

Fig. 8: It was a more accepting time. (Vukas, Iofoto and S.E.W.)

Shakespeare, like the other hyper-overachievers listed above, is believed by many to be the greatest ever in his field. He is acknowledged to have written thirty-seven plays, although some believe it may have been more. Shakespeare's plays fall into three main genres: histories, comedies, and tragedies. He also wrote at least 154 sonnets. In the process of this writing, he coined over 1500 words, among which are "zany," "unreal" and "lackluster"; and invented idioms such as "green-eyed monster," "laughingstock" and "good riddance."

Despite being born toward the end of the Renaissance, Shakespeare was one of the first dramatists to bring its core values to the theater. For hundreds of years, the Catholic Church had suppressed or banned many Classical Greek and Roman texts, but the spirit of the Renaissance had liberated these works and Shakespeare used his knowledge of them when writing his plays. The Shakespeare-didn't-write-his-plays conspiracy theorists cite Shakespeare's supposedly limited education as evidence that he could not have had the breadth of experience to have written the plays attributed to him. So, if he did indeed write these plays (and spoiler alert: he did) then where did he pick up this knowledge?

In his book *Shakespeare*, Bill Bryson outlines what little is known about Shakespeare's education: "It is commonly supposed (and frequently written) that Shakespeare enjoyed a good education at the local grammar school, King's New School, situated in the Guild Hall in Church Street, and he probably did, though in fact, we don't know, as the school records for the period were long ago lost." Bryson notes that the standard of education at King's New School was higher than might be expected (records show that their headmaster was paid more than the headmaster of Eton) and accepted enrolments from any literate local boy. Bryson continues: "Boys normally attended the school for seven or eight years, beginning at the age of seven. The school day was long and was characterized by an extreme devotion to tedium. Pupils sat on hard wooden benches from six in the morning to five or six in the evening, with only two short pauses for refreshment, six days a week." Added to that, discipline was harsh.

Sounds like fun.

While Shakespeare's contemporary and fellow playwright Ben Jonson mocked him for having "small Latin and less Greek," it would appear that Slick Willy may have had a greater facility than Jonson suspected. Grammar school instruction at that time was almost exclusively devoted to reading, writing, and reciting Latin.

Shakespeare's formal education ended around the age of 15 and how he gained his considerable knowledge after that is a mystery. But as we have seen with Leonardo da Vinci, true genius doesn't demand an excessive amount of schooling. And William Shakespeare was undoubtedly a genius. He's probably the greatest ever English-language writer, and his innovations and influence in the world of literature continues to this day.

Galileo: Figaro. Magnifico!

Many people look upon Galileo Galilei (1564–1642) as the "father of modern physics" and with good reason. Galileo is yet another Renaissance polymath, who did much to expand the fields of physics, philosophy, astronomy, mathematics and cosmology. While, contrary to popular belief, the telescope was not his invention, his improved design allowed him to discover the moons of Jupiter, the rings of Saturn, and study the surface of the moon. He had powerful friends and powerful enemies, not least of which were among the leaders of the Catholic Church, who had him arrested in 1616 and again in 1633, for his heretical belief in a heliocentric solar system. During his trial, while being forced to recant his support of the Copernican idea that the Earth revolves around the sun, some accounts report he had the temerity to mutter the words "Yet it moves!" under his breath. He was a genius who didn't know what was good for him and spent the rest of his life under house arrest.

Fig. 9: Whether thunderbolt and lightning were very, very frightening to him is unknown. (Midjourney, and S.E.W.)

Of course, all this genius had to come from somewhere, and with Galileo, it seems his pushy father, Vincenzo, played a starring role. Vincenzo Galilei was a well-bred, well-connected musician, who realized early on that young Galileo was something special. Vincenzo was, without putting too fine a point on it, a bit of a jerk. He sacked Galileo's "extremely vulgar" grammar teacher and decided to home-school him. Only when the father felt he had no more to teach the son, did he send Galileo for instruction by the strict monks in the abbey of Vallombrosa. Later, after Galileo had spent four years at the monastery being taught Latin, Greek, science, mathematics, drawing, and religious studies, he decided to take Holy Orders. Vincenzo got wind of this and swooped into the monastery and took away the fifteen-year-old the monks had been so assiduously grooming to—er—become a monk.

So, no monastery for Galileo. Instead, his overbearing, control-freak of a father had other ideas. After flirting with the idea of Galileo becoming, of all things, a wool merchant, Vincenzo decided he wanted a doctor in the family. And that's how Galileo Galilei ended up at the University of Pisa studying medicine.

Until now, Galileo had had very little agency, but that was about to change. Mathematics was a part of the medical degree, and it interested him like nothing else in his studies. Galileo began skipping medical lectures and ended up approaching the court mathematician, Ostilio Ricci, to persuade his father into letting him drop medicine and pursue mathematics. This wasn't successful, and for a year, Galileo paid little attention to his medical lectures while studying mathematics in secret with Ricci.

By this time, Galileo was exhibiting jerk-like tendencies of his own. He was arrogant and argumentative, upsetting his teachers and being condescending to the other medical students, who nicknamed him "The Wrangler." This was because he would argue with his teachers over almost anything to prove his mental superiority. This all came to a crashing end when Vincenzo could no longer afford his son's tuition fees, which forced Galileo to drop out of the University of Pisa without a degree. I doubt his lecturers or fellow students would have been sorry to see him go.

Then, after years of being pushed around by his despotic father, Galileo finally took control of his own destiny. He made ends meet by teaching mathematics to school children while he pursued his own studies, concentrating on the work of Archimedes. Finally, Galileo approached the famous Jesuit scholar Father Clavius, who recognized his genius and agreed to teach him. Galileo applied (and was rejected) for the position as chair of mathematics in Bologna. Finally in 1589, with Clavius' support, he was appointed to the chair of mathematics at the University of Pisa.

Galileo would later make some modifications to Hans Lippershey's refracting telescope and turn it towards the sky. His observations with the telescope led him to confirm Copernicus' heliocentric view of the solar system, and Galileo's publication of his findings famously brought him into conflict with the Catholic Church.

So, What Kind of Education Makes a Genius?

I suppose it should come as no surprise that there is very little that ties the education of these giants of the Renaissance together. As far as parental influence goes, Piero da Vinci and Ludovico Buonarroti appeared to be quite supportive of their respective sons' artistic careers. John Shakespeare was most likely too caught up in his shady dealings to get very involved with William's education, and Vincenzo Galilei just seemed like an obnoxious combination of a modern helicopter parent and tiger mom.

As far as can be known, Shakespeare, Leonardo, and Michelangelo only attended elementary school. However, Michelangelo spent another two years at the Medici Palace, getting all manner of education. Of these geniuses, only Galileo went to university, and he had to drop out when his dad ran out of cash.

Galileo, Michelangelo, and Leonardo had identifiable mentors who were famous in their own right. Only Shakespeare is not associated with a mentor of note, but this may just be a function of his obscurity during his formative years rather than his lack of a famous teacher. We'll most likely never know.

The only common thread that binds Leonardo, Michelangelo, Shakespeare and Galileo is that they were certifiable, standout geniuses in an era already overpopulated by men of prodigious talent. Although, I'm sure it helped that they lived and worked at a time when it was still possible for one human to have in-depth knowledge about wildly varying fields of scholarship.

It seems there was no secret sauce for a Renaissance man — only spectacular genes and an opportunity to shine.

Machiavelli's Machinations

While political skulduggery has been around since time immemorial, the Renaissance signaled a new complexity in political discourse. Most European states during this time were one of three basic forms of government: monarchies, oligarchies, and princedoms. Larger countries were usually monarchies, with the king ruling by divine right but relying on an increasingly large bureaucracy to manage complex affairs of state. Oligarchies were mostly small city-states ruled by a merchant elite. Princedoms were a little like monarchies, but with very little divine and hardly any right. The prince (or duke, marquis, or count) had often come to power through assassination, bribery, diplomacy, purchase, marriage, or war. Unlike kings, princes rarely wielded absolute power and instead had to rely on political scheming to get things done (and remain in power).

All these types of government required levels of political knowledge hitherto unknown, but given their volatile nature and the complex alliances required to keep them functioning, princedoms were a particular hotbed of political plotting and conspiracy. And one Renaissance figure literally synonymous with such intrigue was Niccolò Machiavelli, the man who is the etymological root of the word "machinations."

Machiavelli (1469–1527) was born in Florence, the son of a rich and influential lawyer. After receiving a comprehensive formal education, he landed his first job as a secretary in the Florentine bureaucracy. Not long afterwards, he witnessed a significant political upheaval as Florence expelled the powerful Medici family. As a direct result, Machiavelli suffered a series of career setbacks, which caused him to ponder the age-old question: can a good politician simultaneously be a good person? The answer he arrived at was, chillingly, no. Not only is it easier for an unscrupulous person to advance their political career, but an effective leader also makes daily decisions at odds with the actions of a good and moral person.

Machiavelli's book *The Prince* does for politics what Sun Tzu's *The Art of War* did for warfare. It's a how-to guide of bureaucratic and diplomatic maneuvering. It's the book in which Machiavelli lays out his ideas such as, "The ends justify the means," and "It's better to be feared than loved." Avid readers of *The Prince* included many internationally famous leaders, including framers of the US Constitution such as Benjamin Franklin, James Madison, and Thomas Jefferson. It also appealed to less savory individuals. Joseph Stalin kept a personally annotated copy, and Adolf Hitler employed numerous Machiavellian concepts to win his way into the Reichstag.

For better or worse, *The Prince* remains the playbook for aspiring politicians the world over.

Fig. 10: Particularly popular among the dictator class (Midjourney and S.E.W.)

Changing Their Perspective

There's a reason that Renaissance paintings look more realistic than their forebears, and it's about more than the relative skill of the artists. One of the main features that sets Renaissance art apart from, say, medieval art was the development of linear perspective. While pre-Renaissance painters such as Giotto attempted to use perspective to a limited degree, it wasn't until the work of Leon Battista Alberti and Filippo Brunelleschi in the 1400s that perspective drawing became an acknowledged artistic method for creating the illusion of distance on a flat surface.

In the wake of the work of Brunelleschi and Alberti, linear perspective took the Renaissance by storm. It wasn't long before artists throughout Italy were representing three-dimensional objects using perspective: from Fra Angelico in the early fifteenth century, all the way up to the masters of the High Renaissance—Michelangelo, Leonardo, and Raphael. While the perspective of da Vinci's *The Last Supper* is a little simplistic by today's standards, it was groundbreaking at the time and remains a textbook representation of how it was done.

Fig. 11: Perspective construction lines in The Last Supper *(Public domain and S.E.W.)*

The story of perspective drawing is an excellent example of the ways collective learning builds human knowledge: In the early Renaissance, it was cutting-edge knowledge and the subject of scientific treatises. Nowadays, eight-year-olds are routinely taught to use single point perspective. But it's more significant than merely improving children's artwork. The work of Renaissance artists in the development of linear perspective directly led to developments of algebraic and analytic geometry, and, less directly, to relativity and quantum mechanics.

Medicine as Art

Perspectives on medicine also changed during the Renaissance. Practices began to improve, although this wouldn't have been difficult. Western doctors still lagged well behind their Islamic counterparts. However, one advantage European medical practitioners did enjoy was the increasing availability of printed medical textbooks, which helped disseminate new (often Islamic) medical ideas.

Improvement was also driven by the spread of humanism. No longer did the Church control the medical profession, and this led to a relaxation of the prohibition of the dissection of bodies. Suddenly, people such as Leonardo da Vinci had more freedom to dissect cadavers and make detailed anatomical drawings. Da Vinci's drawings were, incredibly, only rediscovered 380 years after his death.

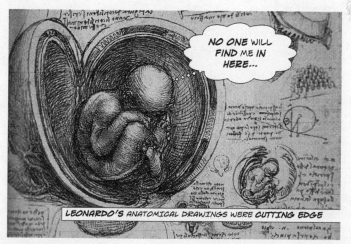

Fig. 12: Unfortunately for you, baby, Leonardo did. (Artspt and S.E.W.)

But accurate and artistic anatomical drawings weren't Leonardo's only contribution to medical research. He wanted to know more about how the human brain processes visual and sensory information and hoped to discover that those processes were connected to the soul. While he (and many others since) failed to find a "soul connection," his studies revealed that nerves fanned out from the spinal cord. Leonardo also discovered that the olfactory nerve was one of the cranial nerves. However, Leonardo's greatest achievement was finding the time to be a cutting-edge medical expert, scientist, inventor, as well as one of the greatest painters of all time.

It's fair to say that medicine didn't advance during the Renaissance as far as, say, art did. This could be because much of the "advancement" during the era was simply a return to classical teachings. In particular, the work of Galen, one of the most revered medical researchers of the ancient world. Galen's complete works were printed in 1490 (nearly a millennia-and-a-half after his death), and became hugely influential on Renaissance medicine. However, despite his many excellent ideas, Galen was often just plain wrong. His conception about how heart and blood vessels work was one such error.

Galen believed that blood leaked from the right to the left side of the heart through tiny holes. He also theorized that the liver's function was to create blood and circulate it through the body. Galen also had misguided ideas about how the brain and nervous system worked, too. It took the work of Andreas Vesalius on anatomy, and William Harvey's studies of blood circulation, to move Renaissance medicine beyond reliance on the 1,400-year-old writings of Galen.

Renaissance Music

A bona fide music historian would appreciate, and be able to adequately explain, the growth of music during the Renaissance.

Unfortunately for you, dear reader, I'm not that historian. However, I'll do my best.

The late medieval period had seen the growth of polyphony (the use of a number of simultaneous melodic lines), and the blending of these intertwining melodic lines further developed to give Renaissance music its rich texture. Importantly, the use of polyphony began to require larger musical ensembles made up of instruments across the vocal range. New instruments were developed around this time, possibly due to these requirements.

One new instrument, the viola da gamba, was a bowed string instrument and forerunner of the violin, even though it had six strings and frets. Along with the viol, European musicians took to the newly invented recorder and the harpsichord; which came in two flavors, the spinet and virginal (the mind boggles). Old medieval favorites, such as the lute and the organ, were also in the instrumental mix.

Like so much else during this time, the growth of humanism also affected Renaissance music, and there were intense studies of ancient Greek writings on music. These works looked at the ways music could tug at the listener's heartstrings through the connection between music and poetry. Thus inspired, the composers of the Renaissance created dramatic compositions that, in time, would inspire the beginnings of operatic music.

One major musical innovation of the sixteenth century owed more to Gutenberg than any musician or composer. In Venice in 1501, Ottaviano Petrucci printed the first collection of polyphonic music, the *Harmonice Musices Odhecaton A*. The success of this publication eventually led to the growth of music printing and publishing throughout Europe.

Renaissance Architecture

Given all our investigations so far, it will come as little shock that architecture, like so much else in the Renaissance, was a conscious response to the architectural styles of classical Greeks and Romans. As in painting and sculpture, Florence was the epicenter of this revival, spearheaded by the work of Filippo Brunelleschi. The Renaissance style quickly spread to other Italian cities, and then across fifteenth- and sixteenth-century Europe.

Fig. 13: Brunelleschi's Duomo (Noppasin Wongchum, Public domain and S.E.W.)

Although early Renaissance was in some ways a slavish reproduction of ancient architecture, by the late fifteenth century, architects such as Donato Bramante and Antonio da Sangallo the Younger mastered the old styles and applied them to create structures strikingly different from those of ancient times. The style of the High Renaissance often added decorative and ornamental features, including domes and cupolas.

Perhaps the pinnacle of this style was St. Peter's Basilica in Rome, but it was far from the work of a single architectural genius. It was also, seemingly, a death sentence. In 1506, Pope Julius II decided to replace the original basilica built in the fourth century by Emperor Constantine. Julius commissioned Bramante for the job, and he continued on the project until his death eight years later. A succession of architects, including Antonio da Sangallo the Younger, continued the work and died while on the job.

It was in 1546 that Michelangelo brought his genius to bear on the building, giving it its iconic shape and adding the tallest dome in the world. Of course, like the architects before him, Michelangelo did not live to see his vision realized. Domingo Fontana and Jacopo della Porta finally completed Michelangelo's vision twenty-four years after his death.

But the work wasn't finished yet.

Pope Paul V decided he wanted to give the building a facelift, and commissioned Carlo Maderno to do a spot of renovation, a task continued by Gian Lorenzo Bernini after Maderno's death. By 1629, over one hundred and twenty years after construction had begun, St. Peter's was seeming like something of a poison chalice. Yet somehow, Bernini (who is also credited with moving architecture into the Baroque period) managed to finish the circular piazza and colonnades in front of the Basilica and complete the interior decoration without falling victim to the curse.

And Speaking of Curses...

As we'll see in a later chapter that the Renaissance saw the beginnings of the scientific method. However, there was still a widespread belief in alchemy and the occult, even among natural philosophers (aka scientists). And when it comes to the occult during this time, one name is still revered by twenty-first-century people fascinated by the paranormal, Nostradamus.

Frenchman Michel de Nostradame (1503–1566) was, like many of the people discussed in this chapter, a man of many parts. He was a physician, apothecary, and astrologer, but his main claim to fame was as a prophet. Nostradamus was studying at the university, but an outbreak of plague shutdown the institution. The disease then took the lives of his wife and two children in 1534, so he traveled through Italy and France, bravely helping tend to plague victims.

Despite devising new treatments for the plague, Nostradamus ultimately could not hold back the sea of death surrounding him. He turned away from the practice of medicine and moved towards the occult. Thus, Michel de Nostradame entered his emo phase. He retreated to his attic and spent untold hours meditating in a bid to see visions of the future, scrawling copious notes and drawings.

In 1547 Nostradamus began to convert the records of his (let's face it) delusions into a form of poetry known as a quatrains, four lines of rhyming verse. He then grouped these quatrains into sets of one hundred which were known as a centuries. In 1555, he published these prophesies in a book which he fittingly called *Centuries*.

Most of Nostradamus' prophesies are frustratingly convoluted and vague, and with a little imagination, can be interpreted in many ways. Some interpretations are said to have predicted major events, such as the Great Fire of London:

> *The blood of the just will commit a fault at London,*
> *Burnt through lightning of twenty threes the six:*
> *The ancient lady will fall from her high place,*
> *Several of the same sect will be killed.*

This does seem to tell of a fire in London, but the Great Fire of London wasn't started by a lightning strike. The rest is gobbledygook, so it's a stretch to claim that this is conclusive proof of his scrying abilities. Other Nostradamus prophesies are said to predict the French Revolution, Adolf Hitler, and the atom bomb (among many others), but not one of these predictions holds up to scrutiny.

The big, bad idea here has little to do with Nostradamus himself, and rather with the growing culture of gullibility, which even now survives in an age of science.

Fig. 14: *Not an actual Nostradamus prediction, but it may as well have been. (Midjourney and S.E.W.)

Something Was Building, but...

During the Renaissance, Gutenberg's development of printing and moveable type, the growth of humanism, the invention of perspective drawing, progress in the development of the scientific method, and the explosion in the adult literacy rate further increased the collective learning of humanity. In particular, the growth of scientific thinking was crucial for further human development, and there were an increasing number of nimble minds prepared to take the next step in learning.

Something was building. Big time.

But before we head towards a brave, scientific future, we take a step backwards and examine the schisms that rocked the Christian Church.

* * *

Losing My Religion

The Reformation

Ground Zero

To understand why the Reformation took place, we need a quick bit of revision.

The Middle Ages had been Ground Zero for religious zealotry. The Church in Rome had grown powerful enough to order kings around. As we saw in Chapter 1, Pope Innocent III (could there be a less appropriate name?) had excommunicated King John and slapped an interdict on the whole of England because he didn't like John's choice for Archbishop of Canterbury. As an interdict effectively meant that the whole of England was excommunicated, the pressure on the king was so great, he was forced to give in to Innocent III's demands. King John then paid a bribe and *voila*, everyone in England could take communion again.

Not to be outdone, in 1302 Pope Boniface officially proclaimed that he was the supreme commander of all the kings and armies in Europe. This move backfired somewhat, as King Philip IV of France, in what may have been a tit-for-tat move, tried to take control of the French clergy. This led to an incident in which Philip IV's forces captured Boniface and held him hostage.

Then there were the "naughty" popes. These so-called Vicars of Christ might bribe electors and murder rich, powerful cardinals to get their money (Alexander VI); exhume the corpse of their predecessor and put it on trial (Stephen VI); torture enemy cardinals, then complain they hadn't screamed loud enough in their death throes (Urban VI); or be murdered by a man who caught them in bed with his wife (Pope John XII). Some popes even ran a kind of religious protection racket for the immortal souls of believers, but more on that shortly.

So, unlike your friendly neighborhood Spider-Man, you could say that with great papal power came great corruption.

But wait, there's more:

In the same way feudal kings bestowed lands and titles upon their toadies, the Pope handed out "benefices" to his loyal religious lieutenants. These were rich land grants, complete with farms and serfs, which were managed by clergymen to ensure they made a living. But these landholdings made more than enough for their owner's upkeep. In fact, the benefices were so lucrative, the Church levied taxes on the income, and they were *still* desirable.

It was a nice little earner. But that was only the beginning of the monetization of the Church.

Pure Indulgence?

Around this time, two religious beliefs came together that helped rich sinners get into Heaven. One was the idea that merely admitting a sin wasn't enough for forgiveness, and that punishment was also required. The other belief was of the existence of purgatory, which was a kind of holding cell between Heaven and Hell whose inhabitants could get to Heaven through good works or the prayers of the faithful.

Luckily, the Church had a fantastic idea that acted like a "Get out of Jail Free" card: the indulgence. The concept was that Jesus and the saints had racked up loads of brownie points for good works, which Pope Clement VI (1291–1352) decreed had been banked in a "Treasury of Merit." All the Church was doing was allowing people to offset their sins with the good deeds of Jesus, rather like how nowadays we can buy carbon credits.

For a small payment (PayPal and all credit cards accepted), sinners purchased indulgences from the Church, which exempted them from punishment and sent them straight to the Good Place. *Go directly to Heaven. Do not pass Go. Do not collect $200.* Those wealthy enough could shell out for the deluxe option: full relief from God's chastisement. Penny-pinching sinners could go for the budget option and still get time off their stay in purgatory.

The poor could burn in Hell as far as the church was concerned. But even then, enterprising churchmen found ways of profiting from forgiveness. In Germany, a Dominican friar named Johann Tetzel, promoted the sale of indulgences for the dead with the pithy couplet, "When a penny in the coffer rings, / A soul from Purgatory springs." Tetzel also claimed that *his* indulgences could absolve the sins of someone even if they'd "raped the Virgin Mary."

Unsurprisingly, this blatant profiteering pissed some people off.

Holy Breast Milk and Foreskins

There was also a great trade in religious artifacts. Few large churches didn't claim to have a chunk of the Holy Cross, the bones of a saint, or in some cases (I can't believe I'm writing this...), the breast milk of the Virgin Mary, who'd appeared to St. Bernard in a vision and cured him with a quick spritz. At a time when churches were the biggest attractions in town, these holy relics were big ticket items that drew crowds and brought in the money.

Fig. 1: St. Bernard had some weird fantasies. (Midjourney and S.E.W)

One of the most venerated (and fabricated) relics was no less than a piece of Jesus himself—his foreskin. Yep, more than a dozen churches across Europe claimed to have possession of the tip of Jesus' dick. The phenomenon was so fascinating that James White of the University of Alberta documented it in his PhD thesis: *Ring of Flesh: The Late Medieval Devotion to the Holy Foreskin.* It took until 1900 for the Church to become so embarrassed by Jesus' foreskin, that Pope Leo XIII threatened to excommunicate anyone who spoke or wrote about it.

Looks like I'm not having communion any time soon.

Fig. 2: And it was all downhill after this…
(Vincenzo Catena, Public domain, and S.E.W)

One Thousand Years of Unity out the Window

After the First Council of Nicaea in 325 AD had begun cobbling together a consensus of Christian beliefs, the Church experienced over a thousand years of relative unity. The first real crack in this harmony came with the Black Death. When superstitious medieval people saw that no amount of fasting and praying could stop the plague, it was a wake-up call.

While most people continued to be God-fearing Christians, some started to question traditional Church dogma. In response to Christianity's failure to protect the faithful, a rather bizarre religious movement emerged in which groups of (over) zealous Christians roamed about the countryside whipping themselves as penance for their sins and the sins of humanity. Unfortunately, while they were begging forgiveness, they were also committing unforgivable sins by stirring up deadly pogroms against Jews and other minorities. While this moronic, murderous, and masochistic frenzy could not provide a long-term answer to a crisis in faith, people had begun to wonder if there were other ways to be Christian.

Like the Renaissance, the Reformation didn't burst forth from nothingness. There had been reformers (or attempted reformers) during the medieval period, such as St. Francis of Assisi and John Wycliffe. Even during the Renaissance, Erasmus of Rotterdam, a humanist and the "greatest scholar of the northern Renaissance" (at least according to *Encyclopedia Britannica*), challenged many of the Church's more ridiculous theological ideas and urged believers to use Christ as a moral compass.

The stage was set for change.

Martin Luther

Few people in history have had such a transformative effect on their world as the former Augustine friar Martin Luther (1483–1546). Priest, theologian, hymn-writer, author, and scourge of the Vatican, Luther was the catalyst of the Protestant Reformation. Protestants lionized him. Catholics demonized him. The truth is somewhere in between.

Luther fought against the corruption and excesses of the Church, causing a schism that has yet to be mended. His views on the Jews were reprehensible and had far-reaching ramifications. He was in equal measure a good guy, bad guy, visionary, and nutjob.

So how did a humble priest of modest background stir up all this trouble?

Thunderstruck?

Martin Luther was the son of Hans and Margarethe Luther. Hans was a local businessman involved with copper mining and smelting. Margarethe was (depending on who you listen to) a respectable working-class woman or a total slut. I've seen a picture of her, and I'd put my money on the former.

Hans Luther was upwardly mobile and wanted Martin to become a lawyer. Martin attended a school which focused on grammar, rhetoric, and logic—an experience he would later liken to Purgatory or Hell. Apparently, Luther was a fan of comparison, because in 1501, he wrote that the University of Erfurt was a cross between a beer-hall and a whorehouse. Somehow, between the drinking and the whoring, he earned a master's degree in 1505.

It all changed one day when Luther was caught outside in a violent thunderstorm. Martin, consumed with paranoia, felt this was God attempting to murder him, and in extremis, he cried out: "Help me, Saint Anne, and I will become a monk!" Of course, Luther survived the thunderstorm and, true to his word, he gave up the law to enter a monastery. For his part, Hans Luther was mighty pissed off with his son. What sane person would exchange a well-paid career for a life of poverty, just because of an electrical storm?

Luther took to the monastery like a priest to a choirboy, studying hard and eventually receiving a doctorate in Theology in 1512. He became professor of Biblical Studies at the university in Wittenberg, then, as academics are wont to do, he published his theological writings, chief among these being the ninety-five theses.

We Need to Talk About the Ninety-Five Theses

Imagine the scene: A hushed crowd gathers as Luther, dressed in monk's robes, marches up the stone steps of All Saints Church in Wittenberg. Arriving at the top step, he extracts a sheet of parchment, a mallet, and some nails from a rough hessian sack. Without ceremony, he hammers these demands for religious reform to the church's thick wooden door. The onlookers gasp, astounded by his sheer audacity.

It would've been a brave, foolhardy, and transgressive act... if it had happened. Unfortunately, there is simply no evidence for Martin venting his spleen at the Church in such a way. There are no eyewitness accounts, and even the man himself, an enthusiastic self-promoter, didn't recall the incident. Yes, he drafted ninety-five theses. Yes, he presented them to the archbishop. But they weren't take-it-or-leave-it demands crudely hammered to a door.

Rather, the ninety-five theses comprised a list of discussion points that Luther would rather like to debate with his ecclesiastical brethren. He couldn't help it if things got a little out of hand... could he?

Things Get Out of Hand

One of Luther's lightbulb moments was the concept of *sola scriptura* (by scripture alone). This was his belief that if something wasn't in the scriptures, it wasn't legit. For instance, the Bible mentions Heaven and Hell, but Luther noted it never mentioned Purgatory. And, of course, this brings us back to the subject of indulgences, because Luther reasoned that if Purgatory didn't exist, then the Church's sin-offset scheme was a massive scam. A scam that Luther could not forgive.

It's difficult to overstate the importance that the printing press played in the wide dissemination of Luther's ideas. When he published the *Ninety-five Theses* in 1517, it was circulated far and wide thanks to printing.

So far and so wide, in fact, that it came to the attention of Pope Leo X.

Luther Refuses to Take the Pope's Bull

Another of Martin Luther's big ideas was that the path to Heaven was solely a gift of divine grace—a break from the idea that humans had agency in their salvation. To an atheist like me, this doesn't seem like a big deal. But this concept, and many of Luther's other somewhat heretical musings, mightily pissed off Pope Leo X, who decided he'd like a bit of chat with him.

This basically meant a heresy trial.

Knowing that such a trial would probably result in Luther's torture and probable death, Frederick III the Wise of Saxony, intervened on his behalf. As it turned out, Frederick was a Luther fanboy and didn't want to see him harmed. He also had some clout in Rome, as the Church needed his money to fund a war against the Ottoman Empire. In addition, his vote was also crucial in the election of the Holy Roman Emperor. On this occasion, Frederick the Wise got his way.

Instead of being summoned to Rome, Luther was told to appear before the Imperial Diet in Augsburg. Once there, Cardinal Cajetan gave him a dressing down and called on him to recant his heresy. Fearing what might happen next, Luther fled at the earliest opportunity and returned to Wittenberg. This was just as well, because Cardinal Cajetan had orders to arrest Luther and drag him to Rome for further "examination." After that, Luther wisely decided to lie low, but his followers weren't so silent.

The Reformation had taken on a life of its own.

By 1520, Pope Leo X had had quite enough of this ninety-five theses nonsense, and issued a papal bull condemning them. But Leo was smart enough to give Luther some wiggle room. If only the obstinate monk would just shut the hell up, it would all go away. But when Leo's papal bull arrived in Wittenberg, Luther drafted a reply entitled: *Against the Execrable Bull of the Antichrist*. He then marched out to the public square and burned Leo's bull, making his subsequent excommunication inevitable.

Luther was summoned to appear before the Diet of Worms to answer for his heresy.

Fig. 3: Martin Luther crosses his personal Rubicon.
(Public domain and S.E.W.)

The Diet of Worms?

Before getting going, let's be clear: the Diet of Worms was *not* a sixteenth-century regimen of eating invertebrates to reclaim your bikini bod. A "Diet" in this sense, is an assembly, rather like a parliament, and "Worms" (pronounced "Vawms") is a city in Germany. So, the Diet of Worms was an assembly of the Holy Roman Empire which took place in the city of Worms.

By 1521, Martin Luther was a wanted man, because the Pope had issued what amounted to a *fatwa* against him. The troublesome priest was to be arrested and executed. Luckily for Luther, Frederick the Wise (who had already refused to carry out the papal bull) realized that Luther might not make it to the Diet in one piece. Frederick provided protection for Luther, ensuring that he made it to his trial unmolested. But once there, Luther's troubles began.

Luther appeared before the Diet of Worms on April 17, 1521. When questioned while standing before a display of his offending books, he readily admitted they were his work. However, when invited to "do a Galileo" and deny his beliefs, he refused. Unless the Church could convince him of his error through the use of scripture or reason, he said, then they could get lost. In fact, he doubled down: "Here I stand, I can do no other, so help me God. Amen." At this, the Diet erupted in turmoil and was dismissed by the emperor.

Nevertheless, Luther knew what was good for him. He bugged out of Worms and went into hiding. The Edict of Worms was issued by the emperor not long after, declaring Luther and his followers political outlaws. Further, it decreed that all of Luther's writings should be burned.

Luther was trying to return home when he was waylaid by Frederick III's soldiers and taken to Wartburg Castle for his own protection. He remained there in hiding for nearly a year, and many believed him dead. But Luther wasn't idle during this time: he translated the Bible out of the customary Latin and into German, which was a *very* big idea.

Fig. 4: Martin Luther asks the question on everyone's lips. (Juulijs and S.E.W.)

Although the Church tried to keep Luther and his followers down, the reform movement was too strong. Dissatisfaction with the Church was so great that once the genie was out of the bottle, it couldn't be controlled. When Luther came out of hiding in March 1522, he returned to Wittenberg to find the place in an uproar due to the pace of change. Luther was, counterintuitively, a conservative, and he was able to slow the speed of reform a little. But by this time, change was inevitable.

In 1524, a peasants' uprising took place in southwestern Germany, which was inspired, to some extent, by Luther's reform proposals. It became known as the Peasants' War, but Luther was not a fan. "(N)othing can be more poisonous, hurtful, or devilish than a rebel," he wrote, which was rich coming from one of history's greatest rebels.

Within a couple of years, Luther's place at the vanguard of religious reform was challenged by other, more radical thinkers, such as Müntzer, Zwingli, and Bucer. Another theologian of the second wave of the Reformation was John Calvin (1509–1564). Calvin was influenced by humanism, which he applied to the study of the Bible. That meant that rather than Bible-bashing his flock into submission, he made a direct appeal to the humanity of the faithful. It was, surprisingly, a radical concept.

I'm Henry VIII I Am...

There is little left to write about King Henry VIII (1491–1547), but I'm going to give it a crack. Born the second son of Henry VII, Henry became heir when Arthur, his elder brother, died in 1502. Tragically, his mother departed this life only months later. Henry's father then passed away in 1509, and young Henry assumed the throne when he was only seventeen. From this difficult beginning, Henry VIII grew to become a towering, controversial, and polarizing figure who was full of contradictions.

We often view Henry VIII as a portly, cranky looking, middle-aged man, largely courtesy of the famous Holbein portrait of the king. However, in his youth he was quite the athlete, excelling in jousting, hunting, riding and real tennis (the half tennis/half racketball sport from which the modern game of tennis developed). He wrote poetry and kept an extensive library. He was also something of a musician and has erroneously been credited with penning the Tudor Top 40 hit *Greensleeves*. Even more incongruously, Henry wrote a treatise condemning Martin Luther, which inspired Pope Leo X to name him "Defender of the Faith." Luckily for Leo, he died before realizing exactly which faith Henry would defend.

As intriguing as all this is, in *Lightbulb Moments in Human History*, we are only concerned with Henry VIII's part in the Protestant Reformation, and how his carnal desires (and desperate need for a male heir) turned England upside down. Of course, these days Henry is rarely mentioned without reference to his six wives. A quick Google search gives a snapshot of the aspects of Henry's life which obsesses the modern mind:

Q Henry VIII   ✕ | 🎤

🖼 Henry VIII
    Monarch of England

Q henry viii **wives**

Q henry viii **children**

Q henry viii **family tree**

Q henry viii **wives in order**

Q henry viii **wives and children**

Fig. 5: It isn't Henry's effect on the English Reformation that people search for...
(Google and S.E.W)

The story of Henry's six wives is well documented, and doesn't fall under our purview (unless one counts misogyny as a "big idea"). Suffice to say that Catherine of Aragon, Anne Boleyn, Jane Seymour, Anne of Cleves, Catherine Howard, and Catherine Parr played varying roles in the story of the fledgling Church of England. All we really need to know is:

King Henry VIII,
To six wives was wedded.
One died, one survived,
Two divorced and two beheaded

However, it's really only the first two wives that figure prominently in Henry's big idea: the birth of the Church of England.

The Spare Becomes the Heir

As a second son, Henry VIII was not expected to become king. It was his elder brother, Arthur, who had been groomed for the throne, but his inconvenient death meant Plan B had to be activated. Henry VII, who'd hitherto paid young Henry little attention, began some Tudor tutoring in kingship. One of his first pieces of advice was for Prince Henry to marry Arthur's widow, Catherine of Aragon, thus securing valuable diplomatic ties with Spain.

Despite being six years younger than his sister-in-law, Henry was very much in love with her. She was refined, beautiful, and had the benefits of an excellent education. But the closeness of the fact they had been in-laws raised eyebrows. This was because the Church viewed Henry and Catherine as brother and sister. The pope granted special dispensation because, supposedly, Arthur and Catherine had never consummated their marriage.

At least, that's what Catherine claimed.

Unfortunately, Henry VII's own death cut short Prince Henry's crash course in Politics 101. Suddenly the callow, seventeen-year-old king desperately needed a mentor. Enter Thomas Wolsey. The son of an Ipswich butcher, he would, despite his low birth, assume the role of Henry's trusted advisor and confidant. Wolsey quickly became invaluable and used his wit, intelligence, and charm to rise to Lord Chancellor and then to Cardinal.

Both Henry and Catherine knew the importance of producing a male heir. But after twenty-three years of marriage, they'd lost five children (who'd either been stillborn or hadn't survived infancy) and had one surviving girl, Mary. Over this trying period, the once beautiful queen had lost her figure and turned into something of a religious nutjob. She even sometimes wore a hair shirt as a means of repentance from sin.

For his part, Henry was becoming increasingly irascible. He was certain that the distressing lack of an heir was God's punishment for the sin of marrying his brother's widow. Henry also belatedly began to question Catherine's claims of virginity after her first marriage, wondering whether marrying his brother's widow had been a great idea after all. Of course, his infatuation with one of Catherine's maids-of-honor, Anne Boleyn, might've had a bit to do with it as well.

Something had to be done to ensure the continuance of the Tudor line (and satisfy Henry's urges). As far as the king's fixer, Thomas Wolsey, was concerned, a dissolution of Henry's marriage to Catherine of Aragon was the only answer. Wolsey appealed to Pope Clement VII for an annulment. He had a few arguments in favor of this action up his sleeve, and for his opening gambit, Wolsey pointed out that the dispensation clearly disobeyed the book of Leviticus:

If a man marries his brother's wife, it is an act of impurity; he has dishonored his brother. They will be childless.
Leviticus 20:21

Wolsey also objected on a technicality, because there was, he claimed, a mistake in the wording of Pope Leo's earlier dispensation. Lastly, Wolsey urged Pope Clement to allow the papal legate in England to make the final decision. As this papal legate was Wolsey himself, the outcome would be a foregone conclusion.

Fig. 6: It also says adulterous women should be stoned to death.
(Georgios Kollidas, Keithburn, and S.E.W.)

Not surprisingly, Pope Clement VII was having none of it. He was quite satisfied that Arthur and Catherine's marriage was unconsummated, and didn't give a hoot about the wording of the annulment. As far as Wolsey's scheme to review the case in England goes, it was just laughable. Clement was probably also motivated by a desire to keep the Holy Roman Emperor,

Charles V (who happened to be Catherine's nephew), on his side. But no one could say "no" to Henry and get away with it. Not even His Holiness.

Wolsey had failed miserably.

D.I.V.O.R.C.E.

Unfortunately for Thomas Wolsey, Henry VIII didn't tolerate failure, and Wolsey's lack of success with the king's "Great Matter" saw him unceremoniously punted out the door of Hampden Court. He was briefly replaced by Sir Thomas More, who didn't last long because he opposed the king's divorce on principle. Henry's next choice for Lord Chancellor, Thomas Cromwell, was far less squeamish about such things, and this suited the king's purposes perfectly. With Cromwell behind him, the king considered a radical option: splitting the English Church from Rome and placing himself at its head.

It would then be a simple matter to grant his own divorce.

Behind the scenes, Anne Boleyn had been winding Henry up. She'd refused to sleep with him without being married, and that had upped the stakes even higher. The pressure was mounting, in more ways than one. Between his ego and his libido, Henry must've been ready to explode.

The appointment of a new archbishop of Canterbury, Thomas Cranmer, made Henry's escape route clearer when he helpfully pointed out that the Bible made no mention of an entity called a "pope." Why *couldn't* a king, empowered by divine right, make his *own* rules? This argument convinced Henry to pull the trigger on the annulment, which was approved by a very obliging Cranmer.

Pope Clement VII was left with little choice but to excommunicate Henry. Not that the king cared much; he had a much bigger plan. When Parliament passed the 1534 Act of Supremacy, Henry VIII became the supreme head on Earth of the Church of England. All ecclesiastical links with Rome were cut, and the English Reformation was born.

The Dissolution of the Monasteries

Despite this severing of ties, the Church in Rome still owned large tracts of land in England and operated over eight hundred monasteries. These monasteries were home to religious communities whose first loyalty was to Rome, but who had served their local communities for hundreds of years. They played a role in education, charity work, and even dispensed what passed for medicine. As we've previously seen, they produced and stored books, and were the repositories of supposedly sacred relics.

Monasteries also owned nearly twenty-five percent of all cultivated land in England, which made them among the wealthiest institutions in the country. Understandably, Henry, who was a bit cash-strapped, coveted their wealth. If he could dismantle the monastic system, he stood to profit whilst removing its papist influence.

For Henry, it was win/win.

The first step was to undermine the credibility of the clergy. To that end, Parliament was presented with a dossier that documented the corrupt morals within the monasteries. Given what we know about the modern church, this probably wasn't *totally* fake news, but it's likely that there were trumped-up charges as well. Two Acts of Suppression, one in 1536 and another in 1539, allowed for monasteries to be closed and have their property confiscated by the Crown.

To rid the monasteries of their holy inhabitants, Henry used the carrot and stick approach: Monks, friars, and nuns who complied with his plans were provided pensions. Those who didn't comply would be executed and have their monasteries destroyed. While this may have seemed a simple choice, there was a catch: members of the religious orders also had to accept Henry as Supreme Head of the Church. This was too much for eighteen monks of the Carthusian order to bear. One of these monks, Sebastian Newdigate, was a close friend of the king and had served on his privy council. This didn't stop Henry having Newdigate chained to a pillar for two weeks, then personally trying to convince him to accept his primacy. Newdigate refused and was put to death along with seventeen other intractable clergymen.

Once free of these pesky monks, the monasteries were sold off to Henry's supporters, which filled the Crown's coffers nicely.

Fig. 7: He knew no limits. (Public domain and S.E.W)

Henry VIII: Fat, Unpredictable, Irritable ... and Lethal

Henry, whose temperament, even in his prime, was unsuited to the Crown, became increasingly secretive, suspicious, and paranoid. He grew unpredictable, irritable, and was afflicted with fits of melancholy. It really should come as no surprise, as Henry suffered from a painfully ulcerated leg and was so fat, he had to be pushed around in a wheeled chair.

He was, in other words, the Tudor Trump.

Henry VIII died in 1547, after presiding over the beginnings of the English Reformation. He had been, in many ways, the quintessential old-school king: autocratic, petty, narcissistic, and lethal to people close to him, such as Thomas Cromwell and Sebastian Newdigate.

Not to mention Anne Boleyn and Catherine Howard.

A Reformation if You Can Keep It.

Henry was succeeded by Edward VI (1537–53), his son by Jane Seymour, who came to the throne aged ten. Edward Seymour, the Duke of Somerset, acted as his regent, and along with Archbishop Cranmer, consolidated the Protestant reforms to the English church. But, unfortunately for young Eddie Tudor, he didn't live long and died at the age of fifteen. After a brief attempted coup when Lady Jane Grey was proclaimed queen, Mary (Henry VIII and Catherine of Aragon's daughter) ascended the throne.

Queen Mary (1516–1558) was a fly in the ointment for the English Reformation. Like her mother, she was devoutly Catholic, and didn't like this Protestant nonsense in the slightest. "Bloody Mary" attempted to return England to the old ways, and burned hundreds of Protestants at the stake to make her point. This sectarian barbeque, plus the controversial marriage to the Spanish heir Philip, did little to endear her to Parliament or her people. When she died without a male successor in 1558, the ascension of Mary's half-sister and Anne Boleyn's daughter, Elizabeth I (1533–1603), was much more to people's tastes.

Elizabeth I was a staunch Protestant, and she arrested the lurch back to Catholicism. Her momentous, forty-four-year reign became known as the Elizabethan era and is regarded as an English "Golden Age," and we'll cover some events of this era in subsequent chapters. Under Elizabeth's watch, the Church of England was officially established, and all seemed right in the Protestant world.

Not so great for her Catholic subjects though, as she killed nearly as many of them as Queen Mary had killed Protestants.

The other Mary in Elizabeth's life was her cousin, Mary, Queen of Scots. She was also a devout Catholic who'd fled from Scotland to England and placed herself under Elizabeth's protection. This was because, for various reasons, she'd pissed off just about everyone north of the border. Not the greatest houseguest of all time, Mary became the locus of a number of Catholic plots against Elizabeth. Eventually, the Queen had Mary executed for treason.

Elizabeth I never married or had children. She didn't even nominate an heir. As a result, she was succeeded by her closest living relative, James Stuart. He became James I (1566–1625) of England, and was already James VI of Scotland... and the son of Mary, Queen of Scots.

James I

In his dual role of king of both England and Scotland, James became the first king of the United Kingdom. Despite his mother's deep Catholic faith, he was a Protestant and had been educated by Presbyterians.

Although James was married and had fathered two sons, he made no secret of his love for handsome young men. According to historian Michael B. Young, James was "the most prominent homosexual figure in the early modern period." He was also the subject of a popular witticism that claimed that: "Elizabeth was King, now James is Queen." But while James' behavior with certain favorites raised eyebrows, it didn't seem to cause him major problems.

What *did* cause James a major problem was Parliament. He believed in the king's divine right to rule, and was convinced it allowed him absolute authority. This came as news to the English Parliament, who didn't see it that way and had control of the purse strings. In an acrimonious address to Parliament, James made it clear that he would "not thank where I feel no thanks due. I am not of such a stock as to praise fools."

James' reign saw the rise of a radical Protestant group known as the Puritans. The aim of the Puritans was to "purify" the church by reducing the bells and smells in church ritual, putting limitations on the power of bishops, and ensuring the clergy were adequately educated. The Puritans lived simple lives based on the concepts of humility and simplicity. They were in favor of frugality, increased education, and empowering the individual, making them popular with the growing middle class of merchants. They weren't going to go away any time soon.

In fact, the Puritans began to lobby for change. They had problems with the two previous English translations of the Bible, and in 1604, King James convened a conference to discuss plans for a new English version which would address these issues. It took seven years for the team of translators and theologians to complete the task, but it was worth the wait. Even today, the eloquence of the narrative prose has caused the King James Version of the Bible to be compared favorably to Shakespeare.

1604 was a busy year for King James, as he also expelled all Catholic priests from England. This intolerance was a motivating factor in the Gunpowder Plot, a Catholic terrorist plan to blow up the House of Lords, while King James I, Prince Charles, and the members of the House were in attendance. However, before the plot could be actioned, an anonymous letter advising a Catholic member of Parliament not to attend was discovered. In the ensuing investigation, an unfortunate terrorist, Guy Fawkes, was captured in the cellars under Parliament alongside enough gunpowder to blow the building to smithereens. He was conveyed to the Tower of London where he was tortured, and although he resisted bravely, he eventually gave up his fellow conspirators.

Fig. 8: It wasn't the best planned act of terrorism... (Midjourney and S.E.W)

The plotters were quickly rounded up and tried, then hanged, drawn, and quartered.

The irony is that because the gunpowder had been stockpiled for months in less-than-optimal conditions, it probably would've been damp and likely fizzled out without the wholesale destruction planned by the conspirators. Despite this inconvenient truth, the Gunpowder Plot is still commemorated in Great Britain on Guy Fawkes Night, which involves community fireworks displays and children burning of an effigy of "the Guy." It was also immortalized in this children's rhyme:

Remember, remember the Fifth of November,
The Gunpowder Treason and Plot,
I know of no reason
Why the Gunpowder Treason
Should ever be forgot.

Although, quite why children were encouraged to light fires, burn effigies, or recite such verses is unclear.

In 1625, James suffered from arthritis, gout, and fainting fits. Within a couple of months, he experienced fevers and then had a stroke. He met an ignominious end on March 27, when he became the second English king in this book to shit himself into the afterlife.

Charles I

Charles I (1600–1649) was a reserved and sensitive man who had a mild stutter. He was deeply religious (some might say, self-righteously so) and had inherited his father's stubborn belief in the king's absolute power and divine right to rule. He was an extravagant patron of the arts and invited the artist Anthony van Dyck to England for the sole purpose, it seems, of painting a number of flattering portraits of him. Charles also collected paintings by Titian and Raphael.

In doing these things, Charles racked up a substantial amount of debt.

It wasn't long after he assumed the crown in 1625 that Charles' problems with Parliament began. Ostensibly, this was because of his frequent requests for money. However, the fact his belief in the divine right of kings clashed with Parliament's belief that he was tyrant, probably didn't help matters. Charles' tax policies, his conservative High Church views, and his marriage to a French Catholic princess, Henrietta Maria of France, made him deeply unpopular. As a part of the marriage contract, the French had insisted that Charles' Catholic subjects no longer be persecuted. For this reason, he was particularly detested by the English Puritans, who were suspicious of his perceived Catholic bent.

Surprisingly, for such a religious man, Charles continued to look to his father's lover and key political ally, George Villiers, the First Duke of Buckingham, for advice. This was a grievous mistake, as the arrogant Buckingham was extremely unpopular with Parliament. Buckingham's foreign policy mistakes increased the tensions that would culminate in the English Civil War. All this time, King Charles was so pissed off with his financial disputes with Parliament that he didn't call one for eleven years, which unkind observers referred to as "the Eleven Years' Tyranny." However, after an ill-fated military campaign against Scottish invaders saw Charles pay off the Scots rather than risk losing on the battlefield, he had a problem. Where was he going to get the money he'd promised? There was only one answer: He *needed* Parliament.

Parliament was recalled in 1640. This resulted in three weeks of stalemate before it was disbanded, ensuring it became known as the "Short" Parliament. The Scottish army then defeated the king's forces again, and more money was required to pay off the invaders. Charles had no choice but to recall Parliament in November 1640. This Parliament became known as the "Long" Parliament.

Parliament knew they had Charles by the short and curlies. This was their chance to wring concessions out of the king and wring they did. The only way Charles would get his money was if a law was passed requiring a Parliament every three years. Further, the monarch would no longer be able to dissolve Parliament at a whim. Parliament also now had the right to approve (or reject) the king's ministers.

Charles I agreed to these demands... with his fingers crossed behind his back.

In 1641, King Charles and Parliament came to loggerheads over the command of the army sent to quell the Irish uprising. John Pym led the Parliament in issuing the Grand Remonstrance, which outlined Parliament's two hundred and four points of objection to Charles' policies. Among many other things, they wanted all bishops kicked out of Parliament and a purging of Charles' flunkies. While the Grand Remonstrance made no accusations against the King, it put forward a conspiracy about a Roman Catholic deep state. Charles was, by implication, a part of such a conspiracy. After all, his grandmother was the Catholic traitor Mary Queen of Scots, and he was married to a Catholic to boot.

Affronted, Charles had his dander up: *He was the bloody king for God's sake, divine right, absolute power, blah, blah, blah.* He marched into the House of Commons to arrest five Members of Parliament, who having been tipped off, had already made a run for it. In response to this outrage, Parliament prevented Charles from entering his own capital by locking the gates of London.

Captain Britannia: Civil War

Charles decamped to Nottingham, where he gathered a Royalist army, which became known to history as the Cavaliers. Parliament did the same, recruiting an army which became known as the Roundheads (purely because the first recruits had short hair). Even though most regular Britons couldn't care less about the whole affair, the battle lines were drawn. For the most part, the west and north parts of England stayed loyal to the king, whereas London and the southeast of England were under the control of Parliament.

There are many excellent histories of the English Civil War, but this book is a history of big ideas, not a history of warfare. Suffice to say that from 1642 onwards, Charles' Cavaliers fought Parliament's Roundheads in the English Civil War. It was during these hostilities, that a commander of Parliament's New Model Army named Oliver Cromwell first distinguished himself. It was not the last time he would come to the attention of historians.

The King was defeated in 1645 and gave himself up to Scottish troops, who then cannily sold him to Parliament for £100,000. During negotiations with Parliament, Charles was given the chance to remain the monarch of a constitutional monarchy, but he flatly refused. After an escape from house arrest in the "hellish gulag" of the Hampton Court Palace, he made it to the Isle of Wight, where he spent a year hiding before being recaptured.

From there, Charles became the focus of royalist rebellions in 1648, and a Second Civil War broke out. But not for long, as it was quickly snuffed out by Cromwell and the New Model Army. In a cross between a Soviet-style purge and a military coup, a detachment of the New Model Army, under the command of Colonel Thomas Pride, blocked one hundred and forty members of the Long Parliament from entering the chamber, thus creating a smaller, more tractable "Rump Parliament." The Rump Parliament was of the opinion that the recalcitrant king was *not* going to see reason. The answer, it decided, was to try Charles for tyranny, high treason, and making war on his own people.

In January 1649, Charles was convicted and sentenced to death, with one of the signatures on the death warrant being that of one Oliver Cromwell. He went to his execution as pompous as ever, and his last words were: "I go from a corruptible to an incorruptible Crown, where no disturbance can be."

Parliament then made haste in abolishing the monarchy and establishing the Commonwealth of England as a republic. This was a lightbulb moment that would have ramifications and influences for centuries to come.

Fig. 9: Cromwell having good old Puritan fun. (Public domain and S.E.W)

The British Interregnum

After the beheading of the king in 1649, the Rump Parliament ran the government of England. However, Cromwell grew increasingly frustrated with their ineffectiveness and in April 1653, he led an armed force into the Commons and dissolved the Rump, reportedly saying: "You have sat too long for any good you have been doing lately... In the name of God, go!" This left what became known as the "Barebones Parliament" which voted to make the 1653 Instrument of Government into law, making Oliver Cromwell the Lord Protector of England.

The Barebones Parliament's next move was to vote itself out of existence, leaving England under a dictatorship. But who was England's new home-grown military leader?

Fig. 10: Cromwell making an offer they can't refuse. (Mannaggia and S.E.W)

Cromwell: Fundamentalist Nutjob or Military Strongman?

Oliver Cromwell (1599–1658) was distantly related through a family connection to Henry VIII's chief minister, Thomas Cromwell. He is a complex historical figure, undoubtedly a military genius and a politician of unique vision. However, he was also a religious zealot, a despot, a regicide, and some would argue, a war criminal.

The future Lord Protector was the son of Robert Cromwell, a country gentleman of modest means, and his wife, Elizabeth. Oliver attended Huntingdon Grammar School and Cambridge University and was earning his living as a gentleman farmer when he experienced a religious conversion. Suddenly, this somewhat religious man of the land became a full-on religious fundamentalist nutjob... a Puritan.

The Puritans had a lot of hang-ups and believed a lot of fun things were wicked. Dancing was wicked. Plays were wicked. Music (other than religious music) was wicked. Parties were wicked. Even a jolly celebration of Christmas was wicked. Let's just say laughter and fun weren't high on their list of priorities. C. John Sommerville in his paper Puritan Humor, or Entertainment, for Children, wrote that even children's entertainment was "tedious if not downright grim" and that "(f)unny Puritans don't exist, almost by definition." These guys were the English equivalent of the Taliban.

Anyway, either by good fortune or by the power of prayer (one guess which the Puritans attributed it to), Cromwell inherited an estate from a wealthy uncle, and his fortunes changed. He became a member of Parliament and, when hostilities with the Crown broke out, he quickly rose through the ranks to command the New Model Army ("New Model" because it was a professional standing army rather than previous armies that had been raised on an *ad hoc* basis). Then, as we have seen, Cromwell rose to become Lord Protector.

Bye, Bye Christmas

As time went by, Cromwell's dictatorial Puritanism began to play poorly across the country, as many normal human activities were outlawed. The celebrations of Christmas and Easter were prohibited. Playing football on a Sunday could result in a severe whipping. Even swearing was punishable by a fine and repeat offenders could be imprisoned. Readers won't be shocked that this caused occasional uprisings, but these were ruthlessly crushed by the New Model Army.

Like all dictators throughout history, Cromwell got a little out of control. Parliament realized this, and offered him the crown, because they felt he'd be more controllable as a constitutional monarch. Cromwell wasn't a fan of the idea, and the army didn't want a new king either. However, Cromwell's second inauguration as Lord Protector was almost indistinguishable from a coronation… It had all the bells and whistles. The only exception was the absence of a crown.

Cromwell now had the world at his feet, but there was one little something beyond his command. His health. He contracted pneumonia, and as he lay dying, he nominated a successor: his son Richard. Oliver Cromwell died on September 3, 1658, and received a state funeral fit for (what else?) a king.

Richard Cromwell took up the mantle of Lord Protector, but really didn't have what it took to maintain the delicate balance between the army and Parliament. After the army threatened to lock Richard up, he renounced the Lord Protectorship. His ignominious fall after only nine months in power earned him the nickname "Tumbledown Dick."

Oliver Cromwell's big idea of an English Republic was ambitious. However, after Charles I's tyrannical ways, replacing one tyrant with another was always going to be doomed to failure. When it came to a replacement for "Tumbledown Dick," a constitutional monarchy seemed like a much better option.

Restoration

Richard Cromwell had handed power back to the truncated version of Parliament, which controlled the country for over a year. However, in October 1659, George Monck, the governor of Scotland, took his army from Scotland and eventually marched into London without resistance. When the Long Parliament was recalled, including the members who'd been expelled during Pride's purge, things were looking up.

Prince Charles, who'd spent Cromwell's reign in exile, then issued the Declaration of Breda, in which he crossed his heart and promised not to be a dictatorial dickhead like his dad or Cromwell. Thoroughly sick of war, tyrants, and Puritans, Parliament proclaimed that King Charles II had really been the lawful monarch all along and invited him back like nothing had happened.

In the spirit of reconciliation, Parliament then passed the Indemnity and Oblivion Act, which pardoned all those who had committed treason against the Crown... except those responsible for the trial and execution of Charles I. The regicides, including the dead Oliver Cromwell, were charged with high treason, and quickly convicted.

That's how it transpired that, shades of Pope Stephen VI, Oliver Cromwell's embalmed corpse was exhumed and hanged. His head was then cut off and placed on a spike attached to a six-meter pole, and displayed above Westminster Hall, where it was on display for twenty-eight years. Until it was, by some accounts, blown down in a storm, to become a curiosity traded among collectors for the next 350 years, until finally being reburied at Cambridge University in the 1960s.

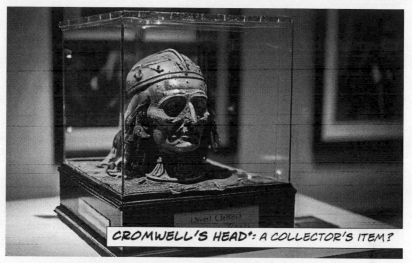

CROMWELL'S HEAD*: A COLLECTOR'S ITEM?

*Fig. 11: * AI artist's impression (Midjourney and S.E.W)*

* * *

The Protestant Reformation began movements that eventually led to modern democracy, skepticism, capitalism, scientific thought, and many other aspects of modernity. During the Reformation, literacy increased throughout Europe, which was a boost to collective learning. Of course, it wasn't all good, and the number of lives lost to senseless sectarian violence over the centuries is incalculable.

However, Europeans weren't just worrying about their immortal souls. All this time, they were also busying themselves with sailing and navigation. We'll now look at how the European powers explored and claimed the planet, each taking their particular version of Christianity and shoving it down the throats of the unsuspecting indigenous peoples, whether they liked it or not.

It should come as no surprise that they didn't.

A Brief Interlude IV

Come Sail Away

In the chapter following, we'll examine the European Age of Discovery, an era that, when viewed in retrospect, can be deeply problematic. While we are quite rightly critical of the many devastating consequences of these voyages (such as Colonialism, genocide, and the slave trade), we shouldn't lose sight of one important point: these were outstanding feats of bravery and navigation performed by the Renaissance versions of Neil Armstrong and Buzz Aldrin.

We're about to look at the adventures, foibles, and (in some cases) crimes of Columbus, Magellan, Cortes, Cook, and company. But before we do, there are other, ancient navigators whose exploits must be acknowledged. These were sailors whose feats of courage and wayfinding matched, and in many ways surpassed, those of the Europeans and Chinese. Such epic voyages were not the doing of a single captain or admiral, and were not recorded at all, other than in legend (and the archaeological record).

These outstanding ancient navigators were the Indigenous Australian and Polynesian peoples.

Aboriginal Australians: The First Human Colonization by Sea

For many years, archaeologists believed that humans arrived on the Australian mainland between 20,000 to 50,000 years ago. However, the most recent evidence suggests that the First Peoples of Australia island-hopped across from South East Asia around 65,000 years ago in what was effectively the first human colonization by sea. No one knows why this epic voyage took place, although it has been suggested that reasons such as human curiosity, war, or famine are likely candidates. Some researchers believe that sea levels may have been lower at that time, exposing more land and making the traverse easier, but we may never know the truth. Whatever the case, Aboriginal peoples still needed to cross over 100 kilometers of open sea to reach northern Australia from Indonesia. With the boat-building technology known at the time, this was no mean feat.

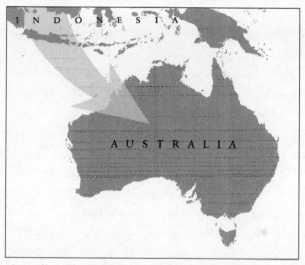

Fig. 1: Australia—The Final Frontier? (Peter Hermes Furian and S.E.W.)

Let's put things in perspective: 65,000 years is a bloody long time. It is 55,000 years *before* Stonehenge was built. Neanderthals were still roaming Europe and would be for another 25,000 years. It was enough time for the Aboriginal people to range across the vast continent of Australia, all the way down to Tasmania, forming over five hundred different nations, with distinctive cultures, beliefs, and languages. This constitutes the longest continuous cultural history of any group of people on the planet.

It needs to be acknowledged.

Polynesian Navigation

Thousands of years later, but no less remarkable, was the spread of the Polynesian peoples across thousands of kilometers of the Pacific, in an area bounded by New Zealand in the west, Easter Island in the east, and Hawaii in the north. The colonization of this "Polynesian Triangle" is all the more astounding because it was achieved using relatively small boats and traditional navigation techniques. Luckily for these Polynesian explorers, unlike the fabled Bermuda Triangle, the South Seas version is not linked with woo-woo inexplicable disappearances of ships and planes.

These gifted navigators sailed in outrigger or double-hulled canoes. However, the word "canoe" doesn't do these vessels justice: these were formidable seagoing watercraft, perhaps not in size, but definitely in capability. The outrigger canoe is, as the name suggests, equipped with an outrigger to prevent it from capsizing. Double-hulled canoes (see below) were constructed with two large hulls of equal length, lashed together parallel to each other, rather like a present-day catamaran. The deck between the canoes provided space for fishing nets, food storage, and weapons, among other equipment. Both outrigger and double-hulled canoes were fitted with triangular sails.

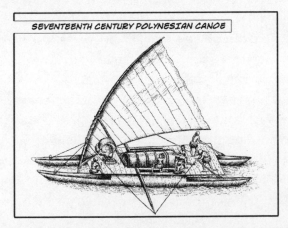

SEVENTEENTH CENTURY POLYNESIAN CANOE

Fig. 2: A Polynesian double-hulled canoe (Acrogame and S.E.W.)

This incredible maritime exploration began around eight thousand years ago, with people emigrating from southern China to Taiwan. Then about three thousand years afterwards, further expansion took place, when indigenous Taiwanese Austronesian-speaking tribes set out by sea and swept across South East Asia (explaining the spread of the Austronesian language family). By 2000 BC, a distinct culture known as the Lapita had taken root on the Bismarck Archipelago in Melanesia.

Then, sometime between 1300 and 900 BC, the Lapita culture was on the move, sailing as far west as Tonga and Samoa. There is archaeological evidence of this, as Lapita pottery has been uncovered in Fiji, Samoa, and Tonga. They were skilled seafarers, who subsisted by fishing the coasts of their islands, although they may also have practiced a limited form of agriculture. The Lapita appear to be the direct ancestors of the peoples of Polynesia.

Early Polynesians are right up there with the best sailors and wayfinders in history. They navigated across the open Pacific Ocean by use of the sun, stars, and interpretation of other natural phenomena. For instance, skilled Polynesian sailors knew that islands block waves and ocean swells, creating a zone of calm water behind an island. Not only that, but islands reflect ocean swells. A navigator steeped in this knowledge can detect the changing ocean patterns these unseen islands create, and navigate to them.

Observation of birds was important for the Polynesian navigators. They knew the habits and flight patterns of Pacific seabirds, and they were able to use this knowledge to help in navigation. It's even theorized that they brought frigate-birds with them, releasing the birds when they felt they were close to land and following them.

Celestial navigation was also used to guide the voyages of the Polynesian people, as well as a large bank of knowledge passed down through oral tradition.

In these oral traditions, the Polynesian navigation pathways were said to resemble an octopus with its head centered in French Polynesia and its tentacles fanning out across the Pacific. Apart from being an apt metaphor for the spread of the culture, the octopus is viewed in Polynesian myth as one of the elemental beings, arising from the primordial ocean to give birth to Fire and Water. In Fijian mythology, Rokobakaniceva, a goddess in the guise of an octopus, defeated Dakuwaqa, the shark god who tried to conquer Kadavu Island. She crushed Dakuwaqa in her arms and he cried for mercy. Whereupon, she pulled out his teeth and released him on one condition: that he agreed to protect her people from shark attacks. Given the number of sharks the early Polynesian navigators must have encountered, such a legend must've been comforting.

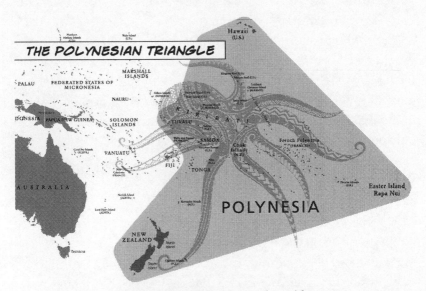

Fig. 3: The Polynesian Triangle complete with octopus
(Peter Hermes Furian, AKV, and S.E.W.)

Sharks and octopuses notwithstanding, it seems Polynesian expansion reached the Cook Islands some time before 1000 AD. From here, they settled Eastern Polynesia, and much later traveled to the extreme corners of the Polynesian Triangle, Hawaii, Easter Island, and New Zealand. It's important to note that the archeological record supports oral traditions of the First Peoples, including the timing of their movements and geographical origins.

The coming of the Europeans to the South Pacific was to have devastating consequences for both the Indigenous Australian and the Polynesian peoples. But as we head into the next chapter about European navigators, we must not lose sight of the stunning achievements of the peoples who sailed before them.

And the price they would pay as a result of colonization.

* * *

—6—

Ship of Fools?

The Age of Discovery

The period between the fifteenth and eighteenth centuries was unified by one big idea: Discovery. The seafaring nations of Europe sallied forth to explore the world. In all cases, this "discovery" came as news to Native Americans, Aztecs, Inca, Maya, Polynesians, and the Indigenous nations of Australia, who justifiably felt they'd discovered these so-called new worlds thousands of years previously.

During this time, European navigators linked the continents of the world and controlled, as historian David Christian puts it: "gateways through which passed the largest flows of wealth and information in human history." This contributed to the collective learning of the European nations. Yet, despite the European's argument that they were bringing Christianity and civilization to the places they colonized, it is arguable they took more in the way of gold, land, and lives than they contributed in "civilizing influence." They also didn't offer the colonized any choice as to whether they accepted the Europeans "help." They certainly didn't let natives decide if they would hand over their land.

For the most part, Europeans joined the navy to sail the world, meet interesting people, and enslave them. And if they couldn't enslave them, they'd assimilate or exterminate them. Whichever came first.

Initially, the Portuguese and the Spanish led the way, with the French and Dutch following, and the English bringing up the rear. As time went on, the cycle of discovery and colonization became a significant factor in European culture. Colonialism became the default policy of European nations.

The Portuguese

The Portuguese were on the cutting edge of maritime exploration, and Prince Henry the Navigator (1394–1460), was a defining figure in Portugal's quest for an empire. Despite his "the Navigator" sobriquet, Henry was less the navigator and more the financier and administrator. Henry wanted to prove his masculinity and defend the Catholic faith in a Crusade against the Moors, and he achieved this by sitting on his ass in Portugal and outsourcing his masculinity and crusading to others. Nevertheless, he is still regarded as one of the initial movers-and-shakers of the Age of Discovery.

One of Henry's greatest legacies was the development of the caravel, a broad-beamed sailing ship much faster and more maneuverable than the trading ships of the day. Caravels had two or three masts, which were rigged with square sails and a triangular sail known as a lanteen. These innovations gave them a greater range and allowed them to sail into the wind, a quality that made them less dependent on the prevailing winds. Possession of state-of-the-art naval technology made it possible for Portuguese fleets to explore uncharted deep-sea waters, as well as rivers and shallow waters.

Fig. 1: A busy Lisbon Harbor (Duncan1890 and S.E.W.)

Not only was Henry responsible for the speedy development of Portuguese exploration, he also helped expedite sea trade with other continents through the exploration of Western Africa and the opening of new trade routes. In 1415, the Portuguese conquered Ceuta, a Muslim port on the North African coast. In 1488, Bartolomeu Dias was the first to sail around the treacherous Cape of Good Hope and into the Indian Ocean. Then in 1498, Vasco da Gama discovered the sea route to India. Trade boomed, along with an increase in cultural capital.

Portuguese sailors continued at the forefront of European overseas exploration throughout the fifteenth century, mapping the coasts of Africa, Canada, and Brazil. They then proceeded to explore southeast Asia, reaching Japan in 1542. It was even claimed by Australian historian Kenneth McIntyre that the Portuguese discovered Australia eighty years before it was first seen by Dutch navigator Willem Janszoon. The cited evidence for this is a sixteenth-century map of the world by Nicolas Desliens, which shows a landmass (that looks very little like Australia) where the southern continent is now known to be. There is also the legend of the Mahogany Ship, a shipwreck which has been reported near Warrnambool, Australia. This now conveniently lost shipwreck is theorized to be that of a Portuguese caravel that discovered Australia by crashing into it. Given the astonishing lack of evidence, this theory is given little weight.

In 1521, Portugal's Ferdinand Magellan transferred his allegiance to Spain over a pay dispute. He then *very nearly* performed the feat for which he would be remembered. Magellan was the first to circumnavigate the world—that is, if you don't consider the fact that he was killed on the beach in the Philippines well before completing the circumnavigation. Given that only one of his ships completed the voyage (under the captaincy of Juan Sebastián del Cano), why Magellan received all the glory beggar's belief.

Fig. 2: But we give him credit for it anyway. (Midjourney and S.E.W.)

The Spanish

Determined to catch up with their titchy neighbors, Spain wanted to get in on the "discovering the world" caper. In another controversial "transfer," an Italian, Christopher Columbus, was commissioned by King Ferdinand and Queen Isabella of Spain, to find an ocean route to the East Indies (and bring back shit-tons of spices). In 1492, the clueless Columbus, whose voyage was based on the misconception that the Earth was much smaller than it actually was, landed on the Caribbean island of San Salvador. He only came ashore in South America in later voyages, and never set foot in North America. Astoundingly, he had no idea that he'd discovered a new continent, believing till his dying day that he had arrived in India.

Another Italian/Spanish turncoat, Amerigo Vespucci, made four voyages to South America. Unlike Columbus, he knew it was a new continent and not the Eastern part of Asia. For this startling insight (and not much else), Amerigo had two continents named after him: North America and South America. Talk about being in the right place at the right time.

Of course, the Spanish didn't really need to import naval explorers. They had many of their own home-grown variety of cruel, gold-crazed, cut-throats. Vasco Nunez de Balboa (1475–1519) explored the island Hispaniola and parts of Central America. In 1513, he and his men walked through the jungles of Panama, becoming the first Europeans to see the Pacific Ocean. Another Spaniard, Juan Ponce de Leon, discovered Florida, now the retirement capital of America, while searching for the Fountain of Youth.

Hernán Cortés (1485–1547) had an interesting way of dealing with his disaffected army and signaling his insane commitment to colonization: He scuttled his own ships, leaving his men with no alternative but to survive by conquest. And conquer they did. After making contact with the Aztecs in 1519, Cortés and a small contingent were invited into their capital of Tenochtitlán by Montezuma II. The Spaniard correctly saw this as the trap it was and turned the tables, taking Montezuma captive. Montezuma was most likely murdered by the Spanish, who barely escaped Tenochtitlán with their lives. After this rather inauspicious beginning, things didn't get much better for the Aztecs. Cortés and his army regrouped and eventually conquered them in 1521.

Not to be outdone, Francisco Pizarro (1471–1541), made his name in a bloody campaign in Peru against the Inca. The Spanish arrived in South America in 1532. and soon captured the Incan capital, Cusco, which they made their base. In what had become the Spanish's signature move, Pizarro invited the Incan Emperor Atahualpa and several thousand attendants to a feast in his honor. During the feast, Atahualpa was pressed to accept Jesus Christ as his Lord and Savior, as well as the primacy of Charles V of Spain. Not a fan of either concept, he refused, unwisely sweeping a Bible onto the floor in the process.

At this desecration, Pizarro unleashed hell, killing many Inca and capturing Atahualpa. Knowing the Spanish obsession with gold, the emperor suggested ransoming himself by filling a room full of gold, a deal to which Pizarro agreed. Yet, despite the Inca filling *several* rooms full of gold, Pizarro welched on his side of the bargain and the emperor was sentenced to be burned at the stake. Offered the choice of being burned alive as a heathen, or being strangled as a Christian, Atahualpa chose the latter. Who really wants to be burned alive?

Fig 3. Atahualpa finds the love of Jesus the hard way. (Acrogame and S.E.W.)

Pizarro then installed Manco Inca Yupanqui as an Incan puppet ruler and things were going fine, until northern Inca cities began to develop tactics to combat the Spanish guns, germs, and steel. Manco Inca Yupanqui decided he wasn't going to take Pizarro's crap any longer; he escaped Cusco and returned with a hundred thousand Incan warriors to besiege the city.

The siege began poorly for the Spanish, as the Inca immediately took Sacsayhuaman, and so held the high ground. From this vantage point, the Inca launched heated stones, which ignited the thatched roofs of the city below. Vicious hand-to-hand battle ensued in the streets. The Spanish launched a daring counterattack on Sacsayhuaman, with a force comprising only fifty cavalrymen and one hundred and twenty infantry, and retook the fortress. After a ten-month siege, the Inca retreated from Cusco and many of their part-time warriors went back to their farms.

It proved to be a tactical blunder, as the Spanish brought reinforcements in from Chile under the command of Diego de Almagro. There was some infighting between de Almagro forces and Pizarro's men, but the Spanish forces were too strong for the Inca. An epidemic of European disease in the Inca Empire didn't help matters. Then Pizarro, understanding that the Inca saw their kings as living gods, adopted the strategy of murdering the king of every region he conquered. With their "gods" defeated, the Inca accepted Spanish rule, and by 1572, the Inca Empire was no more.

*

Unfortunately, the Spanish conquest of South America didn't result in a boost in cultural capital. The Spanish had melted down the art of the Mesoamericans for gold ingots to be sent back to Spain. They'd burned the "satanic" books of the Maya. They'd engaged in the wholesale murder of Inca, Aztecs, and other Mesoamerican civilizations. Their wanton destruction left them with precious little to glean from these once mighty civilizations.

The Dutch Explorers

In the sixteenth century, the Dutch shrugged off their status as a Spanish possession and took their place as a significant naval power. With this change in status came the desire for commerce and trade goods, and Amsterdam eventually rose to be the economic center of Europe, thanks to their bankers and merchants (more of which next chapter). It was in this climate that Dutch sailors took up, with relish, the now ubiquitous European mania for exploration. However, unlike the other European powers who were mostly in it for conquest and colonies, the Dutch had a more pragmatic aim. Their traders wanted to increase their economic power, not by plundering gold like the Spanish, but by increasing trade and by finding additional sources of trade goods. If they settled a few colonies as a result, so be it.

In most respects, the Dutch colonial empire failed to match the empires of Spain, France, and England. However, the Dutch colonies in the Caribbean, South America, South Africa, and Indonesia were selected with care and jealously guarded; these were valuable pieces of real estate. The Dutch East India Company (VoC) was a trading cartel formed to manage Dutch trading interests in these colonies.

The first documented European sightings of Australia resulted from Dutch East India Company's trading in Indonesia. Willem Janszoon's *Duyfken* accidentally made the landfall in Australia in 1606, mapping over 350 kilometers of the western side of the Cape York Peninsula, all the while thinking he was still in New Guinea.

Not to be outdone, in 1616, Dirk Hartog sailed too far south while trying to navigate his way to Batavia and accidentally bumped into Western Australia. He left an engraved pewter plate nailed to a tree on Dirk Hartog Island in celebration of this feat.

In 1642, Abel Tasman, blown by the Roaring Forties (a strong westerly wind which blows around the latitude of 40° south), sailed from Mauritius and, missing the entire southern edge of the Australian continent, made landfall in what is now Tasmania. Of course, he called it Van Diemen's Land, after his boss Anthony van Diemen, the Governor General of the VoC. After Van Diemen's Land had gained a reputation as an island hellhole to rival Devil's Island, its name was changed to Tasmania for marketing purposes. This not only successfully rebranded the island but gave name to the snarling whirlwind Looney Tunes character, the Tasmanian Devil.

Later in 1642, Abel Tasman's ships, *Heemskerck* and *Zeehaen*, carried the first documented Europeans to reach New Zealand. He had such a disastrous first contact with the Maori that he named the site Murderer's Bay, as four of his crewmen were killed trying to land ashore. But seriously, what did he expect?

During Tasman's second voyage in 1644, he mapped the northern coastline of Australia, which he named New Holland. But given the unpromising landscape of the Western Australia coast, and the warlike nature of the Maori in New Zealand, the VoC saw little profit in pressing their claims in the region.

Exploring with the Royal Navy

Don't talk to me about naval tradition. It's nothing but rum, sodomy, and the lash.
Winston Churchill

Despite Mr Churchill's early twentieth-century proclamation, the British Royal Navy also had a tradition of maritime exploration, which was responsible for much of England's colonial glory... and shame. This was less about rum and the lash, and more about colonization, piracy, and slavery. Although, no doubt there was some sodomy as well.

One of the most famous English mariners, Sir Francis Drake (1545–1596), was an explorer, slave-trader, and privateer (basically a government sanctioned pirate). His chief claim to fame exploration-wise was as leader of the second expedition to sail around the world. Drake was knighted by Queen Elizabeth on his ship, *the Golden Hind*. Drake was the scourge of the Spanish, having raided their treasure fleets on the Spanish Main (earning the name *El Draque*—the Dragon), and heroic actions against the Spanish Armada. If the myth is to be believed, he also shagged Good Queen Bess, a task which might easily have required more bravery than circumnavigating the globe and facing the Spanish Armada combined.

If salacious rumors are credited, another lover of the—ahem—*Virgin* Queen was Sir Walter Raleigh (1554–1618). Like so many men of his era, Raleigh was multi-talented: He was a poet, historian, explorer, and popularizer of tobacco... an International Man of Mystery if ever there was one. He commanded expeditions to both the North and South American continents, specializing in founding new settlements such as Virginia, which he named in honor of Elizabeth I (who he allegedly knew firsthand was NOT a virgin).

It is unclear whether he invented the post-coital cigarette.

Fig. 4: This is fake news, unfortunately. (Midjourney and S.E.W.)

Making Up with Queen Elizabeth

Of course, this imaginary love triangle was rumored to have happened before Elizabeth's brush with death. Four years after the Spanish Armada was repulsed, she was struck down with smallpox. It was touch and go for a while, and Elizabeth teetered on the brink of death. Her loyal Protestant courtiers feared what would happen if she turned up her toes, and, horror of horrors, the arch-Catholic, Mary Queen of Scots, ascended the throne.

In the end, their concerns came to nothing. Elizabeth recovered, but was robbed of her natural, smooth porcelain complexion. Although her face displayed some scarring, she was, by all accounts, not overly disfigured. However, even this small amount of pockmarking was too much for her. Yes, she was vain, but also knew the value of her public image as the beautiful young Virgin Queen. That was where make-up came in: She felt it imperative to smooth out the bumps with a thick layer of white, lead-based spackle. She then further "enhanced" her appearance with lipstick in a lurid Hooker-Red. While she believed this was a *fabulous* look, it may appear more like Pennywise cosplay to contemporary eyes.

As we know after our brush with Egyptian kohl in *From Cave to Colosseum*, lead-based make-up is not healthful. In fact, it's downright toxic. While we're not sure of Queen Elizabeth's exact cause of death, some of her symptoms sound suspiciously like lead poisoning. She was highly fatigued, suffered from memory loss, and most of her hair had fallen out. Either Good Queen Bess had acute lead poisoning, or she'd tried to remove the fuel rods from Chernobyl.

A Literary Pirate, Naturalist, and Avocado Lover

William Dampier (1651–1715) was a British privateer, explorer, naturalist, writer, cartographer, and sometime pirate. He was the first man to circumnavigate the earth three times—because, it seems, that no one told him that once was enough. Dampier was also the first Englishman to explore the western parts of Australia, and encounter the indigenous people who he described as "the miserabilist people in the world."

Not surprisingly for a pirate, he was a bit of a bastard. He was dismissed from the Royal Navy after being found guilty of "Hard and cruel usage of the lieutenant" while serving as captain of the HMS *Roebuck*. However, despite his dark side, he was also something of a naturalist. He maintained a journal in which he described unusual creatures such as the manatee, as well as native cultures, plants, and other observations made during his voyages. Dampier was an early adopter of the "avocado" craze, using the word for the first time in English when writing about the preparation of guacamole. He was also among the first people to use the words "barbecue," "cashew," "tortilla," and "chopsticks" in English.

Fig. 5: William Dampier was among other things, an avocado expert. (Public domain and S.E.W.)

Dampier turned this journaling into a book, *A New Voyage Round the World*, which was published in 1697 to popular acclaim. Despite this literary success (his book is *still* available on Amazon), he died penniless in 1715. It's thought his book inspired luminaries as diverse as Charles Darwin, Horatio Nelson, Sir Joseph Banks, Daniel Defoe, and Captain James Cook. All of which probably makes William Dampier the most influential pirate of all time.

The Problem of Calculating Longitude Solved

Marinus of Tyre (70–130 AD) had been the first to use the coordinates of latitude and longitude on the maps he created. The utility of this breakthrough in navigation is obvious, but there was a catch. Latitude, the angular distance of a spot on the globe north or south of the equator, could be determined by celestial navigation, and mariners had practiced this art for centuries. On the other hand, the accurate measurement of longitude, the angular distance east or west, was elusive for naval navigators.

It wasn't as if people hadn't *tried* to solve the longitude problem—even Sir Isaac Newton had had a crack at it with his "lunar distance method." These methods relied on complex astrological observations with reference to a known spot on the map (Greenwich for the English sailors). Unfortunately, these techniques were problematic on a moving ship, because they required an exact knowledge of time in the agreed reference place. The Holy Grail of longitude was a clock that could keep accurate time in trying shipboard conditions.

Many had tried and failed to build this clock, and Newton (for one) believed it couldn't be done. The clock must be unaffected by variations in humidity, temperature, or pressure, and maintain accuracy over long time intervals. It must also be able to work on board a ship at sea, therefore be corrosion-resistant. So important was this clock, that parliament offered a prize of £20,000 to the person who could solve the problem.

It was a self-educated English clockmaker named John Harrison (1693–1776) who designed a "Sea Clock" in a bid to win the Longitude prize. With encouragement from Edmond Halley (of Halley's Comet fame) he developed the design over a five-year period, and the marine chronometer became standard equipment on all Royal Navy vessels.

One mariner who benefited from this innovation was a man named James Cook.

The Voyages of James Cook

Captain James Cook (1728–1779) is one of the most contentious figures of the Age of Discovery. Arguably the greatest navigator of all, he remains a hero to many. He was a brave explorer who, like his near-namesake Captain James T. Kirk (whose creation was inspired by Cook), boldly went where no man has gone before. Two NASA Space Shuttles were even named after his ships HMS *Endeavour* and HMS *Discovery*. By comparison, Captain Kirk only rated one Space Shuttle, the *Enterprise*.

It was Cook who found the solution to the Royal Navy's scurvy problem: ascorbic acid, which he delivered through sauerkraut, lemons and, famously, limes, making him the reason the Brits are referred to as "limeys." Cook discovered the east coast of Australia, which eighteen years later solved the English convict problem. He was also very chummy with Joseph Banks, the chief botanist on the *Endeavour* and eventual president of the Royal Society.

Cook's fame was such that during the American War of Independence, no lesser personage than Benjamin Franklin directed that if Cook's ship were captured that Americans should:

> not consider her as an Enemy, nor suffer any Plunder to be made of the Effects contained in her, nor obstruct her immediate Return to England, [...] but that you would treat the said Captain Cook and his People with all Civility and Kindness, affording them as common Friends to Mankind.

CAPTAINS *COOK* AND *KIRK*

Fig. 6: Star Trek creator, Gene Roddenberry, admitted Captain Kirk was inspired by Captain Cook. (Moonrise and S.E.W.)

Others see Cook as less of a "friend to mankind." This blew-up in a very public spat between two old friends. Australian journalist and historian Peter FitzSimons, whose book *James Cook: The Story Behind the Man Who Mapped the World* is largely admiring of Cook, was attacked by fellow journalist Stan Grant about FitzSimons' depiction of Cook as a man with "great empathy for Indigenous populations." Grant, who says that his "blood is drawn from black and white," said he did not begrudge Cook his reputation as a navigator without equal. However, he pointed out that Cook's first act on Australian soil was to shoot an Aboriginal man, setting a precedent for the next two hundred and fifty years of negative race relations.

To be fair, for all Cook's faults in dealing with indigenous peoples, he treated most he encountered with more respect and less violence than, say, Francisco Pizarro (although admittedly, this is not a high bar). He was an enlightened man by the standards of eighteenth-century sailors. The problem with admiring Cook is when one continues to praise or excuse actions now recognized as negative. Just because Cook wasn't a genocidal maniac, one shouldn't gloss over his faults. For instance: allowing his crew to spread STIs in Hawaii was a poor choice and contributed to a negative first contact between cultures.

So how did an ordinary boy from the north of England go on to become a legend in the South Pacific?

Young James Cook began life in the northeast of England, son of a Scottish migrant farmhand. As James was clearly a clever lad, his father's boss paid for his education up to the age of 12 years, then Cook Junior worked at sea on a collier (or coal transport ship) for eight years. Seeking adventure, he volunteered for the Royal Navy and immediately began impressing his superiors.

So much so that by 1768, when the Royal Society and Admiralty began to plan a scientific expedition to the Pacific, James Cook was chosen to command. The ship he was given was very familiar; an old collier, which was renamed the HMS *Endeavour*. Cook had two primary objectives. The first instructed him to take Joseph Banks of the Royal Society to Tahiti to observe the transit of Venus (in a bid to determine the size of the solar system). His second order was in sealed instructions given to him from the Admiralty, which commanded him "to make discovery of the Continent above-mentioned until you arrive in the latitude of 40°, unless you sooner fall in with it." This order resulted in him mapping New Zealand and discovering the east coast of Australia, then claiming both for England.

Cook's navigational and map-making ability is worth investigating. He honed his skills in Canada during the Seven Years War (1756–1763), mapping the entrance to the Saint Lawrence River and the coast of Newfoundland. The accuracy of his charts brought him to the attention of the Royal Society and the Admiralty, and was one reason he was chosen to command the mission to observe the transit of Venus. On his first voyage to the Pacific, Cook calculated longitude by using Newton's lunar distance method. In subsequent voyages, he created accurate maps of the Pacific with the help of Harrison's marine chronometer. The accuracy of his charts was such that many of them were in use until recently, when satellite images and GPS mapping were available.

Despite being a master navigator in his own right, Cook had a "secret weapon" on that voyage. When the *Endeavour* left Tahiti in 1769, it took on a passenger, a Polynesian man named Tupaia. Up until this point, Cook hadn't been keen on including island people in his crew, but Banks wanted to observe a man in a "state of nature," and being rich and privileged, he got his way.

However, giving in to his rockstar naturalist had some unanticipated benefits for Cook. Tupaia was, in the Captain's estimation, a "Shrewd, Sensible, and Ingenious Man," because Tupaia had extensive knowledge of the islands surrounding Tahiti. He was also able to give Cook insight into the Polynesian methods of wayfinding. In addition, Tupaia was extremely useful in mediating between the *Endeavour* crew and the other Pacific Islanders they encountered.

After mapping New Zealand, Cook, Banks, Tupaia, and company turned west to the unknown, which is where they encountered the east coast of Australia, which Cook correctly identified as New Holland (although he perversely renamed it New South Wales). After sailing up the coast, Cook took the *Endeavour* into a large bay, which he immediately named Stingray Harbor. At Banks' insistence, it would later be renamed Botany Bay.

Alas, Tupaia's ambassadorial skills were useless in Australia, as the local people had had no prior contact with Polynesians.

He was as ineffective at conversing with the Aboriginal people as Cook (although in his defense, at least he didn't fire at the locals). It didn't help that Tupaia was unwell most of the time the *Endeavour* lay anchored in Botany Bay. Unfortunately for Tupaia, his ill health grew steadily worse, and he later died of fever in Batavia.

Cook's second voyage, which was to continue to search for *Terra Australis* (as the boffins from the Royal Society considered New Holland too far north to be the missing continent) had Cook in command of an expedition comprising HMS *Resolution* and HMS *Adventure*. These ships circumnavigated the globe at an extreme southern latitude and made Cook one of the first to cross the Antarctic Circle.

Cook's third and final voyage was to discover a Northwest Passage around North America. He was again in command of HMS *Resolution*, while HMS *Discovery* was under the command of Captain Charles Clerke. In 1778 Cook became the first European to discover the Hawaiian Islands (a discovery he would come to regret). He then sailed north looking for the Northwest Passage, but he could not locate a route through.

It was at that point he returned to Hawaii.

Was Cook Cooked?

The story goes that Cook was initially greeted as a god by the Hawaiians. However, relations soured and after the ship's launch was stolen by natives, Cook unwisely decided to take the king of Hawaii to ransom for the return of the boat. However, some Hawaiians saw Cook trying to entice King Kalani'ōpu'u to his ship and raised the alarm.

Then the shit hit the fan.

In a scene reminiscent of the "chased by natives" trope in movies such as *Pirates of the Caribbean*, hundreds of armed Hawaiians appeared and pursued Cook and his men to the beach. Unlike the movie trope, where the plucky protagonists get away just in time, Cook was not so fortunate. As he tried to help launch the boat, he was attacked and stabbed to death. Cook's body was then dragged away by the Hawaiians.

For many years, there was a general perception that hungry Hawaiians barbecued and ate Captain Cook. The irony of a man named Cook ending up on the menu was lost on nobody. But is it true? Was James Cook the "hero of the meal" in the Hawaiian version of MasterChef?

Well, it depends on who you believe, although no one really believes that Cook was cannibalized.

There are two schools of thought. The "James Cook was worshipped by the Hawaiians" view goes something like this: Despite killing Cook for trying to kidnap their king, the islanders continued to hold the explorer in high esteem. Hawaiian funeral rituals for respected elders were clear: Cook must be disemboweled and cooked. Not for eating, but so that his bones could be preserved and kept as religious relics. The crew of the HMS *Resolution* even had their captain's hands and buttocks returned to them before sailing.

And that was how Captain James Cook's ass came to be buried at sea.

The other school of thought was that "Cook was an evil colonizer who got what was coming to him." This view has been put forward by Hawaiian historian and activist Lilikalā K. Kameʻeleihiwa. In her view, it was all just a big coincidence. Cook had moored his ships in Kealakekua Bay at the same time and place that the Hawaiian people were celebrating the god Lono. As Lono's emblem bore more than a passing resemblance to the spars and sails of Cook's ship, he was understandably mistaken for the returning god. Although the fact he couldn't speak their language probably should've been a red flag.

Kameʻeleihiwa writes:

Rumor has it that Hawaiians worshipped Captain James Cook as a god whom we killed, and then ate, in 1779.

Now it is true that we very proudly killed Cook, who brought Venereal Disease (VD) and Tuberculosis to the Hawaiian people with his disease-ridden men. In fact, we Hawaiians still celebrate every 14 February as Hauʻoli Lā Hoʻomake iā Kapena Kuke, or Happy Death of Captain Cook Day!* But as we Hawaiians preferred to eat fresh fish over people (especially those who bathed only infrequently), we certainly did not eat Cook.

(*Author's Note: I seriously doubt this celebration trumps Valentine's Day in Honolulu.)

However, as Cook was clearly an important chief due to his command of two large ships, Hawaiian tradition "demanded that his body be dismembered, and the bones be put into a [...] casket." When the priests of Lono returned Cook's rump and hands to his ship, Cook's crew were somewhat taken aback, and presumably asked: "Are these just the leftovers?"

And thus, the legend of Cook's cannibalistic end was born.

Fig. 7: Welcome to Hawaii—Cook meets a similar end to Magellan. (Grafissimo and S.E.W.)

The Transatlantic Slave Trade

It's impossible to discuss the Age of Discovery without addressing the Transatlantic slave trade, which is the supreme example of some big ideas being terrible ideas. While the "discovery" that people could profit from the unpaid labor of others had been known since time immemorial, it made a massive comeback in the sixteenth century. In the three hundred years separating the trade's beginnings and its end in the nineteenth century, it is estimated that up to twelve million Africans were enslaved and transported to the Americas. The Portuguese, Spanish, Dutch, French and English all saw the commercial potential in human trafficking on a grand scale and profited from taking part.

The slave traders were infamous for their filthy, overcrowded ships, as well as their brutal treatment of the human cargo. Apart from their loss of freedom, the African slaves suffered other appalling privations: They were chained together in hideously cramped and airless conditions, often covered in vomit and feces. The Africans were only allowed outside on the upper deck for a few hours a day to get fresh air, despite the heat below decks often being unbearable. Under such conditions, it shouldn't be a shock that up to 25 percent of the African slaves didn't make it to the New World and their bodies were jettisoned at sea. This "spoilage" was just considered the price of doing business.

Of course, once the surviving slaves were delivered to their new "home," the horror was only just beginning. The scene is monstrous: Humans being treated like cattle in the slave market and sold to the highest bidder. Humans being chained and whipped in order to ensure their compliance. Human females being raped by their owners and having their children sold away without remorse.

Apologists for slavery argued all this whipping and chaining was overstated, and that slavery was a "natural state" ordained in the Bible. They claimed that slaves were "well looked after" and treated like members of the family. Indeed, some of them *were* family, as it was not uncommon for the child of a master and an enslaved woman to be kept in bondage (we're looking at *you*, Thomas Jefferson).

For most, the horror would never be over, and the ramifications are still being felt.

The Age of Discovery/Age of Colonization

While the Age of Discovery brought the benefits of increased wealth, resources, control, and knowledge to the European powers, the same can't be said for the indigenous peoples who were dispossessed, exploited, enslaved, and exterminated in the name of progress. It didn't help that many of the European explorers of this time were little better than pirates. Arguments about the ethics and legitimacy of the new wave of European imperialism and colonization would have to wait hundreds of years until a less benighted age.

But by that time, the damage had been done.

Whoever you blame and however you look at it, the Age of Discovery was a pivotal period in the history of world geography. In a relatively short period, large swathes of the "unknown" world were mapped, and there had been several significant technological advances in cartography and navigation, as well as a greater emphasis on trade.

Global trade, driven by the random distribution of resources around the world, was a significant consequence of the Age of Discovery. Massive cartels such as the Dutch East India Company (or VoC) and the British East India Company were set up to exploit Western countries' need for resources they did not have at home. Often the VoC and British East India Company literally brought the "war" into trade wars.

And that's where we're heading next.

* * *

—7—

Takin' Care of Business

The Great Trading Companies

Today's world is run by massive corporations which are ever-present in our lives.

I'm writing this book on an Apple computer and using Microsoft software. I research using Google, often wearing Adidas track pants, while drinking a Nespresso coffee (or occasionally a Pepsi). Sometimes, I'll make a phone call on my Samsung Galaxy. Of course, it's not just me that's a slave to the corporations: It's likely you bought this book through one of the biggest companies on Earth, Amazon.com (but kudos if you purchased from a small independent bookstore).

You may be surprised that the size and reach of today's corporations are nothing when compared to the biggest corporation of all time. It's a corporation you won't find listed on the New York Stock Exchange, although it was the first company in the world to be publicly traded. It has an unfamiliar and seemingly unpronounceable name (unless you speak Dutch): the Vereenigde Oost-Indische Compagnie, more commonly referred to as the Dutch East-India Company, or VoC for short.

The word "company" in Dutch East-India Company doesn't really do it justice. It was absolutely humungous. Let's put things in perspective; at the height of its powers, the VoC's net worth exceeded the combined value of Apple, Microsoft, Amazon, *and* Facebook. Adjusted for inflation, its value would eclipse the current GDP of Germany and Japan put together. The VoC also employed over 70,000 people.

Of course, there was a downside.

Google's unofficial motto "Don't be evil," would've been handy for the VoC four centuries ago, because they were, undoubtedly, evil. Although the VoC were initially formed to trade spices with Asia (which one might think was inherently non-evil), they also diversified into commodities such as textiles, tea, coffee, and ceramics. To up the stakes in the evil department, they also engaged in slave trading. Not only that, they were at the cutting edge of colonial oppression, using threats of violence and political pressure to manipulate the Asian countries with which they traded. The VoC had permission from the Dutch Estates General to raise its own military, make treaties with foreign governments, coin its own money, and even declare war.

Can you imagine Microsoft invading New Zealand because their government banned the sale of Surface Pros? No? Well, try to picture it, because the VoC actively waged war against sovereign nations, such as Portugal and Spain. The VoC also treated their staff rather worse than most multinationals treat their staff today. It's almost like the VoC's unofficial motto was "Don't be ethical."

Private companies weren't a new idea, but the high cost and risks associated with outfitting a large-scale trading operation meant that a new way of funding had to be devised. This was how the VoC became the first publicly traded company. However, it wasn't the first company to issue stock. That honor goes to the Muscovy Company, which was chartered in 1555, and had a monopoly of trade between Russia and England. The other company that would rise to rival the VoC was the British East India Company (of whom more shortly) established in 1600, which vied for supremacy in the spice trade.

Spice, Spice, Baby

Trading spices wasn't a new concept. The East had sold spices to Europe since ancient times, and Europeans had become extremely fond of these condiments. Spices had been imported through traders traveling the Silk Road for centuries. However, the advent of efficient sea trading routes meant that there was now a faster way for Europeans to get their fix and cut out the middle-man.

So, what exactly constitutes "spices"? Food preparation across Europe required the use of ingredients such as pepper, ginger, nutmeg, cinnamon, anise, cumin, cloves, and saffron. However, spices were for more than making food taste better. They were used as incense in religious ceremonies, as well as being added to healing ointments and potions. Some were used for food preservation. Spices were also added to wines or eaten in crystallized form like a kind of candy. If you burned just the right spices in the home, they would mask all manner of unpleasant household odors.

Interestingly though, while most spices are obtained from plants, one thing loosely considered a "spice" is produced by secretions from the anal glands of beavers. Sounds disgusting, but "castoreum" as it's known, is a near match for, of all things, vanilla flavoring. God knows what the first person who discovered *that* factoid thought they were doing.

Fig. 1: Great Moments in spice collection? (Midjourney and S.E.W.)

Other than pepper, which was commonly used by rich and poor alike, most of these herbs, spices, and—ahem—secretions were status symbols for the rich (who are entitled to all the anal secretions that money can buy, as far as I'm concerned). Anyway, the point is that spices were extremely lucrative trade items, which the Europeans purchased with silver.

Today the word "spicy" is synonymous with "hot" and, in a metaphorical sense, "sexy." However, a stroll down a supermarket's condiments aisle reveals just how many spices are cheaply available. When I walk down this row, I'm not knocked over by shoppers in the rush for them. Spices such as nutmeg are mundane kitchen items, which generate little excitement with the public or food connoisseurs alike. Nutmeg is neither hot nor sexy.

However, there was a time when a gram of nutmeg was worth more than a gram of cocaine is today, and this comparison isn't as spurious as it might sound. Used in small amounts, nutmeg is a mild food additive, but when taken in large doses, nutmeg can have psychoactive effects. Nutmeg intoxication (there *is* such a thing) comes with side effects such as anxiety, confusion, delirium, and amnesia. Taken in significant amounts, it can cause miscarriages. Nutmeg poisoning can, in extremely rare cases, be fatal.

Fig. 2: *Artist's impression of an imaginary Nutmeg Den*
(Erica Guilane-Nachez and S.E.W.)

Is it any wonder that fortunes were made from the stuff? In fact, the wealth, power, and ruthless legacy of the Dutch East India Company was based on this humble spice.

The VoC: Gods Among Men?

The VoC was established in 1602, when the Dutch government bestowed exclusive rights of trade with Asia upon them. While the VoC was set up to administer the spice trade, they ended up trading many Asian products. Besides spices, the major commodities the VoC shipped back to Europe were fabric from India, tea from China, and coffee from Java. While this may seem pedestrian by today's standards of value-added trade items, in the 1600s this was the big time.

This importance of the VoC in the Dutch psyche of the sixteenth and seventeenth centuries was made clear in a painting by Nicolaas Verkolje, titled *Allegorical representation of the Amsterdam Chamber of the Dutch East India Company*, also sometimes referred to as the *Apotheosis of the Dutch East India Company* (see below). As the word "apotheosis" means elevating someone (or something) to the status of a god, we get a fair idea of the VoC's status in Holland. The work was commissioned to celebrate the hundredth anniversary of the VoC in the early 1700s. In the painting, the figure on the throne, in all her pseudo-classical splendor, is the female personification of the VoC. In her right hand, she holds a laurel leaf (the symbol of victory) and a sword (a literal weapon of war), a signal that this woman meant business and wasn't going to take any shit. She wears a crown of ships, another unsubtle symbol.

Quite why her female attendants are both exposing a breast might at first appear inexplicable, but in the sixteenth century, the exposure of a single breast was an acceptable display of the classical, youthful beauty of women. (Side note: Women of the upper classes didn't breastfeed, so their hooters were "apple-like" and fit for display.) In any event, the fact that the VoC saw themselves in such a grandiose light, explains why they felt they could get away with almost anything.

Fig. 3: The result of a nutmeg overdose?
(Nicolaas Verkolje, Public domain, and S.E.W.)

The Spice Must Flow!

The Banda Islands (in present day Indonesia) had been trading spices for millennia, and for nearly as long, had been known as the Spice Islands. You know, the Spice Islands... the ones that Christopher Columbus had been desperately trying to locate in 1492 when he accidentally bumped into the West Indies over eighteen thousand kilometers away.

In 1511, Portugal conquered Malacca in the East Indies and used this port to dominate trade with the Spice Islands for nutmeg, mace (the spice, not a spray or medieval club), and cloves. The Portuguese enjoyed the fruits of this strategic position for just under ninety years, until the VoC turned their avaricious eyes towards Banda.

In 1602, the Dutch government gifted the VoC a monopoly on the spice trade. This was rather wishful thinking, because the Portuguese already had a stranglehold on trade with the Banda. The Dutch knew in order to get control of the spices, they needed to kick out the Portuguese, and so instigated the Dutch-Portuguese War. But the VoC didn't just fight the Portuguese Empire in the Spice Islands—the theater of war included the West Indies, and Africa.

All in the name of business.

Once the VoC had kicked the Portuguese out of Malacca, the real infamy began. In 1619, the Dutch killed hundreds while subduing the Indonesian city of Jayakarta, which they transformed into the port of Batavia, as a center for administration of the VoC in Southeast Asia. Unfortunately, the difficulty of acclimatizing to Batavia's swampy environment caused it to be labeled as the Europeans' graveyard. Today, Batavia is present day Jakarta.

However, the VoC were not content to merely have an advantage in the spice trade; they wanted the *monopoly* their government had granted them. Whatever it took.

In 1616, the citizens of the Banda island of Rhun "willingly" handed themselves over to the British, as they saw them as being a less evil option than the Dutch. Five years later, the VoC exacted a terrible revenge, destroying the English outpost on Rhun.

The Dutch were mighty upset that the Orang Kaya (the elders of the Banda Islands people) had allowed the English to take nutmeg plants to cultivate in their other colonial possessions. The VoC saw this as damaging to their exclusive rights to the spice. They attacked the Banda Islands with a fleet and over two hundred and fifty Japanese mercenaries. The Japanese were ordered to behead and quarter the Orang Kaya, and the VoC killed or enslaved over ninety percent of the inhabitants of Banda. They then ramped up nutmeg production with large-scale plantations.

A 1619 treaty between the Netherlands Estates General and King James I led to a brief cessation of hostilities between the VoC and the English East India Company. As a part of the deal, both companies agreed to share trading posts and divide the spice market equitably. This situation was uncomfortable at best, particularly with both sides trying to manipulate the local people behind the scenes. The outpost of Amboyna was a powder keg, which exploded in 1623 when ten employees of the English East India Company were tortured and executed by agents of the Dutch East India Company.

The Amboyna Massacre, as it became known, soured Dutch/English relations for decades to come. Given the difficulty the English now had trading in the Spice Islands, and that nutmeg was now growing in their outposts in Ceylon, Singapore, and Penang, they focused more on trade with India.

You've got to know when to cut your losses.

With the English run out of town, the Dutch East India Company finally secured their precious monopoly in the Spice Islands. Batavia became their most important outpost, although this was threatened in 1625, when it was besieged by the forces of Sultan Agung. The Dutch repelled two offensives on the city by the Sultan's forces, and this inspired them to enclose the city with a moat and city wall.

So far, the VoC's venture in the Spice Islands had spilled a lot of blood, but they weren't finished yet.

The Wreck of the *Batavia*

Ten years after the founding of Batavia, the VoC saw fit to name their new flagship the *Batavia*, and it set sail from Holland in convoy with eight other vessels, on its maiden voyage for the Spice Islands. Unfortunately, during the voyage, the 57-meter long *Batavia* became separated from the rest of its fleet, ran off course, and was wrecked on a reef off the coast of Western Australia with nearly 350 people on board.

From the very beginning of the voyage, there'd been problems on the *Batavia*, due to bad blood between its captain, Ariaen Jacobsz, and the fleet commander, Francisco Pelsaert, who was also aboard. It had gotten to the point where Jacobsz and Jeronimus Cornelisz (Pelsaert's second-in-command) had planned to mutiny against Pelsaert, but the *Batavia* struck the reef before they had the chance. Nearly one third of those aboard died in the incident, but for those who survived, worse times were ahead.

The survivors made landfall on Beacon Island, an uninhabited island two kilometers away from the site of the shipwreck. Pelsaert and Jacobsz then decided to take a small party by longboat to the port of Batavia, over 3000 kilometers away, to organize a rescue, leaving second-in-command Cornelisz behind with the other survivors.

Once the two leaders were gone, Cornelisz went all *Lord of the Flies*, and became a bloodthirsty paranoid dictator. Cornelisz believed that Pelsaert knew he'd been planning to mutiny and expected he'd probably be hanged after a successful rescue. He split the survivors into small groups and divided them up among nearby islands.

Cornelisz, one of history's first documented psychopaths, then systematically sent his loyalists out to murder these surviving groups. Throats were cut. Women were raped. Some people were sent out on jerry-rigged rafts to drown. It is believed that one hundred and twenty-five people were killed in this spree, including women and children. Cornelisz is even believed to have personally strangled a baby to death (he's not a documented psychopath for nothing).

When the rescuers returned sixty-three days later aboard ship from Batavia, they were shocked at the carnage. Pelsaert arrested Cornelisz and his henchmen, cut off their right hands, and then hanged them on makeshift gallows. This was cold comfort to two-thirds of the original passengers and crew who never made it to Batavia.

There's no big idea here, but it proves that no matter how far humans have come, our base nature is never far from the surface.

Fig. 4: Return to Psychopath Island. (Public domain and S.E.W.)

Cape Town: The VoC Colonize Southern Africa

In 1648, a Dutch East India Company ship was stranded in Table Bay in southern Africa. The marooned crew were impressed with the area and sang its praises to the VoC when they returned to Holland. Given that the place had plentiful water, fertile land, and was in a strategic position on the tip of Africa, the VoC needed little convincing. Four years later, they sent an expedition commanded by Jan van Riebeek to establish a fort as a waystation for trading ships enroute to the Far East. However, it grew into much more.

While Cape Town had humble beginnings, it didn't remain humble for long. The VoC persuaded the local indigenous people to sell them land in the area. Settlers soon followed, and eventually spread out eastwards. Cape Town soon joined Batavia as one of the first cities founded by a corporation. It wouldn't be the last.

In the early days, Cape Colony was home to around ten thousand, quite prosperous European colonists. These colonists owned slaves, but the enslaved people were not taken from the indigenous Khoikhoi (or as they were called at the time, Hottentot) population. This was because the Khoikhoi greatly outnumbered the whites, and it would *not* have ended well for the settlers. Therefore, the first wave of enslaved people in South Africa were from East Africa, although subsequent slave shipments would come from South and Southeast Asia, and Madagascar.

As we've already seen, the VoC was no stranger to enslavement, having used the local slaves in the Spice Islands. However, it was the Dutch *West* India Company (the VoC's sister company for the West Indies) that was involved in the transatlantic slave trade, and they accounted for, approximately, a 5 percent share of the market.

However, there were other companies who specialized in the trade in humans, one of which had connections in very high places.

The Royal African Company

Europeans, particularly the Portuguese, had been active in the African slave trade since the fifteenth century. In 1660, the "Company of Royal Adventurers Trading into Africa" was established in London to squeeze as much profit as possible from Gambian gold mines. However, its name was changed to the slightly less verbose Royal African Company (RAC), and it became involved in a lucrative and ethically dubious business: The African slave trade.

The "Royal" in the name wasn't just there for show. You see, the Royal African Company was set up and chaired by the Duke of York, who was King Charles II's younger brother, and was the guy who'd succeed him as King James II. In fact, this company transported and sold more slaves than any other during the period of the African slave trade. It was also 100 percent owned by the British Royal Family. At its peak, the Royal African Company transported about 5,000 Africans a year across the Atlantic to be sold as slaves. These men, women, and children would have the letters "DoY" (standing for "Duke of York") branded on their bodies.

In something of a postscript to Chapter 5, when Charles II died, the very Catholic James took the throne. It will come as no surprise that, like most of the Stuarts, he was a bit of a dick. In what seems to be a family trait, he suspended parliament and ruled by decree. Which was a strange choice, considering that James was Charles I's son and had seen *exactly* where being an autocrat could lead. The suspension of parliament and the prospect of James' son (who was also very Catholic) succeeding him, concerned a coalition of English religious leaders, military bigwigs, and parliamentarians. It wasn't long before James was ignominiously deposed in the Glorious Revolution, in which his daughter Mary and her husband, William of Orange, were invited by the same coalition of religious leaders, military bigwigs, and parliamentarians to take James' place as co-regents of England.

This was a modicum of payback for James II's profiting from human misery, and honestly, it couldn't have happened to a nicer guy.

The Glorious Revolution also saw an end to the Royal African Company's monopoly, although in a bid to suck up to the new king, shares in the company were gifted to William III (who didn't refuse them). However, the RAC was never quite as profitable again and went bankrupt in 1708, although it continued to trade slaves until 1731.

The East India Company

To discuss the East India Company (aka the English East India Company, the British East India Company, John Company, or EIC for short) we need to step back in time a little.

In 1577, our old buddy Sir Francis Drake took the *Golden Hind* to plunder Spanish gold in the New World. Once he'd accomplished this aim, he rounded the Horn and set out across the Pacific Ocean, eventually ending up in the Spice Islands. There, he traded his way to a fortune in spices and returned to England in 1580 a national hero. *El Draque* had proven there was a fortune to be made in the East Indies, and it lit a fire under all the Englishmen who enjoyed making money.

Just such a group of avaricious Englishmen met in 1599 to explore a potential East Indies venture, and together pledged the modern-day equivalent of £4,000,000 to the establishment of a company. These would-be spice magnates then applied to Queen Elizabeth I for her blessing, and in December 1600, the "Governor and Company of Merchants of London trading to the East Indies" was granted a royal charter. This meant that formation of the EIC predated that of the VoC by two years.

The royal charter granted the EIC a fifteen-year monopoly on all trade east of the Cape of Good Hope. It also gave the company the right to use military power for defensive purposes or to protect British trading interests. However, the EIC would eventually raise large armies and conquer territory in its own name.

As time passed, the company gradually shifted its focus from spices to calico and silk, and famously, tea. They also tried a spot of drug running, exporting Indian opium to China, but I'm getting ahead of myself. The bottom line is, if the Dutch East

India Company needed Google's "Don't be evil" motto, then the English East India Company needed it even more.

Moving On from the Spice Islands

As we've seen, the East India Company was out-maneuvered in the Spice Islands by the VoC. This left a bitter aftertaste that ensured that the next time the English exploited a country for its natural resources, it wouldn't be half-hearted. So, while the EIC left the Dutch to their own devices in the Spice Islands, they moved on to dominate trade on the Indian subcontinent, other parts of Southeast Asia (such as Burma, Malaya, and Borneo), and Hong Kong.

Initially, the EIC located representatives in trading posts in strategic areas and allowed them to trade for goods. They called these posts "factories," not because they manufactured goods, but because they were bases for their trade officials they referred to as "factors." A treaty signed in 1613 with Jahangir, the Mughal emperor, allowed the EIC to establish its first factory in Surat in Gujarat. By 1623, they had established factories in the west, north, and south of India.

However, the East India Company didn't have things all their own way. Initially, there were problems between the EIC and the Mughal rulers, including issues regarding the fortification of the English factory in Surat, and perceived English collusion with pirates. At one point in the late seventeenth century, the Mughals drove the English out of their factories in Surat, Masulipatam, and Vishikhapatam, and the EIC port in Bombay was besieged. In response, English ships blockaded Mughal ports. But despite their naval superiority, the EIC didn't have strong enough forces to fight their way out of the situation, so they negotiated their way out, paying a fine to the Mughal emperor for the return of their trading privileges.

It was only a matter of time before this power struggle led to war.

The Battle of Plassey

By the mid-eighteenth century, the once mighty Mughal Empire was in decline, the victim of the political and economic machinations of the EIC and the *Compagnie Française Pour le Commerce des Indes Orientales* or French East India Company. Then, after the outbreak of the Seven Years Wars between France and England, both trading companies were also on the brink of a shooting war.

The Nawab of Bengal, Siraj-ud-Daulah, who was no friend of the English, intervened when the EIC refused to halt their military build-up. His forces attacked and seized Fort William in Calcutta, and allegedly crammed 146 English prisoners of war in a dungeon measuring 4.3 meters by 5.5 meters, which became infamous as the Black Hole of Calcutta. After an overnight stay, only 23 people emerged from the Black Hole, with the balance succumbing to heat exhaustion and suffocation from the stifling conditions.

Fig. 5: A.I. artist's impression (Midjourney and S.E.W.)

Despite the undoubted evils of the East India Company, I think we can agree that this punishment was a tad excessive. However, the number incarcerated, and the death toll are disputed by some historians, who believe the figures were overstated to inflame the British public's indignation and thirst for retribution.

If so, the propaganda did its job.

Lieutenant Colonel Robert Clive was dispatched with an East India Company force to take revenge against the Nawab for occupying Calcutta *and* for negotiating with the hated French. This would be no easy task: Siraj-ud-Daulah had 50,000 men under his command, including a 16,000 strong cavalry, and officers on loan from the French marshaling his 50 field guns. By comparison, Clive's forces amounted to around 3,000 men, with a total of ten field guns.

It didn't really look like a fair fight.

The forces joined battle near the village of Palashi (later Anglicized as Plassey), about 160 kilometers north of Calcutta. Siraj-ud-Daulah ordered his field guns to fire before the British were in range, but that was the least of his problems. Torrential rain then began to drench the battlefield. Clive's forces immediately covered their artillery and ammunition with tarpaulins to protect them from water damage. Unfortunately, none of the Nawab's men had the presence of mind to do likewise.

This oversight was to be decisive. Believing that the British artillery could not fire due to the wet conditions, the Indian infantry advanced, only to be met with a withering barrage which set them to flight. The Mughal cavalry commander Mir Jafar, saw the writing on the wall (and a chance for advancement), and betrayed the Nawab, withdrawing his 16,000 mounted troops from the field. With that, the defeat of the Mughal forces was assured.

The Nawab tried to make a run for it, but was arrested and executed as part of a deal between Mir Jafar and the EIC. Unsurprisingly, Mir Jafar was then appointed Nawab of Bengal, a puppet ruler for the East India Company, ensuring the administration of Bengal was effectively in their hands.

Robert Clive was appointed Governor of Bengal, and he proceeded to bleed the region dry through corruption. While Clive's tenure made him an exceedingly rich man, the people of Bengal didn't fare quite so well. Some historians lay the responsibility for the deaths of ten million people at his feet, due to his mismanagement of the Great Bengal Famine. Nevertheless, he was revered by future generations of British colonizers and is known to posterity as "Clive of India."

As for Mir Jafar, his legacy was to become the Benedict Arnold of India—a name indelibly associated with backstabbing and treason.

Fig. 6: Lord Clive meeting Mir Jafar after the Battle of Plassey.
(Francis Hayman, Public domain, and S.E.W.)

Chinese Molasses: The Opium Wars

The narcotic properties of the poppy plant have been known since ancient times. In the *Iliad*, Homer identifies opium as a method of pain relief. The Greek physician Hippocrates believed it was the source of the mythological heroes' power. Even our learned friend from Chapter Two, Ibn Sina, prescribed opium for curing illnesses, both mental and physical.

It's unclear when opium was introduced to India, but a Portuguese traveler writes of its use there in the early sixteenth century. However, it had clearly been around a lot longer. Opium consumption was so ubiquitous in Bengal that, according to one (slightly dubious) source, "Take your opium" was the Bengali equivalent of "hello." Some accounts claim that it was even used to pacify boisterous children, rather like we use Ritalin today.

The East India Company, never big on scruples, had gained a monopoly on the trade in opium after taking control of Bengal. What could possibly go wrong?

Around this time, England had a massive trade imbalance with China. The English public desperately wanted Chinese porcelain, silk, and tea, but the Chinese wanted nothing the British had to offer... except silver. This one-sided trade began to drain British silver reserves. Something had to be done. Besides which, empty British trading ships were arriving in China and leaving full of trade goods. What if the British had *something* to fill those empty ships? It was then that some bright spark in the EIC had a "lightbulb moment"...

What if the EIC became international drug-runners?

As unedifying as it seems, this idea was seized upon by British traders. Thus it was that the East India Company began to export immense quantities of opium from Bengal to China. Before long, the tables had turned and it was China on the wrong end of a trade imbalance, and parting with huge amounts of silver to satisfy the demand for "Chinese Molasses."

The Chinese government banned the import of opium in 1839, impounding and destroying more than one million kilograms of British opium from a Canton warehouse. Undaunted, the East India Company continued the illegal drug trade through third party smugglers. In response, the Chinese blockaded Hong Kong, but a British fleet smashed the blockade and attacked Canton. The British eventually captured the city of Nanking in August 1842, bringing an end to hostilities. The Treaty of Nanking was signed, which required China to give Hong Kong Island to the British and pay them 20 million silver dollars in reparations.

Oh, and the opium smuggling could continue unchecked.

In 1856, Chinese officials boarded the British ship *Arrow* in Canton, detaining Chinese crew members and lowering the British flag. Given millions of pounds worth of opium was involved, things got out of hand and the EIC decided to go to the mattresses. A second Opium War took place in 1858, when the Chinese understandably baulked at British demands for further expansion of the opium market. The British were again victorious. The Treaty of Tientsin of 1858, saw the British give up all pretence of the high moral ground and demand opium importation to China be legalized.

Meanwhile, back in Bengal, opium production increased exponentially.

Fig. 7: Illegal drug smugglers raided by government officials.
(Archivist and S.E.W.)

The Indian Rebellion of 1857

By the nineteenth century, the East India Company's army numbered a quarter of a million troops, surpassing that of many sovereign nations. The officers were (of course) British, but around 96 percent of the army's enlisted men were Indian, as it offered well-paid, high-status employment. The army's equipment and training were a hybrid of European and Indian methods. These Indian troops were known as Sepoys.

In 1857, a big idea took hold of the many Indian people: kick out the colonizers. A major revolt began against EIC rule, which manifested as a series of civic rebellions and mutinies across central India. This uprising is known by different names depending on whether you're a colonizer (the Sepoy Rebellion or Indian Mutiny), an Indian nationalist (First War of Independence), or a disinterested observer (Indian Rebellion of 1857). There are other names as well, but you get the drift.

If you're of Anglo-Saxon heritage, the historic reason given for the "Sepoy Rebellion" is associated with the introduction of the Enfield rifled musket. These new rifles fired Minié balls which were loaded via paper cartridges that had to be bitten open to release the powder. This was a major issue, because these cartridges were rumored to be greased with either beef or pig fat. As cows are sacred to Hindus and pigs are offensive to Muslims, this angered the Sepoys and they rebelled. While this was indeed a partial reason for the insurrection, it was the final straw rather than the sole cause.

If you, dear reader, have been paying even casual attention to this chapter, you'll have seen a number of other potential causes for Indians wanting to rid themselves of the East India Company. It all boils down to the fact that India had been systematically colonized and exploited by the second biggest corporation in the history of the world.

Nevertheless, there were a number of *Boy's Own* adventure tales told of the British response to the rebellion, particularly during the Siege of Delhi and the capture of the Cashmere Gate, and the Siege of Lucknow. There are also stories of atrocities on both sides. The real lightbulb moment is the idea that a colonized country could dare to dream of ejecting the colonizer.

Fig. 8: The defense of Cashmere Gate in Delhi. (Public domain and S.E.W.)

Of course, the rebellion failed. Not all Indian states were in revolt, and many Sepoys chose to return to their homes rather than fight against the British. In the end, 6,000 British were killed during the uprising, and around 800,000 Indians died, either in battle or because of subsequent famine or disease.

Yet, despite the Indians' failure to eject the British, they gained major concessions. The East India Company was dissolved, and the British parliament passed the Government of India Act, which made the British government responsible for the administration of the colony under the British Raj.

Whilst this still left India under the colonial yoke, at least the Raj was less corrupt than the EIC.

*

The End of the Great Trading Companies?

The age of the great trading companies didn't last forever.

Despite the size and power of the VoC, it eventually lost out to the EIC. Financially ruined by a series of Anglo-Dutch wars, the VoC's charter expired in 1796. And as we've just seen, the EIC would only survive VoC by sixty years. The age of massive, cumbersome, monopolistic corporate bureaucracies was over. For the time being, at least. No longer would the VoC or EIC run their respective government's foreign policy. But both companies serve as a warning to governments about the dangers of a lack of regulation of mega-corporations.

A warning that appears to be going unheeded in the twenty-first century.

Amazingly, this didn't signal the end of the capitalist experiment. Freed from the chains of anti-competitive trade practices, it saw the birth of a new wave of capitalism. One where competition was the name of the game. But that story will have to wait for the next book in the *Lightbulb Moments in Human History* series.

* * *

Weird Science

The Scientific Revolution

During the European Renaissance, the momentum of collective learning set off a movement that became a precursor for the Enlightenment: The Scientific Revolution. This period of fundamental change in scientific thought began during the Renaissance and continued through to the seventeenth century. In bygone years, science (or natural philosophy as it was known) had been regarded as a branch of philosophy, but it now became an academic subject in its own right. By the end of the Scientific Revolution, science had split into a number of disciplines, including chemistry, mathematics, physics, astronomy, and biology.

Of course, if Chapter Two of this book taught us anything, it was that the scholars of the Islamic Golden Age had laid the groundwork for the growth in scientific thought, particularly in the fields of mathematics, astronomy, and medicine. If Muslim scholars hadn't preserved and built on the knowledge of the ancients, the Renaissance and Scientific Revolution couldn't have taken place.

Six Degrees of Francis Bacon

The tone for the Scientific Revolution was set by the ground-breaking work of Francis Bacon (1561–1626). He was influential on the development of the scientific method, arguing that humans could only gain scientific knowledge through inductive reasoning and meticulous observation of nature. Although the specific method of scientific investigation he devised, the Baconian method, was later superseded, his concept of skeptical observation and method remained. As a result, Bacon is regarded by many to be the father of the scientific method.

In fact, if John Aubrey's book *Brief Lives* is to be believed, it was Bacon's devotion to practical scientific research that led to his ultimate demise. Bacon had hypothesized that freezing meat would stop it from decomposing. During a coach journey on a bleak winter's day, Bacon explained this idea to a companion on the coach, one Dr. Winterbourne, who scoffed at the suggestion. Dander well and truly up, Bacon had the coach halted, purchased a chicken, and set about performing his experiment in the surrounding snow. In the tragedy that unfolded, Bacon took a chill from this exposure and expired a few days later. So, not only was Bacon the father of the scientific method, he was also the father of frozen chicken nuggets.

Captain Birdseye salutes his sacrifice.

Fig. 1: Bacon makes the ultimate sacrifice? (Acrogame and S.E.W.)

The Revolutions of the Heavenly Spheres

Of course, like all great cultural transformations, the Scientific Revolution wasn't considered a "revolution" as it was taking place, even though many of the concepts generated by this new breed of scientific thinkers were indeed revolutionary. Often in a literal sense.

Renaissance polymath Nicolaus Copernicus (1473–1543) published *De revolutionibus orbium coelestium* (On the Revolutions of the Heavenly Spheres) in 1543, which theorized a model of the "universe" that placed the Sun rather than Earth at its center. Of course, the same idea had been theorized eighteen hundred years earlier, by an ancient Greek astronomer, Aristarchus of Samos, but it's believed that Copernicus conceived the idea independently. We'll give him the benefit of the doubt.

This new-fangled heliocentric model that set off the Copernican Revolution is considered by some to have marked the beginning of this new world of scientific thought, influencing all subsequent astronomers, most notably Galileo. Given Galileo's problems with the Catholic Church, Copernicus probably saved himself a lot of trouble by conveniently dying just after the publication of his work.

Fig. 2: As Copernicus was 70 when he died, this illustration is fake news. (Public domain and S.E.W.)

By this time, of course, astronomers were no strangers to sacrificing for their beliefs. Take the case of Tycho Brahe (1546–1601), a Danish nobleman and astronomer, astrologer, and alchemist, famous for his astronomical observations which proved the Moon was closer to the Earth than the stars, and for his lack of a nose. Unfortunately, on December 29 1566, Tycho and his cousin Manderup Parsberg drank a few too many beers and had a heated debate about which of them was the superior mathematician. Despite the incredible nerdiness of this dispute, these lads then did what any aggrieved mathematicians of the sixteenth century would do—they settled the matter with a rapier duel... in the dark.

By the time the lights were re-lit, the damage was done. The cousins were eventually reconciled, but the same can't be said for Mr. Brahe and his nose. He had to wear a prosthetic proboscis for the rest of his life.

Fig. 3: It was almost undetectable. (Erica Guilane-Nachez and S.E.W.)

Tycho Brahe's name resonates down through history as an astronomer who proved that the heavens were not as unchanging as the ancients believed. However, he also tinkered in the pseudo-science of alchemy and the occult practice of astrology. While the modern world now sees these as the definition of unscientific, Tycho was not alone in his fascination with turning base metals into gold or constructing horoscopes. In fact, some surprising figures of the Scientific Revolution mixed quite legitimate scientific research with ideas that modern science now considers supernatural claptrap.

The revered German astronomer and mathematician Johannes Kepler (1571–1630) was another key figure in the Scientific Revolution. In his early years, Kepler had been Tycho Brahe's assistant, and *Heavenly Intrigue*, a book by Joshua and Anne-Lee Guilder, alleges that Kepler *murdered* Tycho to gain access to secret information. While this is not a mainstream belief, Tycho's heirs delayed publication of Kepler's book *Astronomia nova* through legal disputation, so make of that what you will. In any event, something of Tycho's penchant for the occult rubbed off on Kepler, as he practiced astrology (which in those days was synonymous with astronomy) and is suspected of having been an alchemist.

Kepler's Laws of Planetary Motion built on the work of Copernicus, but luminaries such as Rene Descartes and Galileo had no time for his work. Johannes won out in the end though, as his ideas were highly influential on Sir Isaac Newton's magnum opus, *Principia Mathematica*, widely considered to be one of the greatest scientific works in history.

Sir Isaac Newton: Indistinguishable from Magic?

Even the great Sir Isaac Newton (1643–1727) the legendary astronomer, mathematician, physicist and arguably the greatest scientist of all time, was not immune to the lure of alchemy. Among other alchemical goals, Newton believed he could solve the puzzle of the Philosopher's Stone (which could turn all metals into gold) and create the Elixir of Life. Of the ten million words that survive of his writings, a million of them were devoted to alchemy. Twentieth-century economist John Maynard Keynes, who purchased Newton's unpublished papers in 1936, wrote: "Newton was not the first of the age of reason. He was the last of the magicians [...] the last great mind that looked out on the visible and intellectual world with the same eyes as those who began to build our intellectual inheritance rather less than 10,000 years ago." Keynes' observation appears to be borne out by Newton's proposal to cure the plague by "combining powdered toad with the excretions and serum made into lozenges and worn about the affected area drove away the contagion and drew out the poison." It is an idea which owes more to occult practices than science, and I, for one, wonder why he had used no Eye of Newt(on).

Five hundred years in the future, the science fiction writer Arthur C. Clarke would write: "Any sufficiently advanced technology is indistinguishable from magic." But for many of the natural philosophers of the Scientific Revolution, their primary job was *distinguishing* science from magic and to do that, they had to dabble in many practices we now know to be discredited. The reason we know they are discredited is that through their investigations, these scientists disproved them.

Of course, some people went too far...

Sorcery, Alchemy, and the Devil's Three-Way

Without doubt, the wackiest individual of the Scientific Revolution was John Dee (1527–1608), English mathematician, teacher, natural philosopher, and occultist extraordinaire. Dee's interest veered between legitimate science and the most bizarre manifestations of occult study, including alchemy, sorcery, astrology, divination and my favorite, communing with angels. He was the court astronomer for Queen Elizabeth I, and made valuable contributions to mathematics and navigation.

However, it was his association with the very sketchy Sir Edward Kelley (1555–1597) that proved his extreme gullibility. Kelley was Dee's guide in "magical investigations." This meant conjuring spirits and eventually, conversing with angels. Conveniently, these angels would only speak through Kelley, who also claimed that an angelic entity named Madimi required that Kelley and Dee share everything, *including their wives*. While somewhat taken aback by being ordered by an angel to engage in a three-way, Dee and his wife eventually complied.

Fig. 4: Edward Kelley and John Dee "evoking a spirit."
(Ebenezer Sibly, Public domain, and S.E.W.)

The Royal Society

Freed from the repressive religious strictures of Cromwell by the Restoration of Charles II, and against the backdrop of the Great Fire of London, and yet another bout of the plague, the mid-seventeenth century saw the beginnings of a scientific community. The "Royal Society of London for Improving Natural Knowledge," or just plain old "Royal Society of London," was formed by Christopher Wren (1632–1723) who is best known for constructing St. Paul's Cathedral *and* sporting an epic periwig.

The Royal Society had been preceded by a loose and shadowy sounding group of natural philosophers with links to Freemasonry known as the "Invisible College." With such a name and pedigree, it's not surprising it's been linked to the Illuminati and featured in a Dan Brown novel. The Invisible College comprised Robert Boyle (1627–1691), who was both an alchemist and considered "the father of chemistry," and several natural philosopher buddies. Boyle also sported a periwig of heroic proportions.

Fig. 5: What every well-dressed scientist is wearing…
(L–R) Robert Boyle, Christopher Wren, or Isaac Newton:
(Public domain and S.E.W.)

The Royal Society morphed out of the Invisible College (probably when they realized what a sinister name it was). It was breathed into life during a lecture by Wren at Gresham College, London. This "Colledge for the promoting of Physico-Mathematicall Experimentall Learning" was for the study of mathematics and science, and for all its lofty aims was clearly not a Colledge for the promoting of Correkt Dictionery Speelling. Its stated aim was to "recognize, promote, and support excellence in science and to encourage the development and use of science for the benefit of humanity." In other words, promote collective learning.

The founding members of the Society adopted the motto "Nullius in verba," meaning "take nobody's word for it." Today, the Royal Society's website explains its motto like this: "It is an expression of the determination of Fellows to withstand the domination of authority and to verify all statements by an appeal to facts determined by experiment."

Or, in internet parlance, "Do your own research."

To that end, Robert Hooke (1635–1703), once a lab assistant to Robert Boyle and who became a famous scientist in his own right, was employed by the Royal Society to demonstrate experiments at their meetings. These experiments were performed using Hooke's own methods or methods suggested by members, and ranged across a number of disciplines, including biology, physics, and astronomy. His experiments were often inexplicable and macabre, such as displaying a living dog with an open thorax (the unfortunate pooch was kept alive by having air pumped in and out of its lungs with a pair of bellows). Nevertheless, Hooke was an acknowledged genius that some have dubbed, with perhaps a touch of hyperbole, "the English Leonardo da Vinci."

In the centuries since his death, Hooke's good name as a scientist has often been overshadowed by his reputation for being a prick. This idea is supported by the many adjectives used to describe him over this time: despicable, jealous, unscrupulous, envious, vengeful, cynical, difficult, and irritable, to name but a few. His reputation was not helped by his tendency to claim credit for discoveries that he didn't make.

The World's Most Vindictive Bastard?

The most famed instance of this was Hooke's dispute with Isaac Newton over ideas in Newton's pioneering *Philosophiæ Naturalis Principia Mathematica*. Hooke claimed credit for some ideas expressed in the *Principia* regarding gravitation. Newton, who was something of a prick himself, disputed this in the strongest terms. Hooke also took issue with some of Newton's theories in a manner which so offended Newton that he refused to further discuss these ideas in public.

Such was the depth of feeling that the feud between the two men continued well after Hooke's death. It is claimed that during Newton's time as president of the Royal Society, he deliberately mislaid or destroyed the only known portrait of his nemesis. Robert Hooke's scientific papers also went astray during Newton's presidency and weren't rediscovered for over three hundred years. If even one of these allegations is true, it would surely add the title: *World's Most Vindictive Bastard* to Newton's other accolades.

Newton versus Leibniz

When scientists get into a fight, it can get ugly. When the fight is about alleged plagiarism, it gets even uglier. Multiply that ugliness by ten when the scientists in question are as arrogant and pigheaded as Sir Isaac Newton and Gottfried Leibniz. These two giants of the Scientific Revolution both believed they had invented calculus, the branch of mathematics that studies rates of change, and allows the calculation of the movement of objects.

Calculus was a significant lightbulb moment, particularly for the fields of physics and engineering. It's invaluable in predicting the motion of astronomical bodies, modeling weather patterns, and the movement of sound and light, among many other uses. The advent of calculus has allowed myriad scientific discoveries and inventions. In fact, many of the technological advancements that make modern life possible owe their very existence to calculus.

Newton created his version of calculus in 1665, but did not publish his idea until 1704, supposedly because he previously feared that others would criticize his work. Leibniz invented his calculus around eight years after Newton and published it in 1684. Sir Isaac hadn't seen this coming and smelled a rat: had Leibniz seen an unpublished manuscript of his? Newton's acolytes accused Leibniz of plagiarism. Goaded by flunkies of his own, Leibniz countered these claims, but Newton's relentless campaign took its toll on Leibniz's credibility.

Even though the case against Leibniz was flimsy, Newton emerged from the fight with the credit for creating calculus. This is in spite of the fact that it's Leibniz's notation for calculus which is used to this day. Nowadays, the consensus is that Leibniz and Newton both created calculus independently of each other. Unfortunately, this is too little too late for Leibniz, who died poor and under the cloud of plagiarism.

At least he's vindicated today.

Fig. 6: There's nothing like a good scientific feud.
(Angelov, Orion_eff, Public domain and S.E.W.)

Philosophical Transactions of the Royal Society of London

For all this bewigged small-mindedness, the Royal Society of London was overwhelmingly a force for scientific advancement. In the over three hundred and fifty years since their inception, they published one of the most consequential scientific books of all time (Newton's *Principia*); promoted James Cook's voyage to Tahiti to observe the Transit of Venus (expediting the discovery of Australia and New Zealand); published the first account of vaccination against disease; documented the eruption of Krakatoa; and published all manner of cutting-edge research through *Philosophical Transactions*, which is the oldest science journal in the world.

However, it must be said that *Philosophical Transactions* did not *always* get things right. Adrien Auzout was a French astronomer who speculated in the esteemed journal about what Moon-men might observe of life on Earth. "Methinks, that the

Earth would to the people of the Moon appear to have a different face in the several seasons of the year," he wrote.

Auzout also wanted to build a 300-meter long telescope so he could monitor the behavior of the animals on the Moon. In one of their less enlightened moments, the Royal Society elevated Monsieur Auzout to fellowship on the basis of this bizarre paper.

Fig. 7: Alas, Monsieur Auzout's vision never came to fruition.
(Erica Guilane-Nachez and S.E.W.)

Owner of a Lonely Heart

For over a thousand years, most physicians believed Galen's theory that different types of blood circulated through the veins and arteries, emanating from either the heart or the liver.

There had been some doubters over the years, but it took William Harvey (1578–1657), to conclusively demonstrate the continuous circulation of blood through the human body.

Harvey performed external experiments on living humans to prove his theory, and even dissected the occasional hanged man. He also dissected *living* frogs, eels, crows, and dogs to observe their beating hearts. This obsession with animal cruelty in the name of science, particularly in relation to blood, leads us to some even more monstrous experiments...

A Mangy Dog Story

It also seemed that natural philosophers in the seventeenth century were consumed with the idea of transfusing animal blood between animals, and eventually, into humans. The members of the Royal Society were not immune to this obsession, as several papers published in *Philosophical Transactions* explained how experiments were performed on live dogs, attempting to transfer blood from one to another. In an article with the arresting title, "An Account of Another Experiment of Transfusion, vis Bleeding a Mangy into a Sound Dog," Thomas Coxe began his experiment in the following manner:

> *I procured an old mungrell curr, all over-run with the Mainge, of a middle size, and having, some hours before, fed him plentifully with cheese-parings and milk, I prepared the jugular vein, as we used to do the carotidal artery of the emittent animal, not designing anything further, than to determine by experiment the infection of the recipient's blood.*

Not only did these intrepid scientists explore dog-to-dog transfusion, they experimented with *interspecies* transfusion. In the same issue that Coxe's experiment was described, there was an account of an attempt to transfuse blood from a calf to a sheep.

Of course, French researcher Jean-Baptiste Denys of the Paris-based *Académie des Sciences* was at the *real* cutting edge of interspecies transfusion. His grand idea was to decant the blood of a sheep into a human recipient. In a world where turning lead into gold and the Elixir of Life still seemed within reach, the idea that animal and human blood were interchangeable didn't seem that crazy. However, the experiment didn't go well for either the human *or* the sheep. And while Denys was subsequently found not guilty of murder, the court ruled that such experiments should cease because "the risk that science could create monsters—or worse, corrupt the entire human race with foreign blood—was simply too much to bear."

Fig. 8: History shows it wasn't. (Midjourney Collection and S.E.W.)

Yet despite the Royal Society's early eccentricities, many of which would have had today's animal rights protestors baying for blood, few organizations have done as much to increase the collective learning of humanity. It is the oldest organization of its type in the world, played no small part in the birth of modern science, and remains prestigious and influential to this day. To its credit, the Royal Society owns its mistakes and past atrocities, and their website is where I was able to access much of the detail written above. Over the centuries, famous Fellows of the Society have numbered such luminaries as Isaac Newton, Christopher Wren, Robert Hooke, Charles Darwin, Ernest Rutherford, Albert Einstein, Alan Turing, and Stephen Hawking, to name but a few.

And if Adrien Auzout had been right about the people and animals on the Moon, it would not only have given Neil Armstrong a hell of a shock, but it would also have ensured his name was emblazoned alongside those of Newton, Darwin *et al*.

Alas, it is not.

Samuel Pepys

Samuel Pepys (1633–1703) is remembered today for his comprehensive diary: a fascinating primary source documenting the upper-class life of London following the restoration of Charles II. Although he was not high-born (his father was a tailor), Pepys became one of the most important men of his day by virtue of his education. He attended school in Huntingdon, and finished his schooling at St. Paul's School, London. From there, he received a scholarship to Magdalene College. He received his degree in 1653, not long after having been admonished by the college for having been "scandalously overserved with drink."

Pepys began his working life as a treasurer of the Royal Navy, with little knowledge of the navy or accounting practices. He would later become a member of Parliament, and he was the president of the Royal Society when they published Newton's *Philosophiae Naturalis Principia Mathematica*.

Most academic interest in Pepys' diary is focused on the insight it offers into life in London during this tumultuous era. However, I would be remiss to ignore the light it sheds on cultural attitudes towards collective learning at the time.

There are many references that demonstrate how Pepys' curious nature had made him into a tireless learner. It seemed every social occasion was an opportunity for him to improve his knowledge or contribute to the knowledge of others.

Apart from the joy Pepys had in learning, he often reflected upon his years at "Paul's Schoole." His diary shows that he regularly met up with old buddies from St. Paul's and attended school functions. He also attended functions at his alma mater, Magdalene College, Cambridge. The implication is that Pepys and other men of his class esteemed education for education's sake.

Pepys was the trusted companion both of Charles II and James II, and he numbered Christopher Wren, Isaac Newton, and almost every eminent scholar of the age, among his friends. He also shared their peculiar fashion sense: "I found that my coming in a periwig did not prove so strange to the world as I was afeared it would..."

Yes, like many men of his era, Pepys was a keen periwig wearer. In 1663, he shaved his head and purchased his first wig. However, when the plague hit London, he became concerned about the future of this must-have fashion statement: "It is a wonder what will be the fashion after the plague is done as to periwigs, for nobody will dare to buy any haire for fear of the infection—that it had been cut off of the heads of people dead of the plague." Ever the dandy, Pepys preferred valor to discretion. A diary entry in September 1665 notes that he bought a new periwig even though "the plague was in Westminster when I bought it." He decided that, as it had been "a good while since" the purchase, he could now safely wear his new accessory.

Fig. 9: Samuel Pepys and his not-so-strange periwig (Midjouney and S.E.W.)

A Word about Periwigs

A brief aside regarding the seventeenth century's obsession with the periwig. Nowadays, men endure little stigma for developing male pattern baldness. But this was not always the case. In the early modern era, male pattern baldness was a sign of old age and lack of virility. It made one the butt of jokes. Can you imagine a serious-minded scientist allowing anything like that to puncture his sense of dignity? In the dark ages before head-shaving became trendy, and before the invention of Propecia or Rogaine, there was only one answer: a periwig.

The periwig was an enormous intentionally unrealistic wig worn by well-to-do men during the seventeenth and eighteenth centuries. The early periwigs were often made of horsehair, commonly rendering them uncomfortable for the wearer. To combat this discomfort (and to help ward off lice and odor) men sometimes powdered their wigs. Enormous periwigs were the height of fashion among men of power at this time. They are literally the etymology for the word "bigwig." Competition for the grandest mop-top in the Royal Society must have been fierce, although one presumes the winner was compensating for something.

Perhaps a lack of scientific skill? Or something else...

Of course, there was at least one thing more embarrassing than baldness for the seventeenth-century gent: Syphilis. The "pox" was rife in the 1600s, and its lesser side effects included balding and open sores on the head. What better way to disguise those unsightly and embarrassing symptoms than with a monumental periwig? The bigger, the better. Of course, this cosmetic remedy only went so far. The Center for Disease Control advises that in its advanced stages, syphilis can cause "altered behavior, difficulty coordinating muscle movements, paralysis, sensory deficits, and dementia." At that point, it really doesn't matter how big your wig is.

I know, I know. I'm banging on about periwigs when they have little connection to big ideas. But hear me out: In the seventeenth century, periwigs lent their wearers gravitas and a certain credibility. In short, sporting a massive wig enhanced a man's reputation and guaranteed he would be taken seriously.

So basically, the opposite of what it does now.

Animalcule Magnetism

Dutch cloth merchant Antonie van Leeuwenhoek (1632–1723), was an unlikely candidate to rub shoulders with the demigods of the Royal Society. He came from a humble family of drapers and didn't have a university education. To add insult to injury, he knew no Latin, which was the *lingua franca* of European intellectuals. These setbacks would usually have excluded van Leeuwenhoek from an active role in the scientific community.

It's likely that van Leeuwenhoek was inspired after reading Robert Hooke's book *Micrographia*, which detailed Hooke's own experiments with early microscopes. By 1668, he had learned to grind lenses and had begun to make observations with simple, homemade microscopes.

There's a popular misconception that van Leeuwenhoek was the inventor of the microscope. In actuality, the microscopes had existed for over one hundred years. Van Leeuwenhoek's genius was in exponentially improving the instrument. For the most part, he was self-taught, but this meant he came to his studies unencumbered by existing scientific prejudices.

Van Leeuwenhoek also brought a curious mind and practical skills to his work, and this yielded amazing results. His microscope revealed a world populated with never-before-seen microscopic creatures which he named "animalcules." He was the first person to observe bacteria, protists, blood cells, and sperm cells (history doesn't record where he sourced this).

Eventually, his research brought him to the attention of the Royal Society, and in 1680, they elected him a full member. Eventually, as the illustration below proves, Antonie van Leeuwenhoek got his bigwig, and is now considered "the Father of Microbiology."

Fig. 10: And don't even get him started on the sperm cells...
(Public domain and S.E.W.)

Goodbye Alchemy, Hello Science Denial?

The boffins of the Scientific Revolution had, through the application of Bacon's scientific method, put an end to the "legitimate" study of alchemy and astrology. While achieving this, they forever split the wide-ranging study of natural philosophy into the discrete scientific domains of physics, chemistry, and biology. The sheer number of "Fathers of [insert appropriate area of science here]" mentioned in this chapter is staggering. The rapid scientific learning during this period exponentially increased the pool of human intellectual property and laid the groundwork for the Enlightenment.

And not just the Enlightenment...

Our entire modern way of life, from sophisticated health care to space travel, and everything in between, is only possible because of advances set in motion by the Scientific Revolution. It's deeply ironic that the internet, the miracle of modern technology that is the greatest compendium of human knowledge ever known, is also the most pernicious source of science denial. If the descent into idiocy is not arrested, then my optimistic view of humanity's ongoing growth will be categorically and tragically proven wrong.

Knuckle-draggers, Luddites, and know-nothings have risen before in human history. But knowledge, freedom, and science have always eventually triumphed over ignorance and led the way out of darkness and into the future.

I may be naive, but I believe they will again.

* * *

—Conclusion—

Winds of Change

Colonizer? What Colonizer?

"What the hell?" I hear some readers exclaim. "Where's the chapter on colonization?"

Those who've been reading closely might think I've "pulled a swifty" (to use the Australian vernacular for deliberately deceiving someone). After all, how did I manage to finish this book without fully dealing with the dreaded "C" word? It's a fair question which requires an answer.

After chapters on the Age of Discovery and the great trading companies, a chapter on colonialism might have seemed the next logical step. And yet, while I've mentioned colonization a few times, particularly in relation to South America, the Spice Islands, and India, I haven't examined it in a global context. That's because, for structural reasons, I've decided to leave the chapter on colonization to the next *Lightbulb Moments in Human History* book.

I'm aware, of course, that shunting this burning topic to a future book artificially bolsters my argument. Remember, I'm claiming that humanity is on an upward trajectory. Ending this book on the high of the Scientific Revolution helps foster that impression. It certainly beats ending with a chapter in which the West subjugates and dispossesses the indigenous populations of North America, Africa, and Australasia.

We'll have plenty of time to examine that tragedy in the next book.

Fig. 1: Sleight of hand… (Evgeniy Parilov and S.E.W.)

Nothin' up My Sleeve

Yet, even without this sleight-of-hand trick, I'm confident that I've gone much further towards proving my thesis than I did in *From Cave to Colosseum*. I'm not backing away from my convictions—I believe they are on the mark in the context of the era. For those who haven't read that book, here are the main takeaways.

Over millennia, the ancient world steadily accumulated knowledge. That said, there's only limited evidence that the lives of ancient people improved as a result. Humans had spent millennia developing the killer apps of the ancient world: tool use, language, agriculture, and writing. Once those advances were in place, we saw an explosion of organized religion, philosophy, science, the growth of cities, and amazing strides in artistic expression. Over thousands of years, these lightbulb moments were refined by the slow but sure accumulation of collective learning.

During this time, life expectancy at birth remained stagnant. The day-to-day existence of Bronze Age agricultural laborers differed little from that of Roman farm workers. In fact, researchers now believe that Paleolithic hunter-gatherers worked less, enjoyed better food, and had longer lives than either of those. Yet, our ancient forebears made critical progress in accumulating the intellectual and cultural capital that allowed future progress. *From Cave to Colosseum* had demonstrated human growth. But it was clear, even to a cock-eyed optimist such as myself, that my thesis wasn't fully proven. I had plenty of work to do.

Hence the need for *Lightbulb Moments in Human History: From Peasants to Periwigs*.

From Peasants to Periwigs

Humankind progressed exponentially over the course of *From Peasants to Periwigs*. We began in the Middle Ages, which are generally conceded to be a low point in European history. Then we looked at the Islamic Golden Age, which was the conduit through which Classical knowledge would be reintroduced to Europe to ignite, first the Renaissance, and then a boom in exploration and scientific thinking.

However, it wasn't all one-way traffic towards a bright and shiny future. The underclasses of the time struggled to survive in an overwhelmingly agricultural world, battling poverty, pestilence, and prejudice. The myriad artistic, cultural, philosophical, religious, and scientific advances did little to benefit the poorest people in society.

And yet, there *was* progress.

Fig.2: Alas not for the poorest. (Master1305 and S.E.W.)

The killer app of this era was the printing press. It's impossible to overstate its importance—it quite simply enabled the early modern world to spring into being. Where would we be today without mass produced books? We certainly wouldn't have seen much in the way of medical or scientific advances. And with no way of manufacturing books in large quantities, there'd be precious little literature. Without printed pamphlets, political ideas would take much longer to disseminate.

There'd certainly be no computers or internet.

In fact, without printing, we'd still have rock bottom levels of literacy and be struggling to build collective learning beyond medieval levels. If Buckminster Fuller was correct, and human knowledge did indeed double every hundred years prior to 1900, then the *only* reason that was possible was the printed word.

Over the course of this book, average life expectancy at birth improved modestly, from 35 years to 40 years. While this is nothing to write home about, there had to be certain advances in science and medicine before average lifespans could be significantly extended. That work was done by the natural philosophers of the Islamic, Renaissance, and early modern worlds.

The preliminary work had been completed. Now collective learning was poised to take off in a big way.

When, at the conclusion of *From Cave to Colosseum*, I cited Carl Sagan's famous assertion, "extraordinary claims require extraordinary evidence," I knew I hadn't done enough to prove the "extraordinary claim" in my thesis. In *From Peasants to Periwigs* I invoke Dr. Sagan again, because this time the evidence piling up *is* extraordinary.

So... Have I sufficiently demonstrated my thesis *now*?

If I'm being honest, I believe I haven't proved it beyond a reasonable doubt. There's *still* more work to do.

*

Hold My Beer

So, this ends the second volume of my extended reply to the pub argument I had with C.J.... I'm well on my way to proving my point, and a cursory glance at what's ahead history-wise only reinforces my belief that my case is only going to get stronger.

Would it be petty of me to FedEx a copy to C.J., claiming victory after all these years? Would it?

I can already picture the scene:

A doorbell rings. C.J. opens it to find a FedEx guy, who hands him a book-sized mailing satchel.

"But I didn't order anything." C.J. stares quizzically at the parcel.

"Just sign here, sir."

"Okay, sure." He signs the screen with his finger, closes the door, then starts to rip open the package. It takes a few seconds longer than he expects, because tearing the tough plastic of those satchels isn't easy. Then he reaches in and removes a book... It takes a second to register who has written it. "Why that son of a bit—"

—The End—

Acknowledgements

With a Little Help from My Friends

It's ironic that, despite the solitary nature of writing, the reality is that books aren't created in isolation. This book is no exception. *Lightbulb Moments in Human History: From Peasants to Periwigs* couldn't have been written without a lot of support, both now and in the past.

Way back in the 1990s when the internet was in its infancy, I met Janet Kent from the now defunct Writelinks.com in the #friendlypencil internet relay chat room. She provided invaluable assistance at the beginning of my writing journey. Unfortunately, we lost contact, and over the years I've tried many times to communicate with her, to no avail. Wherever she may be, I pay tribute to her inspirational teaching and encouragement.

I also want to thank Tamian Wood of Beyonddesignbooks. com. She gave me insightful critiques on the cover concepts for both *From Cave to Colosseum* and *From Peasants to Periwigs*, greatly improving both.

In addition, it was through Tamian's wonderful Facebook group, Author's Resource, that I met my editor Jim Bessey, of So Write Editing. Jim did what good editors are supposed to do: he challenged me, and made the book better as a result. He picked up on my mistakes and pointed out places where readers might justifiably want clarification or more information. Having said that, any errors or omissions remain my responsibility. Thank you so much, Jim – two down, more to come!

My old friend (and he *is* old, because he's a few months older than me) Brian Wilkie was the beta reader of *From Peasants to Periwigs* and gave invaluable feedback. I'm particularly indebted to him for reminding me about the Cronulla Public School excursion to see *Chariots of the Gods?* at the Odeon.

Another old friend, Colin Howe, was a constant sounding board. Our irreverent Sunday night chats as we recorded our podcast *What's My Age Again?* (if you haven't heard it, you really should) always made me laugh and ensured I didn't take myself, or this publishing thing, too seriously. Nevertheless, it was Colin's 1996 publication of his book *Diary of a Team* that made me realize that getting my work in print wasn't merely a pipe dream.

Short takes: My friends at Artarmon Public School always offered encouragement, and I appreciate them all. The #writingcommunity of Twitter has also been very supportive, particularly Sheila Young, Mika Paananen, and Terry Melia, who read advance reader copies of *From Cave to Colosseum* and were kind enough to review my work.

Thanks also to the crew at John Hunt Publishing for their vision in backing the *Lightbulb Moments in Human History* series at a time when nobody else seemed interested. I particularly appreciate the ongoing efforts of my publicist, Ben Blundell.

Lastly, to my children, Sarah, Sebastian, and Cate: We're like a single-parent Brady Bunch, aren't we? We all struggle to explain the complexity of our connections (my bad, I'm sorry!), but no matter how unconventional our family is, being Dad to each of you has been the privilege of my life. I love you all very much – this one's for you.

Scott Edwin Williams

Sydney, January 2023

From the Author

Dear Reader,

I hope you enjoyed reading *Lightbulb Moments in Human History: From Peasants to Periwigs* as much as I enjoyed writing it. If you have the time, please consider leaving a review on your preferred online platform. Additionally, if you'd like to stay updated on the next in the *Lightbulb Moments in Human History* series, visit www.lightbulbmomentshistory.com, where you can see news, fun videos, recent blog posts, and subscribe to my newsletter.

Warm regards,

Scott Edwin Williams

Bibliography

"8 Oldest Pyramids in the World." *Oldest.org*, 8 Nov. 2017, www.oldest.org/structures/pyramids/.

Acocella, Joan. "How Martin Luther Changed the World." *The New Yorker*, 23 Oct. 2017, www.newyorker.com/magazine/2017/10/30/how-martin-luther-changed-the-world.

"Act of Supremacy 1534." *Www.parliament.uk*, www.parliament.uk/about/living-heritage/transformingsociety/private-lives/religion/collections/common-prayer/act-of-supremacy/#:~:text=In%201534%20Parliament%20passed%20the.

Adhikari, Saugat. "Top 10 Amazing and Fascinating Facts about Saladin." *Ancient History Lists*, 9 Apr. 2019, www.ancienthistorylists.com/egypt-history/top-10-facts-saladin/.

"a History of Britain in Numbers: Education on Apple Podcasts." *Apple Podcasts*, podcasts.apple.com/au/podcast/education/id766470177?i=1000194651743. Accessed 22 Sept. 2020.

Alfani, Guido. "The Effects of Plague on the Distribution of Property: Ivrea, Northern Italy 1630." *Population Studies*, vol. 64, no. 1, Mar. 2010, pp. 61–75, https://doi.org/10.1080/00324720903448712.

Al Jazeera. "Shock: The First Crusade and the Conquest of Jerusalem | the Crusades: An Arab Perspective Ep1." *Www.youtube.com*, 2016, www.youtube.com/watch?v=HProiNnmGwI&t=147s.

Alter, Robert. "The Art of Biblical Translation and the Eloquence of the King James Version." *ABC Religion & Ethics*, 5 Feb. 2019, www.abc.net.au/religion/the-eloquence-of-the-king-james-version-of-the-bible/10781354.

"Antonie van Leeuwenhoek | the Royal Society." *Royalsociety.org*, 2020, makingscience.royalsociety.org/s/rs/people/fst00039851.

Arkenberg, Rebecca. "Music in the Renaissance." *Metmuseum.org*, Oct. 2002, www.metmuseum.org/toah/hd/renm/hd_renm.htm.

Ashley, Maurice. "Charles I | Biography, Accomplishments, & Facts." *Encyclopædia Britannica*, 2019, www.britannica.com/biography/Charles-I-king-of-Great-Britain-and-Ireland.

Aubrey, John, and Kate Bennett. *Brief Lives*. Oxford University Press, 2016.

Avery, Dan. "13 LGBTQ Royals You Didn't Learn about in History Class." *NBC News*, 18 Oct. 2021, www.nbcnews.com/nbc-out/nbc-out-proud/13-lgbtq-royals-didnt-learn-history-class-rcna3097.

"Aztec Education: Learning at Home and School - History." *History*, 14 June 2018, www.historyonthenet.com/aztec-education-at-home-and-school.

Baker, David. "Collective Learning as a Key Concept in Big History." *Sociostudies.org*, 2010, www.sociostudies.org/almanac/articles/collective_learning_as_a_key_concept_in_big_history/.

—. *The Shortest History of the World*. Black Inc., 2022.

Barlow, Frank. "William I | Biography, Reign, & Facts." *Encyclopædia Britannica*, 20 Dec. 2018, www.britannica.com/biography/William-I-king-of-England.

Barnhart, Edwin. "Lost Worlds of South America." *Www.wondrium.com*, 2012, www.wondrium.com/lost-worlds-of-south-america?lec=19.

Bauer, Susan Wise. *The History of the Medieval World: From the Conversion of Constantine to the First Crusade*. W.W. Norton, 2010.

Baynes, Chris. "Most Americans Say 'Arabic Numerals' Should Not Be Taught in School, Finds Survey." *The Independent*, 17 May 2019, www.independent.co.uk/news/arabic-numerals-survey-prejudice-bias-survey-research-civic-science-a8918256.html.

Beck, James. "SER PIERO DA VINCI and HIS SON LEONARDO." *Source: Notes in the History of Art*, vol. 5, no. 1, Oct. 1985, pp. 29–32, https://doi.org/10.1086/sou.5.1.23202260.

Blakemore, Erin. "How the East India Company Became the World's Most Powerful Business." *Culture,* 6 Sept. 2019, www.nationalgeographic.com/culture/article/british-east-india-trading-company-most-powerful-business?loggedin=true.

Bloudhoff-Indelicato, Mollie. *Beaver Butts Emit Goo Used for Vanilla Flavoring.* 1 Oct. 2013, www.nationalgeographic.com/animals/article/beaver-butt-goo-vanilla-flavoring.

Blumberg, Naomi. "Nicola Pisano | Italian Sculptor." *Encyclopedia Britannica,* www.britannica.com/biography/Nicola-Pisano. Accessed 2020.

Bryson, Bill. *Shakespeare: The World as Stage.* Atlas Books/Harpercollins, 2007.

Cain, Áine. "9 Famous Predictions by Nostradamus Some People Say Foresaw the Future." *Business Insider,* 2018, www.businessinsider.com/predictions-of-nostradamus-2011-12.

"Cannabis (Marijuana) and Cannabinoids: What You Need to Know." *NCCIH,* www.nccih.nih.gov/health/cannabis-marijuana-and-cannabinoids-what-you-need-to-know#:~:text=THC%20is%20the%20substance%20that.

Cartwright, Mark. "Aztec Pantheon." *World History Encyclopedia,* 2017, member.worldhistory.org/article/1034/aztec-pantheon/.

—. "Aztec Sacrifice." *World History Encyclopedia,* member.worldhistory.org/Aztec_Sacrifice/. Accessed 5 Mar. 2022.

—. "Cusco." *World History Encyclopedia,* 30 Jan. 2015, www.worldhistory.org/Cuzco/.

—. "Henry VIII of England." *World History Encyclopedia,* 2020, www.worldhistory.org/Henry_VIII_of_England/.

—. "Medieval Castle." *World History Encyclopedia,* 17 May 2018, www.worldhistory.org/Medieval_Castle/.

—. "Medieval Trades." *Ancient History Encyclopedia,* Ancient History Encyclopedia, 6 Dec. 2018, www.ancient.eu/Medieval_Trades/.

—. "Nazca Civilization." *World History Encyclopedia,* 23 May 2014, www.worldhistory.org/Nazca_Civilization/.

—. "Serf." *World History Encyclopedia*, 4 Dec. 2018, www.worldhistory. org/Serf/.

—. "The Assassins." *World History Encyclopedia*, www.worldhistory. org/The_Assassins/. Accessed 24 Apr. 2022.

—. "The Daily Life of Medieval Monks." *World History Encyclopedia*, 13 Dec. 2018, www.worldhistory.org/article/1293/the-daily-life-of-medieval-monks/.

Cassidy, Cody. *Who Ate the First Oyster?: The Extraordinary People behind the Greatest Firsts in History*. Headline Book Publishing, 2021.

"Ceaseless Motion: William Harvey's Experiments in Circulation." *RCP London*, 24 Oct. 2017, www.rcplondon. ac.uk/events/ceaseless-motion-william-harveys-experiments-circulation#:~:text=Within%20his%20London%20home%2C%20 Harvey.

Chacon, Richard J., and David H. Dye. *The Taking and Displaying of Human Body Parts as Trophies by Amerindians*. Springer, 2007.

Childress, Diana. *Johannes Gutenberg and the Printing Press*. Twenty-First Century Books, 2008.

Christian, David. *Origin Story: A Big History of Everything*. Penguin Books, 2019.

Coleman, John. "Mūsā I of Mali | Emperor of Mali." *Encyclopædia Britannica*, 27 Sept. 2018, www.britannica.com/biography/ Musa-I-of-Mali.

Cole, Michael. "Cross-Cultural and Historical Perspectives on the Developmental Consequences of Education." *Human Development*, vol. 48, no. 4, 2005, pp. 195–216, https://doi. org/10.1159/000086855.

Collections, Special. "Tarlton Law Library: Exhibit – Aztec and Maya Law: Aztec Social Structure." *Tarlton.law.utexas. edu*, 8 Nov. 2018, tarlton.law.utexas.edu/aztec-and-maya-law/aztec-social-structure#:~:text=The%20Aztecs%20 followed%20a%20strict.

Collins, Ben. "How Erstwhile English Pirate William Dampier Helped Undermine Indigenous Australia." *ABC News*, 3 Nov. 2018, www.abc.net.au/news/2018-11-04/william-dampiers-terra-nullius-set-the-tone-for-australia/10420338.

Conocimiento, Ventana al. "Hooke, the Genius Whose Big Mistake Was Confronting Newton." *OpenMind*, 31 July 2019, www.bbvaopenmind.com/en/science/leading-figures/hooke-the-genius-whose-big-mistake-was-confronting-newton/#:~:text=Newton.

Coxe, Thomas. "An Account of Another Experiment of Transfusion, Viz. Of Bleeding a Mangy into a Sound Dog." *Philosophical Transactions of the Royal Society of London*, vol. 2, no. 25, Dec. 1666, pp. 451–52, https://doi.org/10.1098/rstl.1666.0012.

Cybulskie, Danièle. "Courage under Fire: Richard II and the Peasants' Revolt." *Medievalists.net*, 29 June 2020, www.medievalists.net/2020/06/richard-ii-peasants-revolt/.

Dalrymple, Adam. "20 Facts about the East India Company." *History Hit*, 2019, www.historyhit.com/facts-about-the-east-india-company/.

Deacon Keith Fournier. "St. Thomas Aquinas, a Corpulent Man Nicknamed the Dumb Ox Shows Us How to Live for Jesus." *Catholic News Agency*, www.catholicnewsagency.com/column/53436/st-thomas-aquinas-a-corpulent-man-nicknamed-the-dumb-ox-shows-us-how-to-live-for-jesus.

Dean, James M. "Why I Can't Be a Nun: Introduction | Robbins Library Digital Projects." *D.lib.rochester.edu*, 1991, d.lib.rochester.edu/teams/text/dean-six-ecclesiastical-satires-why-i-cant-be-a-nun-introduction.

"Definition of Humanism." *American Humanist Association*, americanhumanist.org/what-is-humanism/definition-of-humanism/#:~:text=Humanism%20is%20a%20rational%20philosophy.

De León, Christina. "Paracas Mummy Bundles." *Www.bgc. bard.edu*, Mar. 2017, www.bgc.bard.edu/research-forum/ articles/358/paracas-mum.

Dershowitz, Idan. "Opinion | the Secret History of Leviticus." *The New York Times*, 21 July 2018, www.nytimes.com/2018/07/21/ opinion/sunday/bible-prohibit-gay-sex.html.

dhwty. "Xochiquetzal: Aztec Goddess of Beauty, Pleasure and Love... but Don't Mess with Her!" *Ancient-Origins.net*, Ancient Origins, 14 July 2018, www.ancient-origins.net/ancient-places-americas/xochiquetzal-aztec-goddess-0010372.

Diamond, Jared M. *Guns, Germs and Steel : A Short History of Everybody for the Last 13,000 Years*. Vintage, 2019.

—. *The Rise and Fall of the Third Chimpanzee*. Vintage, 2007.

Diouf, Sylviane A. *Kings and Queens of West Africa*. Franklin Watts, 2001.

Dreamstime. "Stock Photos, Pictures and Royalty-Free Images by Dreamstime." *Stock Photos, Pictures and Royalty-Free Images by Dreamstime*, 2020, www.dreamstime.com/stock-photos.

Duggan, Lawrence G. "Indulgence | Roman Catholicism." *Encyclopædia Britannica*, 25 Nov. 2015, www.britannica.com/ topic/indulgence.

Durant, Will. *The Greatest Minds and Ideas of All Time*. Simon & Schuster International, 2003.

(Ed: D.S.) Courie, Leonard W. *The Black Death and Peasant's Revolt*. New York: Wayland Publishers, 1972; Strayer, Joseph R., ed. *Dictionary of the Middle Ages*. New York: Charles Scribner's Sons. Vol. 2. pp. 257–267.

"Education in Europe – from the Renaissance to the Enlightenment." *Jrank.org*, 2019, science.jrank.org/ pages/9078/Education-in-Europe-From-Renaissance-Enlightenment.html.

"Escape from Delhi to the Maldive Islands and Sri Lanka: 1341–1344 | ORIAS." *Orias.berkeley.edu*, orias.berkeley.edu/

resources-teachers/travels-ibn-battuta/journey/escape-delhi-maldive-islands-and-sri-lanka-1341-1344.

Eschner, Kat. "350 Years Ago, a Doctor Performed the First Human Blood Transfusion. A Sheep Was Involved." *Smithsonian Magazine,* www.smithsonianmag.com/smart-news/350-years-ago-doctor-performed-first-human-blood-transfusion-sheep-was-involved-180963631/. Accessed 27 Dec. 2020.

Evans, Robert. *A (Brief) History of Vice: How Bad Behavior Built Civilization.* A Plume Book, 2016.

Faruqi, Yasmeen. "Contributions of Islamic Scholars to the Scientific Enterprise." *International Education Journal,* vol. 7, no. 4, 2006, pp. 391–99, files.eric.ed.gov/fulltext/EJ854295.pdf.

FitzSimons, Peter. *James Cook: The Story behind the Man Who Mapped the World.* Hachette Australia, 2021.

Flood, Alison. "Isaac Newton Proposed Curing Plague with Toad Vomit, Unseen Papers Show." *The Guardian,* 2 June 2020, www.theguardian.com/books/2020/jun/02/isaac-newton-plague-cure-toad-vomit.

Ford, Brian J. "Antony van Leeuwenhoek." *Berkeley.edu,* 2019, ucmp.berkeley.edu/history/leeuwenhoek.html.

"Founders Online: From Benjamin Franklin to All Captains and Commanders of Ameri...." *Founders.archives.gov,* founders.archives.gov/documents/Franklin/01-29-02-0057. Accessed 2 Oct. 2022.

Friedland, Gerald. "Discovery of the Function of the Heart and Circulation of Blood." *Cardiovascular Journal of Africa,* vol. 20, no. 3, May 2009, p. 160, www.ncbi.nlm.nih.gov/pmc/articles/PMC3721262/#:~:text=He%20tried%20to%20force%20blood.

Fullagar, Kate. "The Stories of Tupaia and Omai and Their Vital Role as Captain Cook's Unsung Shipmates." *The Conversation,* 29 Apr. 2020, theconversation.com/the-stories-of-tupaia-and-omai-and-their-vital-role-as-captain-cooks-unsung-shipmates-126674.

Gabriel, Richard A. "Muhammad: The Warrior Prophet." *HistoryNet*, 17 May 2007, www.historynet.com/muhammad-the-warrior-prophet.htm#:~:text=The%20idea%20of%20 Muhammad%20as.

"Galen – Used, First, Blood, Body, Uses, Galens Errors." *Www. discoveriesinmedicine.com*, www.discoveriesinmedicine. com/General-Information-and-Biographies/Galen. html#ixzz7bBYes0hT. Accessed 6 Aug. 2022.

Ghosh, Sanjib Kumar. "Human Cadaveric Dissection: A Historical Account from Ancient Greece to the Modern Era." *Anatomy & Cell Biology*, vol. 48, no. 3, 2015, p. 153, https://doi. org/10.5115/acb.2015.48.3.153.

Gilder, Joshua, and Anne-Lee Gilder. *Heavenly Intrigue: Johannes Kepler, Tycho Brahe, and the Murder behind One of History's Greatest Scientific Discoveries.* Anchor Books, 2005.

Gillespie, Susan D. *The Aztec Kings: The Construction of Rulership in Mexica History.* University Of Arizona Press, 2016.

Giorgio Vasari, et al. *Vasari's Lives of the Artists: Giotto, Masaccio, Fra Filippo Lippi, Botticelli, Leonardo, Raphael, Michelangelo, Titian.* Dover Publications, 2005.

Google. "Google." *Google.com*, 4 Sept. 1998, www.google.com.

Gottlieb, Anthony. *The Dream of Reason: A History of Western Philosophy from the Greeks to the Renaissance.* W.W. Norton & Company, 2016.

Grant, Stan. "Between the Ship and the Shore: The Captain James Cook I Know." *The Sydney Morning Herald*, 27 Apr. 2020, www.smh.com.au/national/between-the-ship-and-the-shore-the-captain-james-cook-i-know-20200427-p54ni3.html.

Handwerk, Brian. "Inca Child Sacrifice Victims Were Drugged." *Culture*, 29 July 2013, www.nationalgeographic.com/culture/ article/130729-inca-mummy-maiden-sacrifice-coca-alcohol-drug-mountain-andes-children?loggedin=true.

Harding, Luke. "Kant's Wild Years." *The Guardian*, 12 Feb. 2004, www.theguardian.com/world/2004/feb/12/highereducation.artsandhumanities.

HeritageDaily. "Maya Crypt Contains Cremation Burials Used for Making Rubber Balls in Ritual Ball Games." *HeritageDaily – Archaeology News*, 1 Aug. 2022, www.heritagedaily.com/2022/08/maya-crypt-contains-cremation-burials-used-for-making-rubber-balls-in-ritual-ball-games/144250?amp&mibextid=GwLpAq.

History.com Editors. "Printing Press." *HISTORY*, A&E Television Networks, 21 Aug. 2018, www.history.com/topics/inventions/printing-press.

"History of Information." *Www.historyofinformation.com*, www.historyofinformation.com/. Accessed 21 Apr. 2021.

Hobsbawm, Eric J. *The Machine Breakers.* 1950.

Holmes, Grace, et al. "The Death of Young King Edward VI." *New England Journal of Medicine*, vol. 345, no. 1, July 2001, pp. 60–62, https://doi.org/10.1056/nejm200107053450111.

Horwitz, Tony. *Blue Latitudes*. Hermes House, 2002.

Houtrouw, Alicia Maria. "Forbidden Love in the Andes: Murúa and Guaman Poma Retell the Myth of Chuquillanto and Acoytapra." *Getty Research Journal*, vol. 11, Jan. 2019, pp. 161–84, https://doi.org/10.1086/702752.

"How the King James Bible Changed the World." *Baylor Magazine, Summer 2011 | Baylor University*, 21 June 2011, www.baylor.edu/alumni/magazine/0904/news.php?action=story&story=95758.

Hrbek, Ivan. "Ibn Battuta | Biography, History, Travels, & Map | Britannica." *Encyclopædia Britannica*, 2019, www.britannica.com/biography/Ibn-Battuta.

"Inca Civilization – New World Encyclopedia." *Newworldencyclopedia.org*, 2020, www.newworldencyclopedia.org/entry/Inca_Civilization.

"In Our Time: History: Education on Apple Podcasts." *Apple Podcasts*, podcasts.apple.com/au/podcast/education/id463700741?i=1000377914926. Accessed 22 Sept. 2020.

Isaacson, Walter. *Leonardo Da Vinci: The Biography*. Simon & Schuster, 2018.

Islandculturearchivalsupport. "The Octopus – a Fijian Legend." *Island Time*, 16 Mar. 2017, islandculturearchivalsupport. wordpress.com/2017/03/16/the-octopus-a-fijian-legend/.

"James Cook and the Transit of Venus | Science Mission Directorate." *Nasa.gov*, 2018, science.nasa.gov/science-news/science-at-nasa/2004/28may_cook.

James, Tom. "BBC – History – British History in Depth: Black Death: The Lasting Impact." *Bbc.co.uk*, 2011, www.bbc.co.uk/history/british/middle_ages/black_impact_01.shtml.

Jamieson, Lee. "'The Influence of the Renaissance in Shakespeare's Work.'" *ThoughtCo*, 26 2020, thoughtco.com/renaissance-shakespeares-time-2984986.

John, Terence, and John Russell. "William Shakespeare | Facts, Life, & Plays." *Encyclopædia Britannica*, 20 Oct. 2018, www. britannica.com/biography/William-Shakespeare.

Kameʻeleihiwa, Lilikalā K. "How the Foolish Rumour That Hawaiians Ate Cook Began." *NITV*, www.sbs.com.au/nitv/article/2019/02/14/how-foolish-rumour-hawaiians-ate-cook-began. Accessed 14 Mar. 2021.

Kann, Drew. "Eight of the Worst Popes in Church History." *CNN*, 15 Apr. 2018, edition.cnn.com/2018/04/10/europe/catholic-church-most-controversial-popes/index.html.

Kehoe, Marsely L. "Dutch Batavia: Exposing the Hierarchy of the Dutch Colonial City." *Journal of Historians of Netherlandish Art*, 2015, jhna.org/articles/dutch-batavia-exposing-hierarchy-dutch-colonial-city/.

Kent, Steven. "Of Spice and Men: How Spices Built the VoC." *Epochmagazine*, 30 Nov. 2021, www.epoch-magazine.com/post/of-spice-and-men-how-spices-built-the-voc.

Keynes, John Maynard. "John Maynard Keynes: Newton, the Man." *Maths History*, mathshistory.st-andrews.ac.uk/Extras/ Keynes_Newton/. Accessed 29 Nov. 2020.

Klein, Ezra. "Trump vs. the Media: How Trump Makes the Press into Opposition." *Vox*, Vox, 30 Oct. 2018, www.vox. com/policy-and-politics/2018/10/30/18039990/trump-media-sanders-press-fake-news-enemy-people-bombing.

Knowles, Elizabeth, and Oxford University Press. *The Concise Oxford Dictionary of Phrase and Fable*. Oxford University Press, 2003.

Korff, Jens. "Meaning of Land to Aboriginal People." *Creative Spirits*, 7 Feb. 2021, www.creativespirits.info/aboriginalculture/land/ meaning-of-land-to-aboriginal-people#:~:text=Country%20 is%20family%2C%20culture%2C%20identity.

Korhonen, Anu. "Strange Things out of Hair: Baldness and Masculinity in Early Modern England." *The Sixteenth Century Journal*, vol. 41, no. 2, 2010, pp. 371–91.

Kosloski, Philip. "Why Is the Virgin Mary Feeding St. Bernard with Breast Milk?" *Aleteia—Catholic Spirituality, Lifestyle, World News, and Culture*, 20 Aug. 2019, aleteia.org/2019/08/20/ why-is-the-virgin-mary-feeding-st-bernard-with-breast-milk/.

Lafever, Minard, and WeingärtnerNagel. *The Architectural Instructor: Containing a History of Architecture from the Earliest Ages to the Present Time. Illustrated with Nearly 250 Engravings of Ancient, Mediæval, and Modern Cities, Temples, Palaces, Cathedrals, and Monuments; Also, the Greek and Early Roman Classic Orders, Their Principles and Beauties; With a Large Number of Original Designs of Cottages, Villas, and Mansions, of Different Sizes, Accompanied with Practical Observations on Construction, with All the Important Details, on a Scale Sufficiently Large and Definite to Enable the Builder to Execute the Accuracy; And Further Designs of Churches, Monuments, and Public Buildings: Together with a Glossary of Architectural Terms. The Whole Being the Result of More than Thirty Years Professional Experience.* G.P. Putnam & Co., 321 Broadway, 1856.

Lalor, Ailish. "What Was the VOC? The Dutch East India Company Explained." *DutchReview*, 8 June 2021, dutchreview. com/culture/history/voc-dutch-east-india-company-explained/#:~:text=The%20VOC%20also%20took%20part.

Lekaj, Paul. *Medieval Dead.* Dragonshead Productions.

LeónVicki. *4,000 Years of Uppity Women: Rebellious Belles, Daring Dames, and Headstrong Heroines through the Ages.* Mjf Books, 2011.

Lepore, Jill. "The Myth of Magna Carta." *The New Yorker*, 2015, www.newyorker.com/magazine/2015/04/20/the-rule-of-history.

"Leviticus 20-21 NIV—Bible Gateway." *Www.biblegateway.com*, www.biblegateway.com/passage/?search=Leviticus%20 20-21&version=NIV.

Lewis, Maria. "The Batavia Shipwreck Is the Craziest Australian Horror Story You've Never Heard Of." *Guide*, 2018, www. sbs.com.au/guide/article/2018/08/09/batavia-shipwreck-craziest-australian-horror-story-youve-never-heard.

Lienhard, John. "No. 1375: Newton vs. Leibniz." *Uh.edu*, 2019, www.uh.edu/engines/epi1375.htm.

Luksic, Nicola. "How Jesus' Foreskin Became One of Christianity's Most-Coveted Relics—and Then Disappeared." *CBC*, 2021, www.cbc.ca/radio/ideas/how-jesus-foreskin-became-one-of-christianity-s-most-coveted-relics-and-then-disappeared.

MacDonald, Scott, and Norman Kretzmann. "Medieval Philosophy – Routledge Encyclopedia of Philosophy." *Www.rep.routledge.com*, www.rep.routledge.com/articles/overview/medieval-philosophy/v-1. Accessed 17 Oct. 2020.

"Machu Picchu's Remarkable Water Supply and Drainage Systems." *Omrania*, 21 Jan. 2020, omrania.com/inspiration/machu-picchus-remarkable-water-supply-and-drainage-systems/.

MacQuarrie, Kim. "Why the Incas Offered up Child Sacrifices." *The Guardian*, The Guardian, 14 Feb. 2018, www.theguardian.com/science/2013/aug/04/why-incas-performed-human-sacrifice.

Maranzani, Barbara. "Was Shakespeare the Real Author of His Plays?" *Biography*, 28 June 2019, www.biography.com/news/shakespeare-real-author-theories.

Mark, Joshua J. "Merlin." *Ancient History Encyclopedia*, Ancient History Encyclopedia, 24 Apr. 2019, www.ancient.eu/Merlin/.

Mark, Joshua. "Religious Responses to the Black Death." *World History Encyclopedia*, 16 Apr. 2020, www.worldhistory.org/article/1541/religious-responses-to-the-black-death/.

Mathew, David. "James I | Biography, Religion, & Facts." *Encyclopædia Britannica*, 5 Nov. 2018, www.britannica.com/biography/James-I-king-of-England-and-Scotland.

McKenna, Amy. "Nostradamus and His Prophecies | Britannica." *Encyclopædia Britannica*, 2019, www.britannica.com/story/nostradamus-and-his-prophecies.

Medievalists.net. "10 Unusual Things That Happened during the First Crusade." *Medievalists.net*, 19 July 2015, www.medievalists.net/2015/07/ten-unusual-things-during-the-first-crusade/.

"Medieval Lives – the Medieval Church." *History Learning Site*, www.historylearningsite.co.uk/medieval-england/the-medieval-church/#:~:text=Tithes%20could%20be%20paid%20in. Accessed 12 Jan. 2022.

Menzies, Gavin. *1421: The Year China Discovered the World*. Bantam, 2002.

Merton, Robert K. *On the Shoulders of Giants: A Shandean Postscript*. Univ. Of Chicago Press, 1965.

Michael David Knowles. "Saint Benedict | Biography, Rule, & Facts." *Encyclopædia Britannica*, 4 Jan. 2019, www.britannica.com/biography/Saint-Benedict-of-Nursia.

Millard, F. L. H. *A Short History of Elementary Education in England*. Spck, 1906.

Miller, John. *Early Modern Britain, 1450-1750*. Cambridge University Press, 2017.

"Mischievous Monks and Naughty Nuns." *Just History Posts*, 7 Nov. 2016, justhistoryposts.com/2016/11/07/mischievous-monks-and-naughty-nuns/.

"Moananuiākea – a Voyage for the Pacific." *Hōkūleʻa*, www.hokulea.com/.

Morgan Britton, Luke. "Gene Simmons on Devil Horns Trademark Attempt: 'Bitch, I Can Do Anything I Want' | NME." *NME | Music, Film, TV, Gaming & Pop Culture News*, 18 Aug. 2017, www.nme.com/news/music/gene-simmons-devil-horns-trademark-criticism-response-2126033.

Motta, Cristina. "Renaissance: The Birth of Perspective." *USEUM*, useum.org/Renaissance/Perspective#:~:text=Renaissance%20artists%20focused%20on%20developing.

Mourad, Suleiman. "Understanding the Crusades from an Islamic Perspective." *The Conversation*, 9 July 2018, theconversation.com/understanding-the-crusades-from-an-islamic-perspective-96932.

Movieclips. "Just When I Thought I Was Out, They Pull Me Back In! SCENE – the Godfather: Part 3 MOVIE (1990) - HD." *YouTube*, 27 Oct. 2011, www.youtube.com/watch?v=UneS2Uwc6xw.

Murphy, Andrea, and Isabel Contreras. "The Global 2000 2022." *Forbes*, 2022, www.forbes.com/lists/global2000/?sh=653c25225ac0.

Murra, John. "Inca Religion." *Encyclopædia Britannica*, 2019, www.britannica.com/topic/Inca-religion.

National Geographic Society. "Mansa Musa (Musa I of Mali)." *National Geographic Society*, 14 Apr. 2020, www.nationalgeographic. org/encyclopedia/mansa-musa-musa-i-mali/#:~:text=After%20 the%20publication%20of%20this.

Nevill, Ralph. "Floreat Etona: Anecdotes and Memories of Eton College." *Www.gutenberg.org*, 1911, www.gutenberg.org/ files/53769/53769-h/53769-h.htm.

Niccolò Machiavelli. *Machiavelli*. 1532. Ams Press, 1967.

Oatman-Stanford, Hunter. "Naughty Nuns, Flatulent Monks, and Other Surprises of Sacred Medieval Manuscripts." *Collectors Weekly*, www.collectorsweekly.com/articles/naughty-nuns-flatulent-monks-and-other-surprises-of-sacred-medieval-manuscripts/.

Ofek, Hillel. "Why the Arabic World Turned Away from Science." *The New Atlantis*, 2011, www.thenewatlantis.com/ publications/why-the-arabic-world-turned-away-from-science.

Ohlmeyer, Jane H. "English Civil Wars - the First English Civil War (1642–46)." *Encyclopædia Britannica*, 2019, www.britannica.com/ event/English-Civil-Wars/The-first-English-Civil-War-1642-46.

"Opium – Banglapedia." *En.banglapedia.org*, en.banglapedia. org/index.php/Opium. Accessed 12 Oct. 2022.

Oram, Kirsty. "Charles I (R. 1625–1649)." *The Royal Family*, 30 Dec. 2015, www.royal.uk/charles-i.

Pal, Carol. *Republic of Woman: Rethinking the Republic of Letters in the Seventeenth Century*. Cambridge University Press, 2017.

Palmer, Joy A., et al. *Fifty Modern Thinkers on Education: From Confucius to Dewey*. Routledge, 2001.

Paoletti, John T., and Gary M. Radke. *Art in Renaissance Italy*. Prentice Hall, 2012.

Parsons, Ben. *Punishment and Medieval Education*. D. S. Brewer, 2018.

Pattara, Laura. "10 Interesting Facts about the Aztecs." *Chimu Adventures Blog,* 26 Sept. 2016, www.chimuadventures.com/blog/2016/09/aztecs-interesting-facts/.

Pentecost, Kate. "Barbarism and Brutality: Surviving the Batavia Shipwreck." *Australian National Maritime Museum,* www.sea.museum/2016/06/04/barbarism-and-brutality-surviving-the-batavia-shipwreck.

Pepys, Samuel. *The Diary of Samuel Pepys.*

"Peruke Wig." *Wigs.com,* 2018, www.wigs.com/blogs/news/peruke-wig#:~:text=Nashe%20states%20that%20periwigs%20were.

Pinker, Steven. "Is the World Getting Better or Worse? A Look at the Numbers." *Www.ted.com,* 2018, www.ted.com/talks/steven_pinker_is_the_world_getting_better_or_worse_a_look_at_the_numbers?language=en#t-90606.

Power, Eileen. *Medieval English Nunneries, C. 1275-1535.* Biblo And Tannen, 1964.

Pretl-Drummond, Oliver. "A Detailed Breakdown of How Much It Sucked to Be a Medieval Serf." *Ranker,* 2019, www.ranker.com/list/life-of-a-serf/oliver-pretl-drummond.

Prime Minister and Cabinet. "Communicating with Aboriginal and Torres Strait Islander Audiences | Department of the Prime Minister and Cabinet." *Pmc.gov.au,* 25 May 2016, www.pmc.gov.au/resource-centre/indigenous-affairs/communicating-aboriginal-and-torres-strait-islander-audiences.

Project Vox Team. "Anna Maria van Schurman (1607–1678)." *Project Vox,* projectvox.org/van-schurman-1607-1678/.

Protzen, Jean-Pierre. "Inca Quarrying and Stonecutting." *Journal of the Society of Architectural Historians,* vol. 44, no. 2, 1985, pp. 161–82, https://doi.org/10.2307/990027.

Pruitt, Sarah. "Did Shakespeare Really Write His Own Plays?" *HISTORY,* 2015, www.history.com/news/did-shakespeare-

really-write-his-own-plays#:~:text=Nothing%20has%20
been%20found%20documenting.

Pulp Fiction. Directed by Quentin Tarantino, Miramax Home
Entertainment., 2002.

"Queen Elizabeth I Facts and Myths." *Www.rmg.co.uk*, www.
rmg.co.uk/stories/topics/queen-elizabeth-i-facts-myths.

Rajjak, Shaikh. "Justice and Punishment during Mughal Empire
(Based on Foreign Travelogues)." *International Journal of
Science and Research*, IJSR, 2014, www.ijsr.net/archive/v3i12/
U1VCMTQxMDQ3.pdf.

R Alan Covey. *Inca Apocalypse: The Spanish Conquest and the
Transformation of the Andean World*. Oxford University Press,
2020.

"Rebuilding Notre-Dame, inside the Great Cathedral Rescue."
BBC, www.bbc.co.uk/programmes/m000hbdq. Accessed 6
May 2022.

"Renaissance | Encyclopedia.com." *Www.encyclopedia.com*,
8 June 2018, www.encyclopedia.com/literature-and-arts/
language-linguistics-and-literary-terms/literature-general/
renaissance#:~:text=Renaissance%20states%20had%20
three%20basic.

"Renaissance English History Podcast: A Show about the Tudors:
Episode 102: Education in Tudor England on Apple Podcasts."
Apple Podcasts, podcasts.apple.com/au/podcast/episode-102-
education-in-tudor-england/id326093823?i=1000410036508.
Accessed 22 Sept. 2020.

René Henry Pomeau. "Voltaire | Definition, Facts, Beliefs, &
Ideas." *Encyclopædia Britannica*, 17 Nov. 2018, www.britannica.
com/biography/Voltaire.

Ridgway, Claire. "Henry VIII and the Carthusian Monks –
the Tudor Society." *Www.tudorsociety.com*, 9 June 2015,
www.tudorsociety.com/henry-viii-and-the-carthusian-

Bibliography

monks/#:~:text=Between%20May%201535%20and%20 August.

Rome Museum. "Rome-Museum.com." *Rome-Museum.com*, 2019, www.rome-museum.com/st-peters-basilica.php.

Romey, Kristin. "Exclusive: Ancient Mass Child Sacrifice in Peru May Be World's Largest." *Science*, 26 Apr. 2018, www. nationalgeographic.com/science/article/mass-child-human-animal-sacrifice-peru-chimu-science?loggedin=true.

Roser, Max, and Esteban Ortiz-ospina. "Literacy." *Our World in Data*, 2018, ourworldindata.org/literacy.

Rousseau, Jean-Jacques. *Emile / Translated by Barbara Foxley; Introd. By Andre Boutet de Monvel.* Dent ; New York, 1966.

Royal Society. "History of the Royal Society | Royal Society." *Royalsociety.org*, 2015, royalsociety.org/about-us/history/.

Royal Society of London. "The Method Observed in Transfusing the Bloud out of One Live Animal into Another: And How This Experiment Is like to Be Improved. Some Considerations Concerning the Same." *Philosophical Transactions of the Royal Society of London*, vol. 1, no. 20, May 1665, pp. 353–58, https:// doi.org/10.1098/rstl.1665.0128.

Russell, Eleanor, and Martin Parker. "How the Black Death Made the Rich Richer." *Www.bbc.com*, 2020, www.bbc.com/ worklife/article/20200701-how-the-black-death-make-the-rich-richer.

Salomons, Bobby. "The Dutch East India Company Was Richer than Apple, Google and Facebook Combined." *DutchReview*, 15 Nov. 2021, dutchreview.com/culture/history/how-rich-was-the-dutch-east-india-company/#:~:text=Modern%2Dday%20 companies%20don.

Sanderson, Katharine. "Gunpowder, Treason and Plot." *Chemistry World*, 2005, www.chemistryworld.com/features/gunpowder-treason-and-plot/3004619.article.

311

Scarborough, Vernon L., and David R. Wilcox. *The Mesoamerican Ballgame*. The University of Arizona Press, 1993.

Schlossberg, Tatiana. "The State of Publishing: Literacy Rates." *McSweeney's Internet Tendency*, 2018, www.mcsweeneys.net/articles/literacy-rates.

Science Vs. "Ancient Aliens: Who Really Built the Pyramids? | Science Vs." *Gimlet*, 2018, gimletmedia.com/shows/science-vs/brho25.

Scott, Joe. "The Deadliest Company in Human History | Answers with Joe." *Www.youtube.com*, 2022, www.youtube.com/watch?v=NtCgZmdzWNE.

Sibson, Matt. "Sacsayhuaman as You've NEVER Seen It Before: Excavation Reports and Chronicles | Ancient Architects." *Www.youtube.com*, www.youtube.com/watch?v=2Qwx2jq7R_8. Accessed 6 July 2022.

Snell, Melissa. "Schooling, University, and Apprenticeship in the Middle Ages." *ThoughtCo*, 2019, www.thoughtco.com/medieval-child-the-learning-years-1789122#:~:text=as%20an%20apprentice.-.

Sommerville, C. John. "Puritan Humor, or Entertainment, for Children." *Albion*, vol. 21, no. 2, 1989, pp. 227–47, https://doi.org/10.2307/4049927.

Soutik Biswas. "How Britain's Opium Trade Impoverished Indians." *BBC News*, 5 Sept. 2019, www.bbc.com/news/world-asia-india-49404024.

"STD Facts - Syphilis (Detailed)." *Www.cdc.gov*, 23 Sept. 2019, www.cdc.gov/std/syphilis/stdfact-syphilis-detailed.htm#:~:text=Syphilis%20can%20invade%20the%20nervous.

Stephen, Leslie. "Samuel Pepys, the Dictionary of National Biography Volume 44." *Wikisource.org*, Wikimedia Foundation, Inc., 16 June 2008, en.wikisource.org/wiki/Dictionary_of_National_Biography.

"Stock Photos, Royalty-Free Images, Graphics, Vectors & Videos." *Adobe Stock*, stock.adobe.com/au/?state=%7B%22 ac%22%3A%22stock.adobe.com%22%7D. Accessed 10 May 2022.

"Strange Tales from the Royal Society." *BBC News*, 25 Oct. 2011, www.bbc.com/news/magazine-15445507.

Sunrise House. "Difference between Hashish and Marijuana? | Sunrisehouse.com." *Sunrise House*, sunrisehouse.com/quit-abusing-marijuana/hashish/.

Taylor, Bryan. "The Rise and Fall of the Largest Corporation in History - Business Insider." *Business Insider*, Business Insider, 6 Nov. 2013, www.businessinsider.com/rise-and-fall-of-united-east-india-2013-11.

Tesch, Noah. "8 Masterpieces of Islamic Architecture." *Encyclopædia Britannica*, 2019, www.britannica.com/list/8-masterpieces-of-islamic-architecture.

Tharoor, Ishaan. "7 Wicked Popes, and the Terrible Things They Did." *The Washington Post*, 24 Sept. 2015, www.washingtonpost.com/news/worldviews/wp/2015/09/24/7-wicked-popes-and-the-terrible-things-they-did/.

The British Library. "Timeline of Cook's Voyages." *The British Library*, 2019, https://doi.org/https://www.bl.uk/the-voyages-of-captain-james-cook/timeline.

"The Canterbury Tales by Geoffrey Chaucer." *The British Library*, 2019, https://doi.org/https://www.bl.uk/collection-items/the-canterbury-tales-by-geoffrey-chaucer.

"The Devil's Hellish History: Satan in the Middle Ages." *History*, 30 Oct. 2018, www.nationalgeographic.com/history/history-magazine/article/history-devil-medieval-art-middle-ages.

The Editors of Encyclopaedia Britannica. "Abbasid Caliphate | Achievements, Capital, & Facts." *Encyclopædia Britannica*, 2019, www.britannica.com/topic/Abbasid-caliphate.

—. "Diet of Worms I Germany [1521]." *Encyclopædia Britannica,* 2019, www.britannica.com/event/Diet-of-Worms-Germany-1521.

—. "East India Company I Definition, History, & Facts." *Encyclopædia Britannica,* 2019, www.britannica.com/topic/East-India-Company.

—. "Graphic Design - Early Printing and Graphic Design." *Encyclopedia Britannica,* www.britannica.com/art/graphic-design/Early-printing-and-graphic-design.

—. "Hagia Sophia I History, Facts, & Significance." *Encyclopedia Britannica,* 10 Sept. 2018, www.britannica.com/topic/Hagia-Sophia.

—. "Hans Burgkmair, the Elder I German Artist." *Encyclopedia Britannica,* www.britannica.com/biography/Hans-Burgkmair-the-Elder. Accessed 31 Dec. 2020.

—. "Inca – History." *Encyclopedia Britannica,* www.britannica.com/topic/Inca/History.

—. "Indian Mutiny I Causes, Summary, & Facts." *Encyclopædia Britannica,* 22 Feb. 2019, www.britannica.com/event/Indian-Mutiny.

—. "Lapita Culture." *Encyclopædia Britannica,* 15 Mar. 2016, www.britannica.com/topic/Lapita-culture.

—. "Nostradamus I Biography & Facts I Britannica." *Encyclopædia Britannica,* 2019, www.britannica.com/biography/Nostradamus.

Á. "Opium Trade I History & Facts." *Encyclopædia Britannica,* 3 Jan. 2018, www.britannica.com/topic/opium-trade.

—. "Shaitan I Islamic Mythology." *Encyclopædia Britannica,* 2019, www.britannica.com/topic/shaitan.

—. "Transatlantic Slave Trade Key Facts." *Encyclopedia Britannica,* 23 Nov. 2020, www.britannica.com/summary/Transatlantic-Slave-Trade-Key-Facts.

—. "Woodcut I Technique, History, & Facts." *Encyclopædia Britannica,* 25 May 2018, www.britannica.com/art/woodcut.

—. "Xipe Totec | Aztec Deity." *Encyclopedia Britannica*, www. britannica.com/topic/Xipe-Totec.

The Editors of the Merriam-Webster Dictionary. "Merriam-Webster Dictionary." *Merriam-Webster.com*, 2019, www. merriam-webster.com/dictionary/.

"The English Civil Wars: History and Stories." *English Heritage*, www.english-heritage.org.uk/learn/histories/the-english-civil-wars-history-and-stories/#:~:text=Key%20Facts.

"The History of England: 122 Wycliffe and a University Education on Apple Podcasts." *Apple Podcasts*, podcasts.apple. com/au/podcast/122-wycliffe-and-a-university-education/ id412308812?i=1000305070917. Accessed 22 Sept. 2020.

The National Archives. "John Appeals to the Pope, 1215." *The National Archives*, www.nationalarchives.gov.uk/education/ resources/magna-carta/john-appeals-pope-rome-1215/. Accessed 29 Dec. 2021.

"The VOC and the EIC – the Memory." *Geheugen. delpher.nl*, geheugen.delpher.nl/en/geheugen/pages/collectie/ Nederland+en+Engeland%3A+de+band+tussen+twee+naties/ De+VOC+en+de+EIC#:~:text=The%20East%20India%20 Company%20(EIC. Accessed 14 Sept. 2022.

Titone, Connie. "Catharine Macaulay's Letters on Education." *Teachers College Record*, vol. January, no. 1997, 1997, https:// doi.org/1997.

Toivanen, Otto, and Lotta Väänänen. "Education and Invention." *Review of Economics and Statistics*, vol. 98, no. 2, May 2016, pp. 382–96, https://doi.org/10.1162/rest_a_00520.

Tracy, James D. "Erasmus | Biography & Facts." *Encyclopædia Britannica*, 17 Apr. 2019, www.britannica.com/biography/ Erasmus-Dutch-humanist.

Trueman, C. N. "Building a Medieval Cathedral." *History Learning Site*, 2022, www.historylearningsite.co.uk/medieval-england/building-a-medieval-cathedral/.

Viegas, Jennifer. "Study: Breast Baring Popular in 1600s." *Anthropologist.livejournal.com*, 2004, anthropologist.livejournal.com/230875.html.

Walker, Paul. "Saladin | Biography, Achievements, & Facts." *Encyclopædia Britannica*, 2019, www.britannica.com/biography/Saladin.

Wallace, William E. *The Genius of Michelangelo*. The Great Courses, 2007.

"Wayfinding and Navigation | Manoa.hawaii.edu/ExploringOurFluidEarth." *Hawaii.edu*, 2019, manoa.hawaii.edu/exploringourfluidearth/physical/navigation-and-transportation/wayfinding-and-navigation.

White, James. *Ring of Flesh: The Late Medieval Devotion to the Holy Foreskin*. 2021.

"Why Are Dates Hated by Jinn and Satan?" *World Today News*, 25 Apr. 2021, www.world-today-news.com/why-are-dates-hated-by-jinn-and-satan/.

"Why I Can't Be a Nun | Robbins Library Digital Projects." *D.lib.rochester.edu*, d.lib.rochester.edu/teams/text/dean-six-ecclesiastical-satires-why-i-cant-be-a-nun. Accessed 22 Dec. 2020.

Wikimedia Commons. *Wikimedia.org*, 2016, commons.wikimedia.org/wiki/Main_Page.

Wikipedia Contributors - Various articles. *Wikipedia*, Wikimedia Foundation, 2021, en.wikipedia.org/.

Williams, S.E. *Lightbulb Moments in Human History – from Cave to Colosseum*. John Hunt Publishing, 2023.

Wollstonecraft, Mary. *Thoughts on the Education of Daughters with Reflections on Female Conduct in the More Important Duties of Life*. 1787. Clifton, N.J., Kelley, 1787.

Worden, Nigel. "Slavery at the Cape." *Oxford Research Encyclopedia of African History*, Apr. 2017, https://doi.org/10.1093/acrefore/9780190277734.013.76.

Young, Michael B. *King James and the History of Homosexuality.* Fonthill, 2016.

Ziegler, Joanna E. "Michelangelo and the Medieval Pietà: The Sculpture of Devotion or the Art of Sculpture?" *Gesta,* vol. 34, no. 1, Jan. 1995, pp. 28–36, https://doi.org/10.2307/767122.

Zilberstein, Gleb, et al. "De Re Metallica. Johannes Kepler and Alchemy." *Talanta,* vol. 204, Nov. 2019, pp. 82–88, https://doi.org/10.1016/j.talanta.2019.05.094.

CHRONOS
BOOKS

HISTORY

Chronos Books is an historical non-fiction imprint. Chronos publishes real history for real people; bringing to life people, places and events in an imaginative, easy-to-digest and accessible way - histories that pass on their stories to a generation of new readers.
If you have enjoyed this book, why not tell other readers by posting a review on your preferred book site.

Recent bestsellers from Chronos Books are:

Lady Katherine Knollys

The Unacknowledged Daughter of King Henry VIII

Sarah-Beth Watkins

A comprehensive account of Katherine Knollys' questionable paternity, her previously unexplored life in the Tudor court and her intriguing relationship with Elizabeth I.

Paperback: 978-1-78279-585-8 ebook: 978-1-78279-584-1

Cromwell was Framed

Ireland 1649

Tom Reilly

Revealed: The definitive research that proves the Irish nation owes Oliver Cromwell a huge posthumous apology for wrongly convicting him of civilian atrocities in 1649.

Paperback: 978-1-78279-516-2 ebook: 978-1-78279-515-5

Why The CIA Killed JFK and Malcolm X

The Secret Drug Trade in Laos

John Koerner

A new groundbreaking work presenting evidence that the CIA silenced JFK to protect its secret drug trade in Laos.

Paperback: 978-1-78279-701-2 ebook: 978-1-78279-700-5

The Disappearing Ninth Legion

A Popular History

Mark Olly

The Disappearing Ninth Legion examines hard evidence for the foundation, development, mysterious disappearance, or possible continuation of Rome's lost Legion.

Paperback: 978-1-84694-559-5 ebook: 978-1-84694-931-9

Beaten But Not Defeated
Siegfried Moos - A German anti-Nazi who settled in Britain
Merilyn Moos
Siegi Moos, an anti-Nazi and active member of the German
Communist Party, escaped Germany in 1933 and, exiled in
Britain, sought another route to the transformation
of capitalism.
Paperback: 978-1-78279-677-0 ebook: 978-1-78279-676-3

A Schoolboy's Wartime Letters
An evacuee's life in WWII — A Personal Memoir
Geoffrey Iley
A boy writes home during WWII, revealing his own fascinating
story, full of zest for life, information and humour.
Paperback: 978-1-78279-504-9 ebook: 978-1-78279-503-2

The Life & Times of the Real Robyn Hoode
Mark Olly
A journey of discovery. The chronicles of the genuine historical
character, Robyn Hoode, and how he became one of England's
greatest legends.
Paperback: 978-1-78535-059-7 ebook: 978-1-78535-060-3